CRISIS

MANAGEMENT

IN A
CROSS-CULTURAL
SETTING

D1328548

CRISIS

MANAGEMENT

IN A CROSS-CULTURAL SETTING

Edited by
Patricia A. Burak
and William W. Hoffa

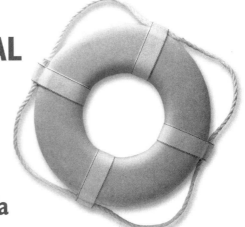

REVISED EDITION 2001

NAFSA: Association of International Educators promotes the exchange of students and scholars to and from the United States. The association sets and upholds standards of good practice and provides professional education and training that strengthen institutional programs and services related to international educational exchange. NAFSA provides a forum for discussion and awareness of and support for international education in higher education, in government, and in the community.

International Standard Book Number: 0-912207-85-X

Library of Congress Cataloging-in-Publication Data

Crisis management in a cross-cultural setting / edited by Patricia Burak and William Hoffa.-- Rev. ed.
            p. cm.
        Includes bibliographic references.
        ISBN 0-912207-85-X
        1. Student exchange programs--United States--Safety measures. 2. School crisis management--United States. 3. Students, Foreign--Protection. I. Burak, Patricia A. II. Hoffa, William. III. NAFSA: Association of International Educators (Washington, D.C.)

    LB2376 .C75 2001
    378'.0162--dc21

                                            2001031204

NAFSA

Association of
International Educators

Copyright 2001 by NAFSA: Association of International Educators, except where otherwise noted. All Rights reserved. Reproduction of NAFSA publications is strictly prohibited without the written permission of the publisher. Printed in the United States.

Table of Contents

Part I. Crises Affecting International Students:
How to Plan and Respond

Part II. Crises Involving International Students on U.S. Campuses

Part III. Crises Involving U.S. Students Studying Abroad

Appendixes. Resources and Forms

Editors, Authors, and Contributors

Editors

Patricia A. Burak, D.A., Director, Lillian and Emanuel Slutzker Center for International Services, Syracuse University and the State University of New York College of Environmental Science and Forestry, Syracuse, New York

William W. Hoffa, Principal Consultant, Academic Consultants International, Amherst, Massachusetts; Adjunct Faculty, School for International Training

Authors and Contributors

Gary Althen, Director of Foreign Students and Scholars, University Of Iowa

David Austell, Ph.D., Director, International Students and Scholar Services, University of South Florida

Ellen H. Badger, Director, International Student and Scholar Services, Binghamton University, State University of New York

Donna Boguslav, R.N., Associate Director of Nursing, Health Center, New York University (retired)

Doug Brown, formerly with the School for Field Studies, Beverley, Massachusetts

James Buschman, Ph.D., Associate Director, Division of International Programs Abroad, Syracuse University

Sidney (Skip) Greenblatt, Senior International Student Adviser, Lillian and Emanuel Slutzker Center for International Services, Syracuse University and the State University of New York College of Environmental Science and Forestry, Syracuse, New York

Terence P. Hannigan, Ph.D., Deer Oaks Mental Health Associates, Laredo, Texas

Jane Howard, Director, International Student Affairs, Mount Ida College, Massachusetts

Peter S. Levitov, J.D., Associate Dean of International Affairs, The International Center, University of Nebraska-Lincoln and Special Assistant General Counsel (Immigration), University of Nebraska

Barbara A. Lindeman, Director, International Center, University of Missouri-Columbia

Peter Maramaldi, C.S.W., M.P.H., Ph.D. candidate and Adjunct Assistant Professor, Columbia University School of Social Work; Social Worker, International House, New York

Stephen Marcoux Nelson, Director of Judicial Affairs, Binghamton University, State University of New York

Melissa Martin, former Director, Office of Study Abroad, Marymount College-Tarrytown

Lester McCabe, Chief Operating Officer, Institute for Shipboard Education, Colorado

Julie Ann Rabaey, International Student Services Coordinator, International Education, Gustavus Adolphus College, Minnesota

Beth Rascoe, Assistant Coordinator, Study Abroad, Office of International Study Programs, Northeastern University, Massachusetts

Lynn Reilly, Foreign Student Adviser, University of South Florida

Gary Rhodes, Director, Center for Global Education, Rossier School of Education, University of Southern California

Brenda Robinson, former Dean of International Affairs, Grand Valley State University, Michigan

Julie Kyllonen Rose, Director, Office of International Student/Scholar/Faculty Affairs, International Education Office, Western Illinois University.

Deirdre Colby Sato, International Student Adviser, SUNY Purchase College, New York

Michael B. Smithee, Ed.D., Associate Director, Lillian and Emanuel Slutzker Center for International Services, Syracuse University and the State University of New York College of Environmental Science and Forestry, Syracuse, New York

Skye Stephenson, Resident Director, Council Study Center, Chile

JoAnn DeArmas Wallace, Dean of International Programs Juniata College, Pennsylvania

Nancy E. Young, Associate Director, Office for International Students and Scholars, New York University

Preface

"What?" "Who?" "Where?" "When?" "How?" and then, "What now?" These are usually the first questions anyone, anywhere, asks when, at home or at work, upon hearing about a crisis situation—always, suddenly, always bringing on a state of shock and disbelief! They are likely standard questions that cross cultures, questions that surface immediately with the immediacy of the news, and with our human need to know all we can about what has just happened. The premise of this book, however, is that responses to such questions may differ from culture to culture, and these variations must be taken into account in setting up the appropriate responses and procedures for high quality crisis management. Indeed, the very definition of what is and isn't a 'crisis' will depend upon its cultural context. The reporting of the event, the urgency of supplying information, the sense of privacy vs. the 'need to know'—all these concerns and many more, determine how one approaches and 'manages' a crisis. *Crisis Management in a Cross-Cultural Setting* is designed to prepare international educators to respond appropriately, expeditiously, and comprehensively to crises that befall students living and learning a long way from where they call 'home.' Its thesis is simple: advance planning and cross-cultural sensitivity can make all the difference.

Understanding culture as an operative component of crisis management is absolutely essential for a professional in international educational exchange. Consider the pastoral country village of Lockerbie, Scotland in the aftermath of the terrorist bombing of PanAm 103. Thirty-five Syracuse University students returning home after a semester of study abroad died instantly, among the 270 killed on board or on the ground. Think about the families of three young women who were killed when their bus careened off the road and crashed on a trip through India during a study abroad program. The several societies within which these crises occurred were active players in the management of these crises. Gentle, caring, family-oriented small-town folk in Lockerbie attended to the matters at hand, helping to find bodies strewn throughout the countryside, carefully marking the places for future reference. The management of the crisis on site was made much easier by the tremendous support of the people, the police, the pastor of the local church, and the rector of the Lockerbie Academy, which served as a center for all activity. These kind, gentle people of Lockerbie, Scotland and their personal approach in a friendly small town stand in stark cultural contrast with the bureaucratic detachment of U.S. Embassy officials in India, after the death of the three students who were on the study abroad program there. The Embassy demanded prepaid repatriation expenses—$3000 each, in 1996—from the stateside families before it would begin repatriation proceedings.

Protocols for on-campus or overseas action; treatment of the survivors; handling of the media; repatriation and legal issues; and much more, are affected by the local reactions, the local "norms," the political and social systems in place at the location of the crisis, and the efficacy of the political system where one is operating in the aftermath of the crisis. Take, for example, another crisis occurring in a country with very hierarchical social structure. In such a society, the son of a prince or the daughter of the tribal leader will not be held to blame under any circumstances. The son of the prince dates a young woman from the U.S. who is studying that semester in his country. They end up in his room, and he takes advantage of her friendliness and affection. "No" does not mean "NO" across cultures. In that society, the behavior that brought her to his room, considering who he was, put the blame upon her shoulders. He was held completely blameless when she filed charges of rape with the local authorities.

Another for instance may be seen when the daughter of a government official who is studying in the U.S. had a car accident, maiming and seriously injuring her passengers and an innocent bystander. She called upon the legal resources available to government officials. Charges of reckless driving and imprudent speed were threatening to curtail her driving activities in the future. Her father's influence and status influenced the situation, and all charges were dropped.

When defining what a crisis is and is not through a cross-cultural lens, the matter of abortion in the United States versus abortion in many other countries in the world is also a good example to highlight major differences. Western society, especially in the U.S., still supports keeping discussion about abortion and its practice "behind closed doors." Abortion as a method of birth control, however, in much of Eastern Europe and Asia, and is a fairly routine medical treatment, or folk treatment. Francine de Plessix Gray (see Appendix A) reports that in the former Soviet Union, abortion is considered to be the most common form of birth control. These differences may not even be brought to the attention of an international student adviser, under normal circumstances. But the cultural conflict arises when a student or spouse from Russia, for example, seeks an abortion in a very open, casual, and routine fashion. The communal nature of the Russian character allows for a more open discussion of this topic, whereas the Puritan ethic inherited by citizens of the United States, either through birth or acculturation, eschews such discussions. In contrast, a U.S. student abroad would bring into her new environment her U.S. reluctance to discuss the issue and a fearfulness of discovery. The stigma attached to unwanted pregnancy is still significant in the United States, and the conflict across cultures that has been exacerbated by this clash in judgment is enormous.

It is the contention of the editors of this publication that the culture component transfigures crisis management in every case. It is the "'culture in our heads'…(the) subjective culture (Triandis 1972) (that) is part and parcel of (one's) personal reality" that affects and injects itself into the crisis at hand. In *Counseling Across Cultures* (see Appendix A), Kay Thomas and Gary Althen present a chart, contrasting assumptions and values between American and other cultures. These contrasting values play a major role in crisis management, and provide some explanation as to why people react the way they do at times of emotional, and often physical, distress. Selected portions of these comparisons apply directly to some of the crises discussed in the chapters ahead, and are reprinted here to guide your thinking:

AMERICAN ASSUMPTIONS/ VALUES	CONTRAST–AMERICAN ASSUMPTIONS/VALUES
People are isolable individuals.	People are integrally related with other people (in groups such as families)
"Professional" people can help other people solve their problems.	One's problems are beyond the control of other human beings.
People can be genuinely interested in the welfare of strangers.	Only one's close friends and relatives can be trusted.
Emotional disturbances have their root in the individual's past.	Emotional disturbances have their root in external forces or situations.
People are (more or less) equal.	There is a hierarchical ranking of people in society.
Males and females are (more or less) equal.	Males are superior.

These examples demonstrate we think that crises affecting students when they are in a culture foreign to their own need to be responded to in a cross-culturally different way. This can only be done via forethought and planning. The immediate psychic disorientation that accompanies a crisis—and not just for those stricken by it—can render any of us virtually unable to think straight and 'do the right thing' instinctively. Developing a protocol or response procedures at the cusp of a crisis is not only often ineffectual, but can make matters worse. All those charged with the responsibility of crisis management need to respond as a 'team.' They thus need to be practiced in 'game plan' and aware of their respective duties.

To assist you in setting up this plan, we have gathered the experiences and expertise of many professionals in the field of international educational exchange, both those who work with international students studying on U.S. campuses and those who work with U.S. students studying in other countries. While U.S.-based and overseas crises will differ often dramatically in their settings and cultural contexts, there are many principles of appropriate crisis management that are the same. Our goal is to be able to enhance and strengthen the ability of all international educators to face the crises that inevitably will come their way. We hope that it will be used both as a guidebook when crises hit, and as a primer for preparing for such a time.

A crisis, by definition, cannot be prevented, but we all can be prepared to handle better whatever may come if we take time in advance to learn from the wisdom and mistakes of others. An old adage, "Forewarned is forearmed" is appropriate here, and it applies to gaining knowledge of different cultural traditions, taboos, religious customs, rituals, values, family and societal hierarchies, political systems, history, holiday observances…the list is endless.

This book presents guidelines and suggestions in each chapter, based on actual crises, whether they happened in the United States (Part II) or abroad (Part III). The unifying subtext throughout—presented in Part I—is that campus protocol set up and overseen by a crisis management team needs to be developed and in place on all campuses and programs which receive students from abroad or send them there. Through the experiences of its contributors, it presents crisis case studies, in both anecdotal and objective formats. By design, the chapters in Part II take up individual types of crises, while those of Part III attempt to synthesize the professional wisdom of practitioners working with U.S. students abroad. The differing chapters cover background and prognosis, review, and the post-crisis analysis. Crises treated explicitly (Part II) or implicitly (Part III) include:

- Health-related topics, such as depression, anorexia and bulimia, terminal illness, pregnancy, rape, and abortion

- Social issues including relationship/domestic violence, alcohol, as well as drug abuse

- Political turmoil and terrorism

- Missing persons, car accidents, accidental death from any cause

- Natural disasters

- International financial crises

- Suicide, murder, and criminal activity

Certain of these crises are signaled by warning signs and can sometimes be treated and resolved with a high degree of success through cross-culturally informed professional counsel and therapy. In such cases, it is possible to prevent the worst-case scenarios. Other crises, such as serious injury and death, begin with something that has already reached the worst-case scenario state, so that the response needed is directed less at the crisis event itself than its aftermath and all those affected by it. These instances require a level of personal and professional response for which no one is ever really prepared, but for which preparation is essential.

Some of the crises that an international educator might face these days seem a product of recent social developments, here or overseas—e.g., sexual harassment, racial and sexual identity crises, prejudices because of race, religion, sexual preference, or political affiliation. Ten years ago, the reasons for the murder of a student such as Matthew Shepherd, the American college student who was murdered by other American college students because he was openly gay, wouldn't have made headline news. International students are even more susceptible to such racist and sexist attacks since they may be unaware of the latent sexism or racism, homophobia, or hate within a community that is new to them. Overseas, the same thing may be true for naïve and uninformed U.S. students.

The invasive role of the media today, responding to the perceived public "right to know," has further complicated the issues involved in crisis management across cultures. How does a privacy-driven culture accept or tolerate public exposure of the murder of their citizen away from home? How does a quiet countryside handle thousands of journalists descending upon it within hours of a disaster? The instantaneous transmission of news and information has had its impact on sharing news with victims' families in a gentle and caring way. In settings where cell phones, faxes, e-mails, and 24-hour television news don't allow for any gentle delay in transmitting bad news across thousands of miles, how does one create time and space for sensitivity in the painful task of notifying next-of-kin? Even in less critical cases, one must be prepared to deal with the aftermath of a startling news release featuring photos of one's burned home in a student's native country, the bombing of an embassy where one's parents worked, or a natural disaster on the campus in which a university's students are enrolled. Before normal person-to-person communications even have a chance to take place, the information has been transmitted. How does one deal with the cultural misunderstanding; the cross-Atlantic or cross-Pacific time lag in reaching a family member; the religious controversy between performing an autopsy on a victim or respecting the wishes of grieving parents? The only answers lie in building better cross-cultural empathy and understanding.

Finally, while we always need to keep ever in mind the pain, suffering, and sorrow endured by the crisis victim or victims, as well as their family and friends, it is also the case that crises can often bring feelings of helplessness and distress to those attempting to 'manage' them as well. In this regard, it is good to be able to remind ourselves that what we do can bring order and clarity, peace and understanding, respect and closure. But the hard-won collective wisdom represented in the following chapters suggests strongly that no open and committed international educator should ever have to go it alone. Indeed, if this volume succeeds in its purposes, it is evidence that we remain students of each other.

The editors wish to thank Steve Kennedy, formerly of NAFSA Publications for the opportunity given us to edit this important and timely pan-NAFSA volume; and to Betsey Lyon and Steve Pelletier for assisting it to its conclusion. We especially want to thank all the many NAFSA colleagues who contributed its professional content and conviction. Without their professional knowledge, dedication, and patience, you would not have this book in your hands today.

Patricia A. Burak and William W. Hoffa, Editors

PART I.

Crises Affecting International Students: How to Plan and Respond

Chapter 1

Setting Up an Inclusive Crisis Management Plan

William W. Hoffa, Patricia A. Burak, and Michael B. Smithee

W hether you are an international program director, a foreign student adviser, a U.S.-based study abroad adviser, or an overseas program director responsible for U.S. students, chances are that one day you will be faced with responding to a crisis involving one or more of your students. When this happens, you will want to be prepared. This book will show you how to start the process of devising a 'crisis management' plan for your institution or program. When in place, it will give you the best chance of responding appropriately and in a culturally sensitive way to crises affecting students living and learning on cultural terms, here or abroad, which are 'foreign' to them. Publications such as *When Crisis Strikes on Campus* and *Campuses Respond to Violent Tragedy* suggest ways American campuses can prepare for most domestic crises. International educators, however, know that 'culture' is a key mediator in interpersonal transactions of every sort. We are likely to be more aware than most of our campus colleagues as to how, in times of emotional and physical distress, 'culture' can transfigure a crisis, and how it conditions why people react the way they do. If your campus already has a routine crisis management plan, sometimes what is needed is simply the addition of a strong cross-cultural awareness dimension to what already is in place. In other instances, planning may have to begin at the beginning. In any and all cases, the cultural components of crisis management are essential and thus are explored fully in this volume.

Whatever the root cause of the emergency, whatever its specifics, and wherever it occurs, it is vitally important, after the shocking first moments, that you and your crisis management team are ready to take quick, cultural-ly-sensitive, and appropriate steps to deal with it. Creating an effective response from scratch is seldom, if ever, better than putting into action what has been thought through in advance and battle-tested. How clear-headed and logical is anyone when the phone rings in the middle of the night, at the end of a wearying week, or when one has just returned from a relaxing social outing? Because mental preparation alone never fully readies an adminis-trator for all of the sudden shocks that most crises bring, being able to act in accordance with preestablished procedures and protocols is the wisest course of action.

You need to have immediate answers to a host of important and detailed questions: Who pays if one of your international or study abroad students needs a medical evacuation? What if you need to evacuate an entire group from an overseas site? If your foreign students are covered domestically under an institutional plan, does this also cover repatriation of remains? If your study abroad students have campus health coverage, does this coverage extend overseas? You should not wait until a crisis erupts to find the answers to these and related questions. Answers need to be provided ahead of time to your students and their families or guardians, who are often ignorant about international insurance coverage. Crisis management planning requires that this information, and much more, be made known to all key members of the crisis team.

Because the administration of international education programs involves such a wide variety of combinations of administrators and faculty, overseas contacts, and campus personnel, no set of policies or procedures will be appropriate for all institutions and no two crises teams will be pre-cisely alike. A campus with significant enrollments of students from abroad and only small numbers studying abroad will need a crisis management plan that looks quite different from that of another campus that enrolls few for-eign students but sends many domestic students to a wide variety of desti-nations overseas. In all successful cases, however, all members of the team will know who they are; they will have been briefed on their responsibilities; and they will know their part in the plan. Although your role may put you at the veritable hot point of crisis management, seldom should you be working alone.

Overview of International Student Crises on U.S. Campuses

The overwhelming majority of the 525,000 international students on U.S. campuses are enrolled in an undergraduate or graduate degree program. They spend, on average, three to five years in the United States, long enough for them to settle in and become part of the American campus milieu. Most have carefully prepared themselves for their extended sojourn and adjust over time to American and campus life. Given the numbers involved, it is impressive how few international students and scholars become involved in a crisis situation during their time in this country. That some bring with them (or subsequently develop) serious personal problems requiring culturally sensitive crisis counseling is also, however, a fact. Responding successfully both to individual and group crises requires foreign student advisers to have protocols in place for on-campus action and for contact with far-off family, friends, and sponsors.

Personal issues that are not uncommon among foreign students, however, include health-related problems, such as anorexia and bulimia; terminal illness; and pregnancy, rape, and abortion. Social issues among foreign students today include domestic violence, alcohol and drug abuse, and political turmoil spilling over from their home countries. Accidental death from various causes, especially automobile and other travel disasters, is not infrequent. Thoughts of suicide are surprisingly common, and occasionally those thoughts are carried out. Questions of repatriation loom large when serious injury or death occur. Legal complications, often transnational, also can arise. Sexual harassment; racial and sexual identity crises; and prejudices related to race, religion, sexual preference, or political affiliation are among the other crises that foreign student and scholar advisers are faced with today.

While the preponderance of crises affecting international students are individual crises, major overseas social, political, or economic developments—such as natural catastrophes, financial crises, and political upheavals—can at times impact all foreign nationals from the affected areas. Recent examples include the Asian economic collapse, which deprived students from many countries of the money they needed to continue their studies, and the hurricanes in Honduras and the Dominican Republic, which devastated the homes and families of students studying here. When a student's studies or finances are interrupted, accommodations need to be made with academic advisers and other faculty. All these matters carry cross-cultural dimensions that need to be made known by the international office and incorporated into any crisis response.

Finally, responding to local or national media attention has further complicated the issues involved in crisis management across cultures. How does a quiet campus handle scores of journalists descending within hours of a disaster, due to local or national media coverage? Cell phones, faxes, e-mail, and 24-hour television news don't allow for gentle delay in transmitting bad news across thousands of miles. How does one create time and space for sensitivity in the painful task of notifying a victim's family? Even in less critical cases, one must be prepared to deal with the aftermath of a startling news release featuring photos of a burned homestead in a student's native country, the bombing of an embassy where a student's parents worked, or a natural disaster on the campus. Before traditional person-to-person communications even have a chance to take place, a mixture of accurate and inaccurate information has been transmitted. How does one deal with the cultural misunderstanding; the time lag in reaching a family member; the religious controversy between performing an autopsy on a victim or respecting the wishes of grieving parents? These are among the many questions and considerations that crises affecting foreign students studying in the United States bring to the work of their campus advisers.

Overview of U.S. Student Crises Abroad

Whereas only some international students on U.S. campuses are directly sponsored by foreign educational institutions (sometimes as part of short-term reciprocal exchange agreements), the overwhelming majority of U.S. students studying abroad are sponsored by their U.S. college or universities and are studying overseas as part of their American undergraduate degree studies. This fact means that both individual and group crises which affect U.S. students are likely to have an immediate impact both on-site overseas *and* on the home campus. If a student is studying on a program sponsored by another U.S. institution (not her or his home campus) the impact will be felt by a third institution as well. However, sponsorship can mean anything from direct program ownership and oversight to affiliation with (or some-times just "approval" of) programs owned and run by other U.S. or foreign educational institutions, agencies, and consortia. Unless a campus allows its students only to participate in it own programs, it must keep track of many students pursuing many different types of educational opportunities in many different countries.

In 1998–99, only 10 percent of the rapidly increasing number of U.S. stu-dents abroad remained overseas for even a single academic year, and more than half were abroad for something shorter than an academic semester. Relatively few American students now enroll directly in foreign educational institutions, participate in training programs, or find volunteer or paid work which immerses them in local life. Most students in this expanding number of U.S. students abroad are thus short-term visitors living in environments that are truly foreign to them. Much of what they experience is circum-scribed by their transience and by the study program or foreign institution that sponsors their stay. Although American students value their new-found independence and some strike out boldly on their own, most remain self-consciously and unmistakably "American students." Their links with their home campus and America are culturally undeniable; those links emerge, often emphatically, when things go awry.

Crisis management planning for U.S. study abroad students thus needs to take into account deep-seated American isolationism and relative igno-rance about the realities of the rest of the world, especially on the part of cit-izens who have not traveled abroad. This lack of knowledge and direct expe-rience can (and often does) readily feed the notion that living and learning in another country is fraught with danger. Of course, there are real reasons for prudent concern over political unrest in many corners of the world, the ongoing threat of terrorism, natural disasters of every stripe, outbreaks of famine and disease in developing countries, road accidents in remote areas, and plane crashes—all of which have affected some study abroad students in recent years. It is often difficult from afar to distinguish real crises from apparent ones.

Complicating matters further, the immediate and graphic visibility of fast-breaking 'news' on CNN and its imitators in the popular media, provide levels of distortion and melodrama that campuses end up having to face. Each of these factors have made crisis management a constant reality in the lives of education abroad advisers, program administrators, and overseas directors. When *USA Today* trumpets on its front page a feature entitled, "The Perils of Study Abroad," anyone who has responsibility for sending students and staff to other countries to live and learn is forced to take notice, and to recognize that confronting perceptions of overseas crises has become part of their job description.

Overseas crises occur when U.S. students are victimized by social, political, or natural circumstances far beyond their program's or their own control—usually as the result of sudden developments. By definition, if such dangers were well known in advance, few students would be studying there, in part because no campus-sponsored opportunities would exist. It is in no campus's interest to send students into harm's way. At such times when national crises occur, whole programs are threatened. This is not to say that poor program planning or oversight cannot sometimes lead to a crisis situation.

It is the experience of most campuses and programs, however, that the majority of crises affect individuals, not groups. In some cases this is due to the vagaries of fate, as students become victims of matters unforeseen, including illness and violence. More often than not individual students themselves contribute to the crisis through their careless or aberrant behavior. In an ideal world where students did not act as students sometimes do— forgetting or disregarding warnings, believing in their own invulnerability, and naively assuming that American norms are universal—many such crises would be preventable. Even good orientation, training, and program oversight cannot entirely prevent such crises from erupting. And it needs to be noted that an individual crisis (e.g., serious injury, emotional breakdown, etc.) can, depending on the circumstances, spread to the entire American group.

As noted, the vast majority of the American students who study abroad take part in programs set up and run by their own or other sponsoring institutions, domestic and foreign—that is, they are not directly matriculated in foreign institutions. This rootlessness often deprives them of the counsel and protection of foreign educational institutions. Therefore, direct communication links between overseas sites and the home campus may not be in place. In the second instance, effective links are less likely to exist, and even where they do, more parties are involved and lapses can easily occur.

The whereabouts of U.S. students studying abroad without home-institutional sponsorship may not even be known to the home campus, especially if the students are considered to be On-Leave. Such students may be directly enrolled in foreign universities or participating in programs hosted by other U.S. or foreign institutions; in either case they may be out of sight and out of mind. Nevertheless, when disaster strikes overseas, the home campus is still likely to be required to make some sort of response to it. Such responses may be especially problematic because of weak communication links and the participation of multiple parties, both conditions that increase the potential for confusion and faltering actions.

When a crisis erupts overseas, even on-site personnel may not always be the first to know about it. Sometimes even those in charge of the program may not be informed immediately or fully, especially if students are separated from each other, missing in transit, or reluctant or unable to come forth. Program participants sometimes contact their family or friends first, who then may contact the home campus before the program director is even aware that a problem exists.

In the case of a more general threat to a group of students, news reports can sometimes hit the home front before overseas staff hear about it. Such media coverage may be sensationalistic or misinformed, or at least not directly applicable to American students or programs. Nevertheless it can set off varying degrees of domestic concern, even panic, and must be countered both on-site and at home with accurate and current information. The point in mentioning these many variables is to recognize fully that crises affecting U.S. students abroad have to be addressed on at least two fronts: where they erupt overseas, in their foreign cultural milieu, and on the home campus in the United States, often in conjunction with other programs sponsors and with parents.

Although crises affecting groups of students may represent a minority of the crises that study abroad personnel may have to deal with (the majority being individual crises), when group crises do occur, they are likely to cause considerable dislocation and receive the maximum of public attention and scrutiny. International threats to entire groups or programs in a given country or region, at a given time, whether due to natural disasters, travel accidents, political instability, terrorism, or economic crisis, usually occur in the public spotlight and can have a variety of public relations and diplomatic consequences. Therefore, the campus response has to be broadly based, politically sensitive, and astute. In such instances, special attention is required to provide short-term safety, security, and sustenance and may even lead to the decision to cancel the program and bring all students home—a decision with a variety of potential logistical, legal, social, and financial ramifications.

Assuming that overseas staff are indeed informed immediately about an emergency—and assuming they work in foreign universities or in large U.S.-sponsored branch campuses or agency programs—they may know precisely what to do, ideally from good training or previous experience. In this case, like foreign student advisers on American campuses, overseas program staff often are able to call upon colleagues and coworkers for support and assistance. They may or may not have need of guidance from the United States. Overseas directors may or may not be in a position to seek it, or sometimes even think about doing so at the moment.

More often than not, however, frontline personnel overseas tend to be American faculty or staff members, in residence with an American group only for an academic semester or year, or traveling with a group of students on a short-term program. Such solitary leaders often have to function entirely on their own, under stress, in an environment not fully familiar to them. It is all the more necessary, in such situations, that program directors have received training in crisis management and that highly dependable communications systems and crisis protocols have been set up in advance so that immediate contact can be made with the students' home campus and, if applicable, with the sponsoring institution.

In sum, whether the crisis happens to an international student on a U.S. college or university campus or to U.S. students studying overseas, at some point the crisis comes home, and the U.S. campus needs to be ready to respond. Since so many of the stakeholders in either situation are likely to be the same campus personnel, it makes sense that a single campus crisis management plan with strong cross-cultural dimensions is in place. This institutional plan of course can be subdivided into sections that focus on crises affecting American students in residence, those affecting visiting international students, and those affecting American students studying overseas. The key is that it should take into account all the ways in which these crises resemble, and differ, from each other.

Executing the Crisis Management Plan

Crisis *management* itself begins at the point after which all that might have been done to prevent harm or injury to students has been done, and after students have been properly warned and thoroughly oriented to their new environs. When, in spite of all possible safety and security precautions have been put in place, something serious happens to a student or a group of students. While the crisis may be on your doorstep or far away, planning for that sudden and always shocking moment can and should begin *now!* A flexible, pragmatic, and comprehensive plan synthesizes into an operational blueprint the wisdom of all institutional stakeholders—defined as those campus offices that are affected directly or indirectly when crises occur. Your own configuration of program sponsorship will naturally influence your approach to crisis management planning. Determining which institutional colleagues are the primary stakeholders in times of crisis is fundamental. Planning for crises and doing your best to manage them when they occur will require working with campus personnel with whom you otherwise may have little or no direct contact. You are likely to discover new colleagues and working partners through the process

The plan should offer general and specific guidelines for each identifiable situation. Its guidance should, very importantly and unambiguously, include the "who, what, where, when, and how" of notification, as well as recommendations for the level and degree of consultation for each decision.

Most international crisis management plans originate as plans for crises affecting domestic students. The first responsibility of the international educator in such cases is to make sure that what currently exists also serves international students—defined here as students living and learning in a different academic, social, and cultural environment from that of their native land. Typically, extra effort must be made to bring this about and to raise consciousness about the special needs and circumstances of international students.

Once the plan has been drafted by a working group of stakeholders, it must be reviewed, accepted, and thoroughly understood by everyone who will have to act or react in an emergency. Ideally, it should go through a formal institutional approval process at the highest levels of institutional administration. Further training and updating is of course essential to keep the plan current. Testing your planning against actual crisis incidents from the past or using case studies as a means of simulating a crisis situation and responding to it can be very useful.

With an effective plan and people adequately trained in its implementation, you and your staff will be prepared to take the best course of action in both the short and long run. You will know what questions to ask; how to make helpful suggestions; whom to call; why and how to record important details; and what phone numbers to have at your fingertips. If everyone is adequately briefed and trained, you will trust that your program's staff will be prepared to perform their roles effectively. The ultimate result will be that your students will get the best care possible, even under the worst circumstances. That is, after all, what they and their parents have entrusted you to provide.

Who Contributes to a Crisis Management Plan?

What follows is a list of the stakeholders who may make significant contributions to the institution's crisis management plan.

The Office of International Programs and Services and the Study Abroad Office. Regardless of campus configuration and programming, international offices always are going to be first on the firing line when international student crises hit. Furthermore, numerous campus policies and procedures need to be informed by the cross-cultural expertise of international educators. For both reasons, the international office has a primary role in setting the initiative for crisis management planning. The office's staff are in the best position to identify potential problems and will in all likelihood also be the command post for the coordination of campus actions. The international office also bears responsibility for deciding who should be on the crisis team for any particular crisis. At the same time, it must work closely with all the other campus stakeholding offices, and of course with parents.

With regard to study abroad students, the responsible office must, first and foremost, set up communications networks between the campus and any overseas faculty and staff directing campus-sponsored programs, as well as provide predeparture and on-site preparation and crisis management training. When the institution's students are participating in programs run by other entities, those tasks become much more difficult to monitor. Still, efforts can be made to understand what is and is not in place and to think through the complexities of coordination that might involve three parties: the overseas program site or educational institution, a foreign or a domestic program sponsor, and the home campus.

Risk Management Personnel. Most institutions have some sort of crisis plan that already has been vetted by the institution's risk managers. If your institution does not have an individual or office responsible for risk management, there is likely to be a standing group that is responsible for assessing risks and responsibilities in various areas, including enrollment policies. If this is the case, then your challenge is to provide information that takes into account the special circumstances that prevail in overseas locations and programs or those that specifically affect international students. A crisis—especially if it receives wide-spread media attention—seldom affects only program participants, so institutional reputation, resources, liability, and overall well-being are always to some degree at stake.

Legal Counsel. One's actions during a crisis, however well-intentioned, may later result in lawsuits against you and your institution. Ask your institution's legal counsel to perform a "legal audit" of your international programs. Keep counsel involved in the preparation of the crisis management plan. Counsel can offer important suggestions on how to protect yourself and the institution before, during, and after a crisis. A word of caution: Finding a middle ground between U.S. legal mandates and foreign practices and cultural norms is seldom easy.

The Office of Student Life. The dean of student life or student affairs is the administrator most closely affected when any enrolled student, domestic or international, is in a crisis situation on campus. Crises are seldom primarily academic. Rather, they involve the student's whole being (and overseas culture, family, and friends); the crisis can affect physical and mental health, social well-being, personal behavior, and economic security. When overseas crises come home, they carry with them not only emotional dimensions, but also logistical ones, such as locating campus housing. Therefore, the dean of student life should be fully involved in international crisis planning.

Academic Deans and Departments. Most personal and program crises sooner or later will require the administrative judgment and oversight of the academic deans. If a student is forced to withdraw prematurely from degree studies or an overseas program, someone will have to determine and approve what credit can be awarded on the basis of work done or what arrangements can be made to make up for work missed. Although academic counseling is seldom the primary need during the earliest stages of crisis response, when the crisis has passed students may need assistance in order to resume their studies. Thus, faculty should be involved in crisis management planning to some degree.

If an overseas program is canceled, provisions usually will have to be made to complete the academic work that has been interrupted, perhaps via alternative arrangements overseas, perhaps at home. If a faculty member is unable to continue leading a program overseas, a successor must be found to continue program oversight. All such decisions affect academic affairs staff, so they should be involved in planning and policy development. In the case of institution-to-institution exchanges, whether of faculty or students, administrative diplomacy may be required after a crisis.

When international students are forced to withdraw from their studies on a U.S. campus, or when an overseas program has to be adjusted or canceled because of the overseas situation, input from specialists in the affected geographical regions needs to play a part in decision-making and crisis resolution. Often, the needed expertise can be obtained from faculty members. With regard to study abroad, coordination with all permanent or rotating on-site staff and faculty directors—and with any sponsoring institution or foreign university that enrolls your students—is absolutely crucial. These professionals know the students better than anyone else on campus. They may already have faced emergency situations and have developed on-site expertise to handle them.

Counseling Center. The administrative line between assistance offered by foreign student and study abroad advisers and that available from professionally trained campus psychologists working in the campus counseling center is not always easy to draw, nor are such relations consistent from campus to campus. But because few international educators are professionally qualified to deal on their own with the severe emotional health problems that sometimes unfold under the stress of living and learning in a foreign culture, far from family and friends, one should work as closely as possible with those who are qualified to provide such counsel. On the other hand, their help may not be readily available; even if available, it may not be readily accepted by students seeking to avoid the stigma of apparent mental illness. Most students will turn first to family and friends; others will gravitate toward the advisers they know best. This means that foreign student advisers on U.S. campuses and overseas program directors are often asked, perhaps obliquely, to provide personal counsel. By consulting campus health counselors in the crisis planning stages you can prepare yourself to make appropriate referrals at moments of stress.

Most serious crises will have emotional repercussions, not only for the students immediately involved, but also for other students, their friends, and their family at home. Professional counselors should be prepared to advise administrators and help students deal with the emotional sequences of a traumatic international crisis.

Campus Ministry. Most campuses have an interfaith or spiritual life center as well as one or more chaplains. Such resources can be important in times of major crises, and they should have a role in drawing up the crisis management plan. Campus clergy or religious leaders from the local community can assist in dealing with an unfolding situation or with the aftermath of a crisis. It is not the campus's own identification with matters of the spirit that is at stake at times of crises, but that of participating students and their families. Preplanned alliances with religious institutions and personnel can provide spiritual guidance and comfort when the need arises.

Public Relations Office. When you are in the midst of an emergency, the last thing you want is to worry about saying the wrong thing or projecting the wrong image to the press. A public relations debacle, moreover, can be more damaging than the immediate crisis. Press coverage reflects on the entire institution and its community and will be taken very seriously by students, parents, alumni, donors, politicians, your colleagues, and the university president. Public relations professionals, who work with the media for a living, generally are better equipped than you are to represent the institution in times of crisis. Work with the public relations office to set up systems for sharing information, making public statements, tracking down rumors, and putting out the easily ignited fires of journalistic sensationalism. Take steps to route press inquiries through a single point.

Campus Security. Unlike most campus offices, campus security usually can be reached 24 hours a day, seven days a week. Security personnel are trained to handle crises. They are often the first to get word of a problem and thus function as a trigger for the crisis management plan. They are ideally situated to notify all concerned parties and assemble the crisis team. Work with campus security to develop protocols for their switchboard operators and become involved with their training to prepare them for this responsibility. Some issues to consider are accepting international collect calls, determining if a call involves one of your students, and contacting other university officials in the event of an extreme emergency. Utilizing campus security can be an excellent option, enabling the numerous one- and two-person international education offices to provide constant coverage.

Example: Crisis Sequence for Responding to the Death of a Student

The context and setting of an incident will naturally affect greatly how the crisis is handled. The particular crisis that generated the analysis presented below involved the murder of an international student in her off-campus apartment. The assailant was arrested the same night, and bail was not granted. The murder came at a time when more than five rapes and one other murder had been reported on the campus in the previous two months. Although there was no evidence that rape occurred in this incident, the fact that a violent crime had been committed in the midst of other violence certainly resulted in a heightened sense of vulnerability and anger among the women on campus. The family of the murdered woman had to travel from afar to attend to the details of the death.

The crisis sequence described below exemplifies how complex crises are and how much needs to be done when they occur. Events, players, and resources surrounding other crises will determine how many more or fewer tasks need to be completed. This crisis is discussed in full in the chapter on "Death of a Student" in Part II, where other scenarios and responses related to deaths of students are shared.

- *Notify the authorities.* Those who first become aware of the incident should notify campus security and the local police.

- *Verify the incident and ascertain the victim's student status.* If the victim proves to be an international student, the international student office (ISO) should assist the authorities by reviewing the student's files for emergency contacts, family details, language capabilities, and insurance coverage. Assist in identification of the victim as needed. Leaders or members of the victim's national or ethnic group on campus may be able to provide support for the ISO and the victim's family.

- *Inform the family.* Notification will not be easy. Consider language issues, cultural traditions, and time zones. In light of the circumstances and available resources, decide who should make the call. If the institution has the name of an emergency contact in the United States, consider notifying that person first and asking about the best way to notify the family. If there is no local contact person, and the institution is not familiar with the culture or is concerned that nobody in the family speaks fluent English, the embassy may serve as a valuable resource. In all cases, it is important to think out the process and its variables before making the call.

Often the authorities will notify the student's embassy directly, and the embassy official will designate an officer to handle details. The ISO should maintain close contact with the embassy. Gather basic information on the incident for dissemination to the crisis team. Once the victim has been positively identified, notify the victim's embassy, if the authorities have not already done so.

- *Convene the crisis team.* After notifying the crisis team pursuant to the crisis management plan, confirm lines of communication, contact times, and methods. Confirm responsibility for components of the crisis both within the team and within the ISO. Coordinate and redistribute ISO staff workload.

- *Identify a liaison to the family.* Establish a phone and e-mail reference list for use during the crisis, and begin a log of events and people contacted or involved in the crisis. Identify and ensure observance of culturally sensitive issues and traditions related to the victim. Other members of the crisis team, in addition to those discussed above, may include the university switchboard, representatives of the victim's embassy, and experts on the victim's culture recruited from among the faculty, community, and student body.

- *Coordinate the university's public response.* Make sure all members of the crisis team and relevant others understand that all requests for public statements and interviews are to be handled by a single university representative, usually within the university relations office. Identify that representative. Coach others on how best to refer press and parents to that person. In some cases, parents may learn of the incident prior to official notification, or the media may seek a response or interviews prior to official identification of the victim's family. Refer all callers to the designated spokesperson. Prepare a statement to be made to the family by telephone and in writing soon after official notification of the incident. The statement should be made by the highest university officer available; it should be done with the assistance of interpreters and the ISO. Prepare a statement for the media and begin to accumulate further information and resources to use in responding to follow-up requests. Agree within the team on an information management strategy.

- *Coordinate your planning with the victim's family.* Obtain information regarding the family's wishes for disposition of the body, and ask the family to identify a spokesperson. That person will become a key contact for the crisis team. Determine whether the family will travel to the United States to take care of the victim's affairs and accompany the body home.

    Should the family decide to travel to the United States, preparations should be made to receive and host them. Form a delegation to meet the family at the airport. Inform airport security (through campus security or local police). Arrange for a private room to meet with the family upon arrival. At this time, condolences can be offered, a brief overview of the situation can be given to the family, and the immediate wishes of the family can be determined. Preserve the family's privacy. If the family is to be registered at a hotel, it is recommended that the room be reserved in the name of someone other than the family. Media and well-meaning community members often intrude on family. The development of a daily schedule for the family will depend on family's wishes, the cultural issues involved, and the extent of the cultural resources the ISO has been able to marshal. Should the family or kin not wish to visit, work with the family and the embassy for disposition of the body and estate. Rules and procedures differ from state to state regarding the disposition of property. Normally a death certificate is required along with proof that whomever disposes is a family member. The presence of a member of the ISO helps to speed such business because the language needed is sometimes complex. Suggest and contact a funeral home, assist with funeral arrangements, and help the funeral director and the family understand cultural differences regarding funerals. Repatriation is an act usually conducted by a funeral home. The ISO, if there is one, may need to assist, plan, or make such arrangements. Contact a reputable moving company and help the family negotiate shipping arrangements.

    Advise the family about the victim's insurance coverage and offer to help with formalities. Help the family understand applicable U.S. judicial procedures. (Before doing so, however, consult with university counsel.) The procedures of our country may not make sense to those of another. In criminal matters, ask the district attorney to meet with the family.

- *Work with the community.* As soon as you are able, involve students from the victim's national or ethnic group as part of the crisis team. Meet with leaders of the group to review the impact of the death on the community. The meeting should cover facts of the incident; safety issues; the availability of counseling; the family's wishes; and planning for a memorial service. In the case of a violent death, students and parents will raise questions about violence in the United States. Authorities and experts should be invited to speak publicly on these issues. Alert the speakers regarding language, bluntness, and slang. It is important that the ISO staff listen closely to what is being said and how it is being said. While the language may be clear to an American and even to students from the nationality group, the intent and the rationale behind the statements may not. Staff of the ISO should be prepared to "interpret" these statements to members of the nationality group.

  Send a letter to the entire international student body explaining the circumstances surrounding the crisis and offering assistance and counsel. Ask the campus media to provide information about the crisis without infringing on the privacy of the family or those working to resolve the crisis. Retain and update the distribution network for future dissemination of information during the resolution of the crisis.

  Maintain contacts with local officials. The relationship between the local officials and the crisis team is one of mutual help. Local officials rely on the ISO for interpreters, access to the family, and information of a cultural nature. The ISO relies on officials to provide information to the family and to assist with certain legal and logistical aspects of the crisis.

- *Plan a memorial service.* A memorial service is important in the resolution of the crisis, because it gives the campus, community, and the family an opportunity to pay respects to the deceased and to begin resolving their feelings about the events. However, such a service may be rejected by the family at first. Let them know that in our culture a memorial service is a sign of respect and honor, not an event to draw unwarranted attention to the deceased. The memorial service, if offered on campus, should focus on helping the campus come to terms with its grief. The funeral is a more intimate setting of saying farewell to the deceased.

- *After the crisis.* Request the registrar and faculty to remove the name of the deceased from current lists to avoid embarrassing correspondence from being sent to the family. Assign a team member to monitor bills and payments, and maintain contact with the family. Consider gathering and binding mementos from fellow students and from the memorial service. Create an appropriate campus memorial for the student. Convene the team to assess the lessons learned from the crisis and to make any necessary modifications to the crisis management plan.

Conclusion

Given the many different types of individual and group crises that can and do occur, it is imperative to think through, in advance and in general, what sorts of preparations need to be made to anticipate any and all emergency situations. Campus, organizational, and overseas planning begins by drawing up—or modifying and extending an existing institutional plan—a Crisis Management Plan that takes into account the cross-cultural dimensions inherent in crises affecting students living and learning far from home. The plan may be seen as an abstract document until a crisis strikes, when it will prove its worth in providing the rational guidance needed to set up an operational crisis response team appropriate to the particulars of a given situation; then clear, pragmatic guidance during the evolving phases of the crisis; and finally, when the dust settles, a means of evaluating what worked and what did not, in preparation for the next crisis, even if it is a vastly different set of circumstances at a much later date.

PART II.

Crises Involving International Students on U.S. Campuses

Chapter 2

Preparing for and Responding to Specific Types of Natural Catastrophes or Disasters

Julie Ann Rabaey

There are all kinds of natural disasters, and most of us think they won't happen to us: from extreme heat to frigid cold; parched and barren dry earth from droughts; soaking, overflowing rivers from floods; scorching fire; destructive earthquakes; and every possible variation of these occurrences. The experiences of international educators who have lived through these disasters with students under their wings will help prepare and guide any adviser or program director facing a natural disaster.

Scenario

"When you think of natural disasters you think, we'll escape or we'll bus students somewhere." This reflection, provided by Anneke J. Larrance, International Student Adviser at St. Lawrence University in upstate Canton, New York (see Appendix B), expresses the attitude many of us have. We think that there will always be "a way out." Larrance and her colleagues learned a different lesson, though, in January 1998, as they lived through an ice storm of unprecedented meteorological history. She reported to Julie Ann Rabaey, "Those option— 'escape' or 'bus students somewhere'—were not available to us because of the ban on traveling. It wasn't that we could say, 'let's get students someplace where there was water and electricity. That wasn't an option. The option was how to keep them warm right where we were.'"

Responding to Natural Catastrophes

When natural disaster or catastrophe occurs on your campus or around your campus community, there are many implications for international education areas. International students often do not have family in the host country. The international education staff—or on large campuses, leaders of country-specific groups—are often called upon to be the students' support network, tasked with finding alternative places for the students to stay if they are not allowed to remain on campus, providing transportation, and providing supportive services from resources within those groups or communities.

These are areas that may be your direct responsibility as an international education professional. You may communicate to officials that the needs of international students may be quite different than those of domestic students. Students' finances may be very strained, since federal financial assistance is not available to international students in the United States. You may need to intervene when there are cross-cultural misunderstandings. It may be appropriate to provide ceremonies or special recognition for or on behalf of the international community.

For students who are on study abroad programs, the crisis will affect them as well, even if they are not physically present on campus. You may need to communicate to students and exchange partners abroad after the event and during the recovery period.

Considerations in the Face of Disaster

International Students May Be Displaced

In the event of an evacuation, international students most often will not have a place to go to within the United States for the days or weeks after a natural disaster. You may find yourself taking students into your own home, relocating them to a neighboring community shelter, or finding alternative housing for them on a short-term basis.

Insight: Preparation during orientation. "Our campus has the policy of trying to evacuate as many students as possible within 48 hours of a possible strike when we are under a hurricane warning. Based on this, when our international students first arrive we ask them to make "contingency" plans in case this situation should arise. We suggest that they connect with their host family, student mentor, or an American student that lives "inland" so that they have someplace to go or someone to travel with to a safe place. Our office assists students that are unable to find someplace to go during an evacuation.

"When a hurricane occurred, a few students stayed with us and we found that our home became a gathering place for students in the vicinity. It became clear that it was important for the students to maintain contact with each other. Upon reflection, it was possibly a critical support network for them since they were staying in homes with people they didn't know that well and were unable to be with family and friends from their home country."

Insight: Students at a temporary shelter. "We were very lucky because the ice storm hit during a vacation [break period]...But many of our graduate students who were international students, were in the village...There was a huge area where the electricity was completely knocked out several days and so anyone who lived in the village in an apartment didn't have any way to heat their apartment. It was quite cold; they didn't have any way to keep food because the electricity was off. But Clarkson University [a nearby university; ed. note] had some generators set up and so students, international and American students, were allowed to come to campus to sleep in the Student Center. Many of the international students did. They were given food there as were any people in the community. They were able to...stay warm that way."

Insight: Students staying with volunteers and/or in neighboring communities. "...we enlisted local community organizations and advertised in church bulletins and also through the University of Iowa staff publication and on e-mail and also through the university hospital asking for volunteer, temporary volunteer host families to help students...put them up for a few days or weeks until they were able to get into housing... we offered information sessions for potential host families for new international students and tried to clarify expectations and what role they might play. As best we could, we reviewed the potential host families to screen out any poor or inappropriate matches."

Insight: Provide information to displaced students. At Gustavus Adolphus College, when we attended meetings, campus administrators suggested that a mailing be sent to parents as a way to keep them informed of decisions. We needed to remind officials that the families of international students may not receive these announcements for possibly a week or longer.

International Students May Not Seek Traditional U.S. Counseling

During or after a crisis, international students, who may be unfamiliar with or hesitant to use counseling services, may not seek out the multitude of opportunities to "talk out feelings" with on campus counselors, volunteer psychotherapists, or representatives from various social service, volunteer, and/or religious organizations. International students may not seek such assistance from a perceived stranger. They may not feel comfortable walking into a counseling center. Peer groups may need to be organized and other alternative methods to reach out to members of the international community.

"We had meetings with all the resident assistants as well as the students. We had people come over from Psychological Services and Residential Education. They kept saying, 'in two or three weeks you're going to start feeling it.' Suddenly an RA stood up and said, 'I'm fed up with this. This was a little earthquake; nobody was hurt. Nobody was injured and yet you're making it into this big drama and you're telling everybody that in three weeks they're going to come down with some depression and you're just kind of making them do that.'…Instead of saying let's get back to normal and if people need to talk, we're here; you're projecting on them a depression that they probably won't have."

There was an All-Student Orientation scheduled for all students as they returned to campus. "Gustie chats" were scheduled by counselors and described as "opportunities to talk about how to cope with loss, deal with stress, and adjust to a new academic schedule and changes in living conditions." Student Affairs staff inquired if we would want a specific meeting for international students. In consultation with counseling staff, an International Student Gathering was held at an alternative time during orientation. The intention was not to detract international students from the opportunity to attend a "Gustie chat," but to provide an alternative that was intended to be informative as well as consoling.

International Students May Experience Unexpected Financial Losses

Students unable to travel back to campus may face unanticipated hotel bills. They may have to purchase additional clothing to prepare for the weather or to replace damaged items. If the students are evacuated, they may be unable to legally work if the campus is closed.

One experience: "Students typically were renters. They didn't have renter's insurance. One student lost his dissertation because the disks were destroyed...they lost their books. There was profound loss of property. I think probably the most serious impact it had was that because there were so many displaced U.S. citizens, the newly arriving [international] students found a totally changed housing market because the housing prices just about doubled overnight."

"...Many of the students who come are also not necessarily wealthy...I think around the world you can get cotton clothes pretty easily, but cotton sweaters are not necessarily popular around the world. Sweaters to most people means wool. How do you tell somebody from Norway to bring a cotton sweater? Just as in Arizona wool is more expensive, cotton is more expensive in some of these countries. How many students go out and buy a new wardrobe? Buying a wardrobe for hot weather is also weird...How many students leave their winter coats at home, and then are financially unprepared to buy those extra things..."

Insight: International students excluded from federal financial assistance. Regulations for Federal Emergency Management Agency (FEMA) financial assistance changed in 1998, and no longer provide relief for nonimmigrants legally in the United States.

One experience: "We immediately worked with FEMA because we knew FEMA had a compensation program for disasters...We were able to do a fairly good job of working through their bureaucracy to get compensation for most of our residents for loss of goods...The FEMA folks I talked to seemed pretty disgusted that tax dollars were going to non-U.S. citizens."

International students in the United States do not qualify for financial assistance from FEMA according to "Response and Recovery Directorate Policy No. 4430.140 C: Policy of Verification of Citizenship, Qualified Alien Status and Eligibility for Disaster Assistance" [3/2/98]. The change in policy was to provide guidance for implementing Title IV of the Personal Responsibility and Work Opportunity Reconciliation Act of 1996, P.L. 104-193, which complies with the intent of Congress to prohibit "federal public benefit" to persons who are not United States citizens, non-citizen nationals, or "qualified aliens." It is to be applied to all disasters declared on or after February 28, 1998. All FEMA Regional Offices, National Processing Service Centers, and Disaster Field Offices are expected to follow this policy.

It is important that affected institutions are aware of these legalities, so that financial assistance for your students can be obtained from other sources: (e.g., donations, the campus insurance policy, and relief organizations). The assistance of others needs to be obtained so as to develop a fair system of distribution of funds. Communicate to the students the process of filing for assistance.

Insight: Receiving donation funds to assist students. If funds to assist international students are received, the international office should assist in the development of criteria and a method to distribute the money that will be perceived as "fair" by all students. Include others on a committee to help make decisions and determinations of awards.

One experience: "We...got a donation from a private agency for $500 and we used it to pay for two scholarships for students that had been affected to purchase books. Then I think we did things on a one-on-one basis...with students that had been affected, to try to find solutions to their specific concerns..."

Insight: IRS provisions. If the disaster occurs around filing time for federal (or state) income tax, there are filing implications. An Internal Revenue Service representative should be invited to conduct a session for international students on how to file late returns. Students should be advised as to how to claim and recover losses on tax forms.

As far as IRS provisions for recovery, the intent of claiming losses is to reduce the amount owed to the federal government. Unfortunately, for most foreign/international students who have not paid federal income tax, the IRS will not provide reimbursement for losses claimed. Therefore, in reality, students will not have monetary benefit from the IRS for their losses.

International Students May Lack Sufficient Transportation

Without a U.S. driver's license or a car, it may be difficult to evacuate when necessary and return when it is clear to do so. Sometimes students are expected to clean out personal belongings at set times and you may need to arrange transportation for them to return. You may wish to let others know of the limited transportation options for students to enlist volunteer drivers. At Syracuse University, after a devastating microburst thunderstorm characterized by devastating wind shears, when it was time for the 440 students (and family members) living in hotels to move back to campus, a systematic move-in was organized, with resident advisers helping the move-in process at both ends. Buses, chartered by the university, departed on a regular schedule. All the students were notified the previous night as to the time of their scheduled departure. The organization made a very difficult process much more palatable.

Explaining Cross-Cultural Differences at Times of Crisis

"..The [International Programs and Services] office was asked by the director of the Malaysian Student Services office in Chicago to intervene with a county coroner on behalf of the family of a Muslim student. The student had been transferred to another hospital and had died there. Because the fire was arson, the resulting deaths were potential homicides. The coroner in that county wanted to do an autopsy, which would have been a violation of Islamic principles. However, the case was made that the cause of death (smoke inhalation) had already been determined, so no autopsy was needed. Thus the family's wishes were followed with no interference in investigative procedures."

At the University of Iowa, cross-cultural differences resulted in serious misinterpretation by the media and the community. A Chinese student and her two friends attempted to retrieve artwork necessary for her application to a Master's degree program. They saw a canoe nearby with the University of Iowa name on it. They grabbed it, understanding that they were University of Iowa students and this was on university property, so they could use it. They got in it and started down the rapidly flowing river. The boat capsized. The students were floating down the river, holding on to the boat. It was a very serious situation, made more difficult for rescue teams because of communication difficulties. The students were rescued. The news TV teams were there, taking pictures of...what they called the "joy ride." The Chinese students were embarrassed because they had lost face in front of the community. The police arrested the students and had them stay overnight in jail because boating on the river was not allowed. It appeared that the students were laughing when being rescued. The immigration specialist at the University intervened to inform the police that in 'Chinese culture its proper to laugh when you're really embarrassed.'

After a major fire at one campus, cultural differences hindered the investigation process. "Several [International Programs and Services] staff members noted that some of the investigative team members (all Americans) were not aware of cultural differences that caused them to be misunderstood by internationals and vice versa. For instance, one detective, in interviewing a Japanese female, continued to talk very fast, even though he was asked twice to speak more slowly. The student kept her eyes lowered, as a sign of respect, but an American interviewer could very well interpret that reaction as a sign of nervousness, or question avoidance, or guilt, or lack of cooperation."

Arranging Memorials or Special Events of Recognition

"You can imagine the feeling that they had evacuating, leaving their things behind and as scary as that is and then not to know how graduation would take place...when school began in the fall, two Norwegian students came back to salvage what they could of the belongings that had been left behind for all of them and we went to our president and he said, 'we will come and graduate you in Norway.' He went and they graduated them on Labor Day of 1998 which was wonderful because then all of the parents and aunts and uncles could be there for the graduation in Norway...we sent a box of gowns and diplomas and it became a wonderful replacement for the official ceremony."

Contacting the Embassy

Keep phone numbers, e-mails and fax numbers for Consulates and Embassies at home as well as at the office. When one cannot enter your office, it is important to have contact possibilities from home.

Assisting Students with INS Petitions

International students may be severely affected financially since they may not have sufficient insurance to cover property losses and they are excluded from FEMA financial assistance. Also, students have limited work options. If evacuated from campus, they will not be able to work. You may wish to assist individuals apply for work permission based on economic necessity.

"What we found was that our students that had been affected needed emergency assistance to work and they needed to be relieved from the full-time course load requirement...We made the list of the counties in Florida and the parishes in Louisiana that had been affected and we went to the Immigration and Naturalization Service...our proposal was...that they establish an emergency provision for students that are hit by a crisis… they could work if they documented that they had been affected by the hurricane. They could work more than 20 hours a week; they would be eligible for off-campus employment authorization and they could reduce their course load to a part-time course load."

In one case, a student had submitted his optional practical training application to INS prior to the tornado. He was living off-campus and had listed that address on the application. The tornado extensively damaged the residence and he had to find an alternate place to live. When I heard of this change in address from him, I knew that he would not receive his Employment Authorization Document (EAD) since the Post Office is instructed not to forward legal documents from the INS. I contacted the Student and Scholar Regulatory Representative (SSRR) and our District INS representative to change the address on the pending application.

Assisting and Communicating with Students on Study Abroad Experiences

You may need to help the students who were not present during the disaster to comprehend the damage. You will also prepare them for their eventual return. Communicate and provide information to students and exchange partners abroad.

"What we did … was to collect newspaper articles and mail those to the students who were abroad and a number of them commented that that was extremely helpful to them, that it had all seemed too unreal and they didn't have enough information to understand the extent of the damage. By actually having a newspaper in their hands that they could read really helped…."

During the ice storm, a study abroad student briefly returned to campus to take care of bills and to confirm her independent study plan in Paris. Because of the storm, she had to remain on campus and did not return to Paris in time to take final exams for the first semester. "And that meant that I had to write a letter in French to explain this later, and would they please take her back. But it means we didn't get grades for her first semester because she didn't take the final exam and most of the grades are based upon an exam. Because it was my program…I was able to look through all her materials and give them to a colleague in the French Department and we gave her credits anyway. So we worked it out, but it could have been worse…But it was a lot more complicated in anxiety producing, certainly."

"…We did communicate with our exchange partners to reassure them that their own particular exchange students were safe. But I think we did that a little later than they might have liked. With hindsight I think we would have done that sooner because some of them contacted us…. Because we knew everyone was okay, we didn't feel the same urgency they did."

Preparing in Advance

Supplies

In preparation for many categories of natural catastrophes/disasters, the following supplies are recommended to have on hand:

- Flashlights and extra batteries

- Portable, battery-operated radio and extra batteries

- First aid kit and manual

- Emergency food and water

- Manual can opener

- Essential medicines

- Cash and credit cards

- Sturdy shoes

Access to Supplies and Possessions

- Some of these disaster supplies may be available to international students in a centralized location that should be communicated to them in advance.

- Students preparing to go abroad should bring items with them and retain them in their residences in the event of an emergency.

- Students should be reminded to keep all essential documents in a safe place (e.g., passports, immigration documents), easily and quickly accessible during a storm, fire or other disaster. Copies should be on file elsewhere, such as in the international education office.

- Recent campus-wide disasters, such as the tornadoes that struck the Gustavus Adolphus College campus and city of St. Peter in 1998 suggest that copies of all crucial documents should be kept with a family member or friend in another city as well, in case the students' own originals and copies are lost in the disaster.

Immediate Response to Disaster

- Turn on a battery-operated radio or television to get the latest emergency information. Be certain that the international students and U.S. students abroad know which local channels carry the best emergency broadcasts.

- Remember to help others who may require special assistance— infants, elderly people, and people with disabilities. Give first aid where appropriate. Do not move seriously injured persons unless they are in immediate danger of further injury. Call for help.

- If evacuation is necessary, inform someone outside the affected area where you are going.

- Take pictures of the damage for insurance claims.

- Ask out-of-state relative or friend to serve as a contact. After a disaster, it's often easier to call long distance.

Implications for International Education Areas

- During orientation, provide instructions on how and when to call 911, police, and/or the fire department.

- Prepare students for weather "test" alarm sounds that may occur on a periodic basis versus the sounds that may signal an actual emergency.

- International students and students abroad most often do not have relatives or friends "out-of-state." Some alternatives for communication purposes at time of crisis:

    ☞ *Establish a way to have your students to contact you in the event of an emergency. You may wish to have your home phone number listed within the phone directory. If you have an unlisted phone number, you may want to consider an emergency communication plan with other staff.*

    ☞ *If you have a cell phone, distribute that number for emergency use only. The purchase of a cell phone for office use only (paid for by the office operating budget) may be a worthwhile investment. Be sure it goes home with the "on-call" staff member each evening, weekend and holiday period.*

    ☞ *Consider host/friendship families, leaders of student groups, and campus emergency numbers for such an emergency communication plan.*

    ☞ *Have e-mail addresses for all students on file both at home and in the office. If electricity is available, keep students informed via e-mail.*

    ☞ *Record cell phone numbers for students and keep them on file both at home and in the office. When electricity fails, cell phones should still be operable.*

Crisis-Specific Insights and Recommendations

Earthquakes

Insight. "Virtually every structure on campus received damage. The collapsed parking structure was the most visible symbol, which was published around the country. The campus had over 350 million dollars in damage and has been ranked as the single largest disaster to befall an institution of higher education in the United States....In this earthquake, everything that could break, broke. Fires damaged the Science buildings, and numerous buildings were condemned. Students were killed in an apartment collapse across the street from campus. All of the campus dorms were ordered to vacate…"

"…We had to evacuate the entire dorm.…I had about 330 students in the dorm, all undergraduates, a number of them international.…[when returning to their room to collect medicine and essentials], we told them to.. put the message on their answering machine straight away saying that they were okay and that they would make contact with parents and family members as soon as they could..[to say that] there has been an earthquake; I am okay; I will call you when things settle down."

Extreme Heat

Insight. "Students were coming in at the middle of August, many of them from northern Europe. They have never had experienced 117-degrees heat. We had to remind them…drink water, not soda; put a wet cloth around your neck so the blood in the jugular vein is cooled off as it goes up to the brain; wear hats; wear long sleeved clothes…How do you wear long sleeves in that kind of heat? The sunburn factor is tremendous, especially for pale skin.…use an umbrella to shade yourself from the sun…the dehydration factor… headache factors… all have to be anticipated."

Impact to international education areas: "We actually had one student go home; she was from Scotland, and part of her problem was dealing with this kind of heat. She could not take it."

One response: Arizona State University provides information during orientation on heat related illnesses. The information includes the prevention, causes, and symptoms of as well as treatment for heat cramps, heat exhaustion, and heat stroke.

Fires (House and Building)

Insight. "I received a call from the campus police telling me that our building…was completely engulfed in flames. I called my staff; we all ended up going on campus and watch [the building] burn to the ground. We had immediate questions, first of all, whether or not anyone had been in the building…Next morning the building, parts of it were still standing…Most of the second floor had fallen on to the first floor. There was one office on the first floor that was completely destroyed…They let us go in the building before they tore it down to see if there was anything they could salvage....We spent the weekend sorting through papers, everything we had salvaged from the building. Computer disks were destroyed...computers themselves just melted. So we were able to salvage nothing that had been on the computer. We salvaged a lot of paper. It was unusable because it had either absorbed water or the smell was so phenomenal that we didn't want to go near it...Unfortunately most of our student records had been completely destroyed. They were in an office that burnt completely. Anything archival had went. So we were left with all kinds of paper, but much of it wasn't anything you'd want..."

"...One or more arsonists set fire to a three-story, off-campus housing unit in Carbondale, Illinois....occupants on the third floor were trapped, with the result that five university students died and eight other residents suffered various injuries, including three who jumped from third floor windows...Since all the injured had been transported to the Emergency Room of the local hospital, the [International Studies and Programs] director and assistant director went there to coordinate activities that might require information from students' records. IPS involvement was important because a majority of the residents affected by the fire were international students at SIUC."

Implications. There was a need to recreate files following the fire. Consider that students might be able to provide photocopies of various documents that were in the files.

As part of orientation for international students and scholars, be sure to discuss evacuation of buildings during emergency situations.

Floods and Flash Floods

Insight. "...The University of Iowa was affected by [the flood] because the Iowa River flows through the center of campus.... The international population...the most effect was upon newly arriving students for the orientation program in the beginning of fall classes because the campus was partially underwater at the time, temporary housing which had been arranged for the students in the dormitories was unavailable because the dormitories were flooded and so we didn't have as many places for people to stay as we had planned.

Insight: Health risk. "They made certain that people were there to give us tetanus shots because we all had to have the shots because we had been sandbagging and there was concern for our health."

Impact to international education: "A lot of phone calls would come in from all over the world actually to find out about people. Information was getting out. We had parents calling from other countries wondering about their students. Sometimes students called their parents and their parents hadn't heard about it ..."

Response Considerations

- The International Office has to maintain contact with students and assist them to find places to stay at such times of crisis. Since homes of community volunteer friendship families might also be damaged, students may need to stay on a nearby university campus or with volunteer families in neighboring towns.

- International applicants for the next year should be notified of the crisis. Due to the expected shortage of housing for the next academic year, applicants may need to be told to defer their admission for a semester.

- Study abroad students may wonder what the campus was like, what could they do to help. Information about the crisis needs to get out.

- Efforts must be made to communicate with parents.

- Information dissemination may not seem like high priority initially, when people are isolated and taking care of basic humanitarian needs is critical.

What to Expect After a Disaster Recovery

The University of Wisconsin-Extension, Department of Cooperative Education provides "The Disaster Handbook," designed to help county extension agents provide immediate assistance. In it are described four phases associated with disaster recovery: historic, honeymoon, disillusionment, and reconstruction (see Appendix H). While it is interesting and important to understand the theoretical background to such phases, most pertinent to this publication are the implications for international education areas. Several aforementioned educators have provided insights that are helpful to anyone who finds themselves "recovering" after a disaster. As one goes through the historic, the honeymoon, the disillusionment and the reconstruction stages, let them understand that their experiences are not unique or unwarranted. These first-person accounts will provide some assistance in that regard.

Historic Phase

"The thing that happens in a disaster is that not only are your international students in a disaster, you are also...as an international student advisor, you may not be able to respond the way that you would have thought you would respond because you also may have your own personal family, and your own personal problems. In my case I had my own home that I had to keep warm so that pipes didn't freeze. My home was turned into a mini-shelter. There were five other people besides my family living there so I had responsibilities at home to deal with...The lesson to be learned in my particular case is that although you may have every plan right down pat, you may not respond the way you'd like to because of your own circumstances."

"Practically every individual working on campus or attending school experienced personal hardship and loss. It's a good thing the school closed temporarily to give everybody time to recover and clean up their own personal 'mess'...and also recover psychologically and emotionally. The first week or so everyone was numb with the magnitude of clean up."

The assistance you provide may take a tremendous amount of your time and energy. You may be called upon immediately to respond and assist. "When a disaster like this happens you have to put everything aside. I was spending 20-hour days for three weeks on this issue." "I found...that there is a psychological exhaustion that comes with these things while you're experiencing them and just survival seems to take a little more energy."

Communication is often difficult. You may find that you may not be able to receive messages or contact others due to the extent of damage. It may also be difficult to find out information on decisions being made for coping, and recovery efforts planned. "When the tornado hit Gustavus, it also hit the town of St. Peter and my home being near the campus, I found that I was in a kind of information vacuum so that I felt estranged from the campus. It was unusual to be so near and yet so far. We didn't have any television to watch, so we didn't actually see the national or local reports…Communication seems to be the hardest thing. When your phones are down and you have to actually walk the streets lined with fallen trees and downed power and phone lines, trying to find something out, but knowing you probably won't, it is a very discomforting thing."

Honeymoon Phase

For "survivors," there is a strong sense of having shared with others a dangerous, catastrophic experience and having lived through it. Supported and often encouraged by promises of many kinds of help, clean-up efforts begin. There is anticipation that more help soon will be available. Preexisting community groups and emergency community groups are especially important resources during this period.

A common theme for almost all crisis recovery situations is the generosity and outpouring of help including food, clothing, and donations of necessary goods. There are heroic efforts and volunteers to provide assistance to those affected. One may be overwhelmed with the amount of offers to help.

"[The international students] were amazed at the emergency response. They said that 'in our countries all these people would be dead because they don't have the emergency response like that.'"

Students may be involved in helping others: "…there were volunteers who came and our international students joined those groups…and I think that was very satisfying for them to be involved, instead of just sitting around, feeling lost."

"This was a national disaster so there were groups from all over the Northeast and other areas coming in, electrical crews to try to put power back on line and so they were actually being housed in the Student Center as well. There was another shelter in the town. So the impact really for international students was minimized by the fact that the disaster was so great that the whole community was responding and there were things available for everybody in the community…"

Disillusionment Phase

"…We felt it important that we deliver the services. So we started delivering services in our temporary space. Four years later we were still delivering services in that space because while initially everybody said, 'oh my, my, aren't you wonderful,' what that boiled down to was, 'oh my, my, my these folks can work anywhere.' So we worked in rather bizarre conditions for about four years….Some of people were doing a lot of working at home or renting office space from somebody else a week at a time…We ended up with files in one location, people in another location…If we had to do it over again, we would have immediately thrown up our hands and said, 'we can't do anything.'"

"Given the size of this flood, the size of the damage that occurred, we were somewhat lost in the limelight of things…But the folks at International House felt very marginalized because…they were the only folks in the campus community who were affected. Their living environments were affected. …the university was not overly excited about promoting too much of the negative aspects of the flood…Through time more and more press appeared but it wasn't that much. Any time there was an article posted we posted it all over the building so the people could be aware of what was going on …"

Reconstruction Phase

"We are in the reconstruction stage. There are several international students who have since graduated or completed their exchange program. Frequent questions include the appearance of the campus and how we are functioning during the continual rebuilding efforts. In a sense they need to maintain the contact and hear our progress to gain a feeling of recovery. Our office had been moved to a trailer for many weeks so we readily inform them that we have returned to our original office space and have new carpet, painted walls, and new furniture. The students have a sense of loss from the destruction of the international residence hall, but we inform them plans are in place for rebuilding a new international house.

Coping

"…An international office is not really a key component in a disaster recovery operation. It's the engineers, construction workers, physical plant operations people...they're the ones who make the difference...and all those who know communication technology. We study abroad advisers and foreign student advisers just cope day to day, and try to make everyone's life a little more cheerful by keeping a positive outlook and a sense of humor!"

"I think one of the big issues that affects professionals in international student service when there is a crisis is that resources are siphoned off to be used for the crisis. You have students coming in with regular problems that they would have come in with the week before. You're so tempted to say to them, 'I can't deal with you now.' It's very important to have a plan in place so that if there is a crisis, a certain percentage of time will be still allocated in some way for more routine problems that don't "seem routine" to the students that are affected by them. They seem important even though they are not the earthquake, the hurricane, or the flood. They still seem critically important to those students....I can remember needing to refer a student to the Counseling Center and the Counseling Center was totally inundated with people who had lost their homes. This student who was going through a different kind of personal concern just seemed to be the lowest priority."

Conclusion

Show by words and actions that you care. A friendly arm around troubled shoulders or a few words of support can help tremendously. Offer specific types of help or ask how you can help. Don't be afraid of saying or doing the wrong thing. And keep helping. Even small, kind deeds will mean a lot to others.

Amid hugs going around during the recovery, physical contact may be uncomfortable for some international students. Provide other ways to express your support. In some cases, students will be frustrated by unanswered questions. Attempt to follow up with key administrators to resolve difficulties. At times, you cannot provide answers to all questions, but be willing to offer help.

If a catastrophe occurs on your own campus or nearby community, you as an international educator will cope much better during the shock of the occurrence if you are prepared. The impact of such an event on your life and the lives of your students will always be with you, but the experiences of others who have been through similar disasters can be a valuable resource in your time of need.

Chapter 3

Advising Students Facing Political and Financial Crises Back Home

Sidney (Skip) Greenblatt and Julie Kyllonen Rose

Scenario 1

May 3-4, 1989. Peiming is distraught. She spent the whole night watching CNN's coverage of the massacre in Tiananmen Square. She was inconsolable, couldn't eat, couldn't sleep, couldn't move from the TV set. The world seemed to have been turned upside down. The People's Liberation Army, the people's own army, had opened fire on the very ones they were supposed to protect.

Kanwu lived far from Peiming, but he too couldn't eat or sleep. How could Deng Xiaoping, China's best hope for a brighter future, have brought such shame on the nation? He felt that shame deeply and personally, and he was paralyzed by it. He wanted to dig a hole in the floor and disappear.

Right around the corner, Ting Ling and Zhang Zu were huddled together in tears. They had to do something right away. They packed a few belongings, leapt into the car and drove all the way to JFK Airport in New York, hoping to catch the next plane back to Beijing. They had decided to add their lives to those already sacrificed at Tiananmen. They were turned away at the ticket counter and forced to return to campus, where they didn't answer the phone for fear that the Chinese consulate in New York already may have sent agents to campus. Word was out within three days that some students on campus were agents of the government surreptitiously taking notes on the behavior of their fellows. The Americans seemed concerned, but they were blissfully ignorant of the true dimensions of the tragedy. What to do? Where to go? Would they be exiles for the rest of their lives?

Scenario 2

The appearance of the young woman who has come to see you is shocking. She is pale and very thin, and her clothes hang on her. She reveals to you that she has lost 30 pounds in the past six months, and is down to 88 pounds. She cannot register for the semester until she repays significant outstanding debt to the university. Her department is willing to provide a graduate assistantship for the following term, provided she repays. She has no food, "but a friend is sending her some money soon." She hasn't paid the university health service fee, isn't registered, and has no health insurance. Her parents do not want her to return home because the Asian financial crisis has seriously strained their finances. The student is desperate yet proud, talented and hard-working, but doesn't know what to do. What can you do to help her?

Handling Political and Economic Crises

While the political and economic dimensions of crisis are rarely addressed in the literature on the advising and counseling international students and scholars, they have been with us from the beginning of educational exchange. Recent events have drawn this reality into sharp focus.

In these times, the electronic lifeline of international educators, the INTER-L listserv, has been swamped with inquiries about the special relief provisions of immigration regulations stimulated by financial crisis in Asia and a score of other political, economic, and social crises affecting international students on our campuses and U.S. students abroad. These crises range from chronic concerns over the viability of Boris Yeltsin and his administration to the after-effects of NATO's accidental bombing of the Chinese embassy in Belgrade.

Such cases face international educators with an even larger need to keep abreast of world events, economic and political, and to prepare contingency plans for natural and other disasters that will personally impact their students. Reading several national, regional, and a local newspaper for balance, is wise, since different editorial philosophies present different "takes" on what is occurring and how it likely will impact the United States. A solid grounding in U.S. government and recent U.S. diplomatic history are also important to help judge what may happen next.

Many of the myriad events unfolding around the world affect one or another segment of the international populations we serve. The political crisis engendered by the takeover of the U.S. embassy in Iran in 1978 reverberated into the depths of international education. Iranian students had to report, in person, to the district offices of the Immigration and Naturalization Service to be accounted for and counted. Confusion about frozen funds frayed nerves to the point of breaking. The Gulf War in 1991 brought animosities and hatreds to the surface on U.S. campuses, igniting clashes between Arab and Israeli students, Muslims and Jews, and Americans and citizens of the Arab World.

Helping Students Sort Out Their Situations

International educators have learned firsthand that political, economic, and financial crises can devastate their students. The Asian financial crisis that began in 1997-98; the Gulf War of the early 1990s; the Iranian "assets freeze" in 1979-1980; and the Nigerian student payment problems in the late 1970s and early 1980s have all affected large numbers of students throughout the world. For those international educators who have all they can do just to keep up with ever-changing U.S. immigration laws and counseling in instances of personal crises on their campuses, these larger crises have come as a shock and have required heightened resourcefulness and problem-solving skills.

A crisis produces both personal and social reactions that rattle and shake whatever momentary stasis individuals and groups have reached in their efforts to deal day-to-day with host cultures and environments. Some individuals lose sleep, stop eating, become severely agitated, depressed, and withdrawn. Others are stimulated to action, reassess their relationships, search for new alliances, and take separate or joint measures to address the crisis at hand. Some groups fracture; others form new coalitions along fault lines that are always tentative. Some of those alliances and fractures, either inadvertently or by deliberate intent, cross the boundaries that lie between American hosts and their international guests. One cannot but note, however, how utterly insulated most hosts are from the tribulations to which their guests are subject.

The Social Ecology of Crisis

Assessing the social terrain on which crisis is unleashed is essential if we are to understand who needs or wants help and whether, how, and by whom it should be provided. The Asian financial crisis serves as a good example of the differential social impact of a series of traumatic events over a wide range of countries. Students from Malaysia, Indonesia, Thailand, Hong Kong, and Singapore were the first to be identified as victims, soon to be followed by students from Korea. Grouped together by a political and economic crisis, the students were identified as "alike" in their adversity. Their needs were different, however, and advisers' knowledge of those differences offered comfort in a time of great distress.

For example, knowing the social history of Chinese immigration into Malaysia, and the social hierarchy of Chinese-Malays versus the Bumi Putra made advising Malaysian students a complex affair. The political situation in Indonesia, especially between ethnic groups distinguished by their heritage (Chinese or indigenous), affected the options exercised by Indonesian students seeking solutions to both the Asian financial crisis and their political dilemmas at home. Indonesian students of Chinese descent, fearful of anti-Chinese bigotry and angry over reports of rape and other brutalities against Chinese women in Indonesia, sought redress from the People's Republic of China (PRC), the United States, and world opinion. Indonesian students whose families occupied posts in the Suharto regime responded to reports of raids on their homes and other property by seeking to extend their stays in the United States. The 1997 turnover of Hong Kong to China influenced the prognosis of financial stability or instability for students from Hong Kong.

The Differential Impact of Political and Economic Crises

The media often tend to overstate the extent of a crisis. While it often appears from media sources that whole countries are mired in fiscal disaster, the actual impact of events may differ considerably from one enterprise to another, one region of the country to another, one neighborhood to another, even one family to another, and all of these may vary from one day to another. Jittery investors stepped out of the Asian market even though many of the enterprises with which they were engaged were financially healthy and in no immediate danger of collapse. No one can lighten the burden of the unmitigated violence that attends political crises, but in that case too, not every corner of a given universe is affected in precisely the same way. It is a very unusual and frightening realm in those instances where the disaster equals or exceeds media reports of the situation, as in the killing fields of Cambodia and Rwanda or the famine in the Sudan.

Getting a fix on the variability that usually attends crisis means that advisers must have their ears close to the ground; that is, close to where real human beings from the affected regions are located. Some students from Korea, for example, were supported by parents whose funding came from dollars invested overseas, principally in the United States. While their resources were diminished by the crisis, they were not cut off by the Korean government's attempts to halt the outflow of scarce dollar reserves, at least not in the earliest stages of the crisis. These were students who needed to adjust their lifestyles—sometimes in difficult and abrupt ways—to account for new financial realities, but they were not faced with destitution.

Others, however, were courting disaster. Their parents were bankrupted by the crisis. Younger siblings left behind in the home country were withdrawn from school, marriages dissolved, properties were confiscated, and the students on our campuses became the sole source of hope for destitute families that, a few short weeks before, had been in the ranks of Korea's upper middle class. Affected students from face-saving cultures confronted by these conditions tried not to reveal the impact of the crisis, drained their own bank accounts to send money home, maxed out credit cards, starved themselves and, in a few cases, ended up hospitalized. When arriving at the international office to apply for loans, they indicated that they were "OK" and "able to get by." Probing, then, is an essential tool for interested advisers and counselors to learn about critical situations and needs.

Researching the Truth

There are times when resourcefulness among international offices can play a major role in allaying student fears in a crisis. For example, first impressions after U.S. President Jimmy Carter announced the Iranian assets freeze were that all funds coming out of Iran would be "frozen" and that the thousands of Iranian students in the U.S. would be without funds. The result to U.S. educational institutions would be substantial, since some of them had enrolled hundreds of Iranian students. An enterprising foreign student adviser in the Midwest took it upon herself to research the "freeze" with three U.S. federal entities: the White House, the U.S. Treasury, and the U.S. State Department. The most effective response came from the Undersecretary of State for Political Affairs who advised her to contact Bank Melli Iran in New York, the official conduit for funds from Iran, and the agency where officials know the rules. The answer? There would be no effect on flows to private individuals in the U.S., including students at U.S. educational institutions. Only Iranian government funds were frozen.

A More Difficult Problem

Earlier difficulties with Nigerian student funds were more complicated to resolve. After substantial numbers of member schools experienced significant problems obtaining both Nigerian government and private funds for students, NAFSA: the Association of International Educators appointed a nationwide troubleshooter to visit the Nigerian consulates and the embassy. With substantial cultural, economic, and political factors affecting the outcome, the only clear solution for U.S. institutions was to demand one year's fees in advance for each prospective Nigerian student. This action served to guarantee financial security for a student in the first year of study in the U.S. It also satisfied the guidance in U.S. immigration regulations, which states that a U.S. educational institution "must be assured" that sufficient financial support is and will be available to the student while in the U.S.

In subsequent similar cases where financial support verifications from particular countries have been questionable, U.S. institutions have resorted to requesting an advance payment for part of a year's tuition and fees, or even for the whole first year's expenses. Such measures are a great help to students already coping with cultural and educational adjustments of no small measure.

Advisers need not rely only on their own sensitive ears or probing questions. Our offices can draw on ties to student leaders of the various country and regional groups on campus (1) to canvass their members about matters of pressing or passing concern, and (2) to reflect the needs of individuals and families within their communities. However, care has to be taken to assure that barriers of generation, status, and gender are not accidentally built into mechanisms for communication and that confidentiality is protected. Undergraduates may be unwilling to speak frankly to graduate student leaders; women may be quite resistant to sharing their concerns with men when trauma threatens; and the fear of loss of face looms large for many people both within and outside their own membership group.

This issue is important when it comes to applications for financial relief in the form of departmental assistantships. Students from Asia, suffering the weight of fiscal crisis, may be excellent academic performers but too "quiet," as perceived by faculty, to warrant selection as teaching or even research assistants. Although they may seethe inwardly with energy and commitment, they are not socially aggressive and rarely engage in face-to-face confrontation or competition to meet behavioral standards that some faculty and administrators regard as prerequisite for assistantship support. Combined with reticence about the extent of their need, such characteristics leave many deserving candidates in the lurch.

Bringing Resources to Bear

One of the functions that foreign student advisers can perform in crisis situations is to bring as many resources as possible, from locations both on and off campus, to bear on the resolution of critical situations. Since we know our own campuses best, it is important to list those resources and rank them in terms of priority for critical, foreseeable scenarios. In financial crises, the university's bursar and vice presidents for financial and student affairs, approached appropriately through the offices of the deans to whom international offices report, are the most likely candidates for measures of immediate relief including tuition waivers, deferred tuition payment plans, short or long-term loans at low or no interest, facilitated bank loans, and financial counseling. To minimize the trauma with which students are confronted, the ability to put relief packages together in a timely way serves not only to ameliorate the crisis, but also to reassure the community of the university's commitment to its constituents.

It is essential to introduce your students to financial management and planning. On any given campus, a show of hands among first-time international students at new student orientation will show most have never before had full responsibility for handling their own funds. They will need training on how to make choices (not an easy effort with the bombardment of advertising we all receive in the United States, particularly on television), how to budget their money carefully from term to term, how to record their spending, and how to adjust if they are overspending in any particular area. While U.S. college students would probably not regard such a warning with much interest or will, international students, for whom education is generally their primary objective, will follow advice about finances.

Counseling for financial crisis is not a simple matter. In the early stages of the Asian crisis on one campus, students and the personnel of the bursar's office were headed for a standoff. Students were asked how much they needed, and the bursar's staff was asked how much they would give. Neither shared a protocol for dealing with the other. With a little prodding and a few simulations, students learned to assess and express their own needs, and staff learned to probe for relevant answers. Interestingly, introducing financial counselors from the community is not necessarily a productive option. Financial counselors tend to assume that our international students follow patterns typical of American undergraduates, and neither the style of discourse nor the content clarifies matters for the internationals in our midst. However, the forms consultants use for establishing a long-term record of assets, liabilities, income, and expenses are helpful.

The support provided by colleagues in the divisions of the university that address student issues is inestimable. Housing officials can help ease financial readjustment by releasing students from housing and meal contracts, modifying their contracts, or providing temporary shelter. When crisis strikes, health and counseling services, and the chaplains on campus can help in a crisis, provide reassurance, and link students to the larger community. Culturally sensitive and politically or economically informed counseling are rare on- or off-campus, so such counseling should be treasured and rewarded when found.

Senior administrative personnel are key links in the relationship between the university, the nongovernmental (NGO) sector, the home governments, and countries from which students come, and our own government's agencies. Apart from legitimizing activities we and our colleagues undertake in the face of crisis, their role should be reserved for those situations where power and authority make a difference. And, as in all such cases, the imprimatur of senior officers is best exercised when the chances of success are reasonably high. Pulling on the coat strings of the powerful is risky and alienating if it is a strategy that is repeatedly used to no avail.

Senior officers may be willing to advocate on behalf of international students and scholars using their connections to alumni, trustees, donors, congressional representatives, and government officials. As advocates, they add to the voices seeking special relief for students from countries affected by political or financial crises. That role can be extended beyond U.S. boundaries. During a recent visit to Malaysia, our chancellor aired on television his commitment to a long-term relationship to his counterparts there. His appearance and the tenor of his remarks assured his audience that our institution regards these relationships as intensive and long-term, and the effect was pronounced both in Malaysia and at home.

Preparing senior officers for advocacy and intervention requires good advance groundwork. Knowing who's who in the government sector, keeping current with current and changing policy perspectives, and having a sense of how large-scale events affect our student population are prerequisite.

Foreign embassies and consulates, as well as sponsoring and placement agencies, may be helpful in signaling changes in policy such as the withdrawal of students from the United States prior to completion of their degree programs, rules governing the export of cash reserves, assistance in contacting family and relatives in times of crisis, and providing emergency passport requests and visa waivers.

In some instances, however, the embassies and consulates are part of the problem. The embassy of the PRC played a nefarious role during and after the massacre in Tiananmen Square. Agents were dispersed to harass students, scholars, and their dependents in the United States and then swamped the Chinese student community with propaganda when human rights activist Harry Wu appeared on campus. That agitation helped to exacerbate fissures in the ties between PRC students and students from Taiwan, and the conflict leaked into the ranks of Americans responding to events in China.

Political crises in Latin America, Central Europe, and the Middle East have stimulated similar patterns and responses. The student population in the United States can follow much of the agitation in the discussion pages on the Internet before it takes physical shape on the university campus. The staff of the Office of International Services at Syracuse University recall sitting in the office lounge on the day the embassies in Rwanda and the Sudan were bombed. The Taliban allegedly was connected to the terrorist activity. When questions surfaced regarding this organization's history and current structure, a student from the Middle East, who had been seated in the lounge, volunteered to check their web site: http://www.taliban.com was at the tip of his tongue!

It is incumbent upon leaders in international education offices to reassure anxious campus communities that they are on safe territory when it comes to expressions of concern, but that rules of free speech and responsibility hold sway on campus. The best approach to galvanizing support for legitimate causes lies in an even-handed, sober, and nonideological approach to the underlying causes of (and cures for) political violence, nationalism, and irascible conflict. The Chinese Embassy operates today in a much more transparent manner than it did in 1989, in part because a dialogue on human rights, however tentative, is underway.

Developing Assistance for International Students

Both the Gulf War and the Asian Financial Crisis bring to light a deficit in the infrastructure of most U.S. educational institutions: the lack of substantial financial assistance for nonimmigrant students who are caught in the midst of sudden and unexpected financial crises. Most U.S. schools, particularly public institutions, reserve the bulk of their financial aid for U.S. citizens and U.S. permanent residents. What "loan" funds exist are primarily short-term, to meet immediate needs for food and shelter, and must be paid back by mid-term to ensure timely registration for the next term, or, at minimum, must be repaid by the beginning of the next term. Scholarship funds are in short supply, too, and, in most cases, are something that one must apply for a year ahead of time; not a likely prospect for students immersed in their scholastic and personal endeavors and not fully aware of impending crisis.

International Student/Scholar Offices, through their institutional reporting lines, must devote attention to substantial fundraising efforts to strengthen student retention despite periodic financial crises. This author was fortunate to have worked at a large public midwestern institution that received a substantial bequest when a faculty member with an interest in international students died. A portion of the substantial funds was set aside for grants to financially needy students, another portion was set aside for long-term loans, and a third portion was used to fund a work-study program similar to federal "work-study," to encourage on-campus employers to hire an international student. New work opportunities opened up in campus offices where employing international students had not previously been considered, and the campus profile was substantially broadened. Certainly, most international students have the potential to repay long-term loans made available to them—if not too great an amount—during the INS-approved one-year period of post-graduation practical training employment.

On-Campus Employment

Just as in the areas of taxes, immigration law, and health insurance, international educators need to be ready to help international students assess their financial viability and begin part-time work well before their situations reach crisis proportions. Does your campus have sufficient opportunities for on-campus employment? If not, does your community offer sufficient openings for part-time employment and is the community receptive to international students holding these positions? These questions can be more important in small, conservative and rural areas where the solution is not always readily at hand, as it may be in urban settings. A substantial amount of personal lobbying may be necessary to open doors in campus and community offices/businesses.

Of course, occasionally we will be unable to assist or "save" our students. As in the Asian Financial Crisis, our best advice may very well be "Go home for now. Save your money. We will welcome you back whenever you are able to return in the future." This is the best advice for students who are just beginning their educations in the U.S. or for those who have little or no funding coming from usual funding sources that there is no hope of continuation of their education at that time.

There are other avenues to pursue, but one must be diligent and resourceful in researching such options. During the Asian Financial Crisis, NAFSA: Association of International Educators, and the Institute of International Education (IIE) offered both loans and grants to qualified students. Although it was a competitive process, the students who were the beneficiaries of the awards were enormously grateful. In some cases, it was the only thing that kept them in the United States.

Individual donors, especially among university alumni and board of trustees, can sometimes be a resource. The University of Oregon collected $50,000 to assist Asian students in 1998 during the worst of the crisis. The International Office developed a loan/grant application process, and numerous students were the lucky recipients. Other universities, like Syracuse University, deferred tuition and housing payments until the end of the semester, and even longer under extreme extenuating circumstances. A key component to the support of this effort was the teamwork strategy employed when the chancellor set up the ad hoc Asian Financial Crisis Committee. An effective, aggressive and active leader, the vice president for student affairs, was assigned to lead this group. The group reached consensus as to the appropriate actions, and the student population was informed via a letter from the chancellor. Universities were able to retain many students with these efforts who otherwise would have returned home.

Realms of Ambiguity

Beyond the reiteration of rules of engagement and expressions of concern lies more ambiguous territory. Should our offices express sympathy to the Chinese community over the alleged rape and murder of Chinese women that may have occurred during recent riots in Indonesia? This particular "crisis" mobilized Chinese students from around the globe, and the expression of the anxiety, anger, and fear that it generated, reverberated across the Internet and in demonstrations in cities throughout our country, China, and Taiwan. Indonesian officials denied the charges and described the evidence presented on videos as anti-Indonesian propaganda aimed at the government, police, and armed forces. Historical evidence of violence against the Indonesian Chinese community is undeniable, a fact that rendered the charges credible. However, expressions of sympathy for one community may be viewed as zero-sum withdrawals of sympathy for another. On the other hand, many find silence intolerable. In this case, we chose to express our concern and to indicate that the charges were "alleged" not proved. Others might have elected a different response.

About "Face"

Because Asian students comprise such a substantial proportion of our international student population, the concept of face, shared by many societies, deserves acknowledgment. Loss of face is not only an individual phenomenon; families lose face as do whole nations, and the extent of the loss can be measured in the enormous moral burden that falls on the shoulders of those who feel that loss. To put it in slightly different terms, the more extensive the loss, the deeper the chasm into which individuals fall, and the harder it is to relieve the depression and despair that are its consequence. The concept of face puts an edge on trauma, its symptoms, and its outcomes. When it is attached to financial crisis, boundary lines of the merely fiscal are eclipsed by the depression that comes in its train. When it is enveloped in political and ideological garb, it can lead to total withdrawal or unleash anger against the self or others. Sensitive listening is, then, a very critical skill, and affording the time to listen, especially since crises often strike at times when we are least prepared, warrants priority. Matters involving face ought to give us pause.

Advisers are best equipped to deal with political and economic crises when certain resources and skills are present. We all can endeavor to obtain adequate information about international events and their probable impact on the communities we serve. In choosing our sources of information and in evaluating the information we receive, we need to acknowledge that diversity is not merely a buzzword, but a key to the composition and dynamism of all of the groups that are subsumed, often out of ignorance or expediency, under various national or regional labels. We need to use all the resources we can muster to relieve anxiety and assure our students' and scholars' safety and academic progress. Some of those resources are material, but some are derived from sensitive listening, advocacy, and sustained emotional support. Advocacy is particularly important to prevent regulations and the policy prejudices that sometimes underlie them from adding to the toll taken by political and economic crises.

Entire communities are affected in one way or another by a political or financial crisis. It certainly helps to know who can be helpful, and in what way, before the crisis hits. New advisers can seek advice from colleagues across the country. Many rescue boats for your students are floating on the water; it is a matter of swimming out to one and riding it to shore.

Chapter 4

Mental Health Issues of Students Who Cross Borders

David Austell, Donna Boguslav, Patricia A. Burak,
Terence P. Hannigan, Lynn Reilly, and Nancy E. Young

International students are examples of our human capacity to adapt to new situations and environments. The majority of international students adjust to their new lives away from home with remarkable effectiveness, although most of them experience stress in the transition. International educators play an important role in guiding students in transition to maintain good mental health while they adapt and thrive in their new environments. One of the most important outcomes of the international sojourn may be gaining the self-knowledge that one can live successfully in a foreign culture. Once this vision bolsters the student's self-concept, it provides an element of self-assurance that can last a lifetime. By contrast, a psychological crisis that sends the student home prematurely may leave the student full of self-doubts about adapting to life elsewhere that can last a long time.

Sources of psychological illness vary as much as do sources of physical illness. Recognizing signs of illness and knowing how to respond to signs of psychological distress can be much more difficult than with a physical illness. Many individuals bear the full burden of their mental illnesses without any recognition for a long time, often until the symptoms become too severe to overlook.

International educators describe their experiences helping foreign students through psychological illness requiring medical evacuation, through the devastating effects of eating disorders, and through mental anguish that can lead a student to disappear.

When Medical Evacuation Is the Best Option

Scenario

A male graduate student approaches a foreign student adviser (FSA) in the International Office seeking assistance. The FSA immediately senses from the student's body language (stooped shoulders, eyes staring at the floor, unusual difficulty in speech, trembling hands), from the tears streaming down the students cheeks, and from the student's few struggling words, "I'm having a difficult day," that the student is deeply troubled emotionally. Though he came to the International Office of his own volition, the student is unable to articulate what he wants or needs, but the tears continue to flow. The few words that he is able to articulate focus on his "unhappiness" and "loneliness." Fairly quickly, the FSA feels the need for assistance from professional staff trained in psychological counseling, and gently persuades the student to go to the Counseling Center. The student agreed to go if the FSA will accompany him.

At the Counseling Center, the student apparently becomes very frightened and loses control. The psychologist assisting the student feels compelled to call the campus police, who forcibly restrain the student. Since the psychologist perceives that the student is a threat to either the public or to himself, she authorizes the involuntary committal of the student to a local private mental hospital. The student is preliminarily diagnosed with "schizophrenia accompanied by severe psychosis and delusions." Since there is no local support network for the student sufficient to assist him in this crisis, the family decides to have the student return to his home country immediately.

Key Elements of Medical Evacuation

Medical evacuation is in order when a student or scholar is very ill, physically or emotionally, and chooses to return home for treatment. The decision to return home is generally not an easy one for the student who often feels that illness has derailed or at least postponed academic progress. Returning to an extensive and supportive home environment can be extremely helpful to a student in a health crisis. A decision to return home can be a cost-effective way to manage the expense of health care, and so can be a tremendous relief to the student and the family. Realistically, however, these concerns are inevitably weighed against the quality of medical assistance received in the United States as opposed to that available in the home country. It is not unusual for a foreign student adviser to be asked to take part in the decision-making process, often as a facilitator.

The Role of the Support Team. There may be times, especially related to students who are physically or emotionally incapacitated, when the FSA will want to convene a support team of close family members, friends, the academic adviser, trusted community persons who can advise on the home culture, and medical personnel. The FSA will need to be sensitive to Family Educational Rights and Privacy Act (FERPA) concerns, and to seek release from the student (if possible) or a responsible family member to openly discuss the crisis with this support team. The purpose of this team is to reach consensus regarding the advisability of home return and to plan for the student's medical evacuation. Details of the student's withdrawal from the institution can be planned for and coordinated through the support team. For example, there may be an apartment to vacate, bills to pay, and bank accounts to close. Family members and friends can assist in this process. It is important to keep in mind that friends of the ill student want to help, but if they are students themselves, they must be advised not to compromise their own academic success out of compassion for the ill student. The support team can help keep this kind of outcome in check. The team can also be very helpful to the FSA, to the student, and to the family, in planning for the student's possible return to school to continue study after he is well.

Insurance. The FSA will need to help review the student's insurance policy to see if it covers medical evacuation. If so, the insurance company usually will want to confirm: 1) that the student has been hospitalized for at least five days; and 2) that there is a physician's letter recommending that the student be sent home in order to get needed care and rest. The insurance company presumes that the day-to-day care of the student, and the rest that the student needs, are usually best facilitated by family and people in the home community.

The insurance company usually will cover airline ticket costs. The FSA should check to confirm the student's policy's benefits for this coverage as well as for possible coverage of a person to accompany the medical evacuee. If a student is disoriented or otherwise incapacitated, and a family member is unable to fly with the student, a nurse or other professional should accompany the student.

Withdrawing From the Institution. The student in the throes of a health crisis may need to formally withdraw from his academic institution. The FSA will want to make sure that the academic adviser is involved, and that the institution is officially notified, either by the student or by an immediate family member. Institutions vary procedurally regarding withdrawal from class, and the FSA should review these specific procedures with the student or family member as appropriate.

Home Concerns. While an international student's return home for health reasons can be fundamentally positive, there are aspects of home return for illness that can be extremely stressful to the student, and sensitivity is required.

The student is likely to be concerned and disappointed that his academic progress has been set back and perhaps derailed. As much as appropriate, the FSA can help the student and academic adviser with appropriate planning for a possible return to school when the student is well.

Many cultures do not embrace western society's open discussion of psychological disorders. Religious or social backgrounds can lead some students to feel that discussion of their illness is taboo. Even if the student has become more accustomed to western ways, the student's family may not share the student's new thinking. Some cultures attach enormous stigma to an emotional or psychological disorder that can compromise the entire family. For this reason, the idea of returning home may not be as pleasant a scenario as the FSA might hope. Instead, the decision to return to the home country might be fraught with intimidation and anxiety, faced by a person whose mental functions are already compromised. The FSA should be aware of the difficulties for an ill student and the family back home, in cases involving depression, mood disorders, psychosis, or other mental conditions.

Prevention: What to Do to Lower the Risk of a Mental Health Crisis on Your Campus

The international educator can play a major role in facilitating counseling and mental health services for students who cross borders to pursue educational goals. There is advice for the professional in this role: be aware and think about prevention!

Research indicates that a significant percentage of international students are not personally well adjusted—DeArmand (1983) (see Appendix C) reports that approximately 25 percent are not, while Thompson and Bentz (1975), as quoted in Zwingmann and Gunn (1983), report that only 33 percent have a personality score associated with "good mental health"— suggesting that the international educator should improve the campus atmosphere in order to provide support for students from overseas. Mental health issues are most acute during the first semester and first year of the sojourn, when the student is least knowledgeable about the host culture and is still grieving the loss of contact with the home culture. A student at this stage of the sojourn is not familiar with options and resources in the new

SUMMARY OF MEDICAL EVACUATION ISSUES

✓ Advise the student or appropriate family member, if the student is incapacitated, regarding withdrawal from school according to the institution's policy.

✓ Communicate with the health insurance company about medical evacuation benefits covered by the insurance policy.

✓ Review medical evacuation procedures with the student or family member.

✓ Make sure the student is appropriately accompanied on the journey home.

✓ Remember to get written release from the student if possible to discuss the case openly with persons who will assist with the medical evacuation, such as health insurance representatives.

✓ Assist the student with any planning related to a future return to school.

✓ Review with the student any pertinent immigration regulations governing re-entry to the United States after an extended absence.

✓ Convene a support team to assist the FSA, the student, and the family, in matters related to the medical evacuation.

✓ Be aware of student and family concerns about the home country perception of the student's illness and the effect of this perception on the family. ●

environment, and feels the loss of friends, family, and home more acutely than during later stages of the journey.

Clearly any number of factors increase or decrease the risk that a student will experience serious cross-cultural adjustment difficulties. One factor is the degree of cultural similarity between the student's host country and home country. Canadian, British, Irish, and other students from English-speaking nations will probably have an easier time in the United States than will students from countries where other languages are native. Western Europeans also would have a relatively easy adjustment, with Latin Americans, and Middle Eastern students falling midway on the adjustment continuum. Asian and African students generally have the most difficult time due to the larger cultural leaps they must make to adjust. Students from these regions are also physically different from U.S. citizens, a factor that may make the transition more challenging, in spite of our often-cited American melting pot image.

Factors that make the adjustment difficult include: financial strain; bias against the student's homeland; differences in dress, climate, and religion; fear of losing one's cultural identity; shifts from rural to urban environments (and the reverse); and whether or not there is a common ethnic community for the student on campus or nearby.

Often international students feel like outsiders on U.S. campuses. To compound their feelings of isolation, they can feel that they must toe the line with their compatriots by not mingling with members of ethnic groups considered adversarial back home. Failure to play by their cultural mores may make them feel like outsiders with not only their hosts, but also their compatriots. The international educator also needs to be sensitive to the few students from one national or ethnic group who feel ill at ease because they encounter many members of an antagonistic group on campus or in the neighboring community.

International students arrive in the United States with some general awareness that racism is an issue. At home, the same tensions may occur along class or religious lines. International students of color are part of the race issue in the United States whether they want to be or not, and may find themselves the victims of racism. (See the section on racism later in this book.)

Another dynamic that keeps international and U.S. students apart occurs when American students are viewed as superficial and hard to get to know. The perception is that American students rarely take the time to invest in close, ongoing relationships. As with all stereotypes, there is at least a grain of truth to this one: Americans, with their highly mobile lifestyle, are used to the coming and going of friends as they are uprooted for reasons of employment or education. Americans often see students from overseas as bookish and having difficulty with English conversation. There is a double barrier of mutual stereotyping.

Alexander, Klein, Workneh, and Miller (1981) stress that there is a relationship between the level of traditional values held by the international student and the level of intimate involvement with U.S. students. The more traditional the outlook of the international student, the more likely the student will interact with compatriots and the more likely the student will have few or no interactions with U.S. students. Less traditionally-minded students tend to move more freely across the cultural barrier on U.S. campuses. Self-confidence seems to be another key ingredient in crossing this barrier. It also is related to better English language skills, a better sense of well-being, less loneliness, and more academic achievement. In essence, these authors imply that a cultural and personal defensiveness may lead to congregating with compatriots rather than with host country students. By contrast, willingness to seek out new experiences may be a key ingredient for success on an American campus.

It is good preventative mental health care for the international educator to be sensitive to these factors so that there is a sense of how much risk each international student carries. International educators should ask recently-arrived international students about the events that led up to their coming to the United States. In general, this can help educators understand the pressures the international student is under to succeed in the United States. It is important for international educators to be aware of this "emotional baggage" that students carry and how it may be manifested. Headaches, stomachaches, tiredness, and changes in eating and sleeping patterns, are possibly signs of stress about culture shock and pressures carried from the homeland.

Suggestions for Mental Health Baseline Assessment

When evaluating whether or not the student is experiencing adjustment problems and to what extent, consider:

- How well does the international student speak English?

- How interested is the student in meeting other compatriots...or in not meeting them?

- How interested is the student in meeting Americans or international students from homelands different from their own for sightseeing, socializing, and other group activities?

- Is the student studying in the United States because of outstanding academic performance?

- Does financial privilege allow the student to study in the United States?

New Students—Orientation

New students are often at higher risk for mental health problems, and the international educator should spend time with these students in prevention activities. Orientation programs should, of course, include information on cross-cultural adjustment. Students should be made aware that it is common to be homesick and doubt the decision to study abroad during the first year of the sojourn. Once orientation has been completed, the international educator should check in regularly with high-risk students. Students may be responsive when encouraged to stop by to see personnel in the office on a regular basis.

The typical student from overseas is not here to learn about Americans and their culture, except perhaps to learn English, frequently seen as an important tool to succeed—a means to an academic end. Even if students do socialize, they may feel guilty about what is frequently seen as a "waste of time," given the considerable academic demands they face and the fact that reading and writing in English may take them longer than their American counterparts.

You may need to train international students to use their contacts with Americans in recreational activities as a means of moving away from their work temporarily so that they can return to their studies more energized and effective. It may take constant reiteration of the theme, "Don't work hard, work smart," before the student is able to accept this counterintuitive advice. Gary Althen, in an article in the *NAFSA Newsletter* some years ago, wrote on the subject of teaching foreign students how to socialize at parties. This article is worth sharing with international students at orientation and at different times during the year when they would benefit from taking a break from their academic work to gain perspective and to recharge.

Adjustment Issues

As the semester unfolds, it will become clear which students are adjusting well and which students are not. This may be the time to press for regularly scheduled sessions with a counselor. Struggling students should be given the option of inviting a friend or fellow student to counseling sessions. Consider offering the option of two or three brief sessions weekly. A key goal for these sessions is to assist the student in replacing the sense of loss that results from a major transition.

Cognitive behavioral approaches may be ideal for the student because they are easy to understand, address the behaviors that are problematic, and can lead to improvement after a few sessions. In this method, the therapist and the student enter into an alliance in which they decide the behavior and thoughts the student wants to change. A schedule of activities and a plan is developed for the student. Often the therapist may provide brief readings or may be available by phone if the student is having a particularly difficult time. These techniques are especially helpful for the depressed student, because she leaves the session with a way to address the difficult situation with support from another person.

One ongoing task that needs constant work is the development of a community contact list of ministers, mental health professionals (including psychiatrists, psychologists, psychiatric nurses, and social workers), community events, services, restaurants, etc. that cater to the needs of the students from overseas. It is important to know which faculty members have served in the Peace Corps and where they have served, and if anyone else on the campus and in the community has lived and studied overseas, and where.

Psychological Trouble

Alexander, Klein, Workneh, and Miller (1981) state that when students are in psychological trouble, they experience themselves as deviant in both the host and home cultures. Students feel out of control, which leads to unhappiness, anxiety, concerns about their American hosts, and a self-conscious perception that all their mistakes, linguistic and behavioral, are obvious and the butt of jokes.

These authors talk about depression caused by loss of social anchorage, status, or any familiar routine in which events can be easily predicted, and breaks in the ties with loved ones, friends, and family. It is also noted that it is rare that sojourners cross borders without losing most or nearly all sources of self-esteem. All of this sets the stage for homesickness, an area that psychologists have only recently begun to investigate seriously (Van Tilburg & Vingerhoets, 1997).

The international student is faced with the loss of peers and family members. Where there is less external stimulation from friends, there is an increase in internally generated stimulation, sometimes in the form of self-consciousness or paranoia about how the host country students view the stranger. This heightened sense of one's own feelings may explain why somatic complaints may occur. The distressed student is not distracted enough to overlook emotional and physical discomforts.

The international student may maintain a guarded and passive role that makes the U.S. therapist feel ineffective or that the cross-cultural gap is too great to bridge. When matters become serious and the international student is distressed, it is important that the therapist take a directive role that is supportive. Keep in mind that one of the major stresses for international students is the unpredictability of life in the new setting. One can gain confidence with a frightened international student by explaining what will come next, such as what the mental health practitioner will ask, what a mental status examination is and how it is conducted, the possibility that medications will be prescribed and how they can help the student, and what the side effects are of any medications prescribed. If the helping professional can serve as a guide, the international student may be willing to use the services provided. The student may need a list of ways that the problem would be resolved in the host culture. The international educator might respond, "Ah yes, we have a counselor (lawyer, gynecologist, mullah) who works with our students who have this problem all the time." Such an intervention "normalizes" problems and offers reassurance that resources are available to resolve the difficulty.

Clearly the strategy is to gain the student's confidence early by being accessible and reliable, and by dispelling the belief that the counselor or psychologist undoubtedly will have the student committed or sent home. This may involve identifying agencies or individuals whom the student recognizes as helpful. Of course, if this is done early in the relationship, when a major crisis occurs, the international educator has the credibility he or she needs to be accepted as a helper *and to act with authority to make decisions with, or for the student, who may not be able to do so.* Once their trust is mutual, the student and educator can focus on the problem at hand.

Providing Support During a Mental Health Crisis

If the international educator has done this preventive work, the difficult process of managing a mental health emergency will be easier. Making the effort to meet and to get to know international students as a matter of course can greatly ease any crisis that arises. Any familiar face can be comforting at a time of crisis.

When an international educator encounters a distressed student, it is best if the student and educator retreat to a quiet office, such as the International Education Office, where the student can be shielded from curious eyes. If a close friend is available, the student may welcome that person's presence. Ideally, the distressed student should be positioned near the door with the educator positioned in the room facing the door. This way you can have an assistant outside the door ready to respond if help is needed, and to serve as a gatekeeper to the room. It is particularly important that this person not let emergency medical technicians (EMTs) or other personnel arrive in the room unannounced. By facing the door, you will be able to see when emergency personnel have arrived, and can quietly inform the distressed student of their arrival. It is a good idea to tell the student that you are going to go out to talk with the assisting personnel and plan to return with them.

It is especially important that the distressed student not feel tricked or ambushed. Very likely, you will be seen as an adversary if you do not inform the student in advance about the arrival of additional personnel to assist. If you say little or nothing to the student, it is likely that you, the international educator, will be perceived as part of the band of assistants who may need to intrude and possibly press to have the student go to the hospital.

It is also possible that the student simply needs a "time-out" and a chance to talk about a precipitating event that may have caused the difficulty. In this situation, it may be possible to provide the necessary counseling on the spot or to call for assistance from the counseling center. If the crisis does pass, and the student is assessed as able to leave, a backup plan is needed. The plan should consist of a hotline number; a clear and precise "check in" time for the student to contact an appropriate helping professional; and the name of a key contact person, perhaps a close student friend who can be reached if there is more difficulty. Frequently, it is best to specify that it is the student's responsibility to stop in or call to let a specific person know that her situation is manageable. This puts the student in control and builds an alliance that shows that she is managing the problem with the helping professionals. However, make it clear that if the distressed student does not check in, you will assume that all is not well and campus personnel will contact her. If the crisis is not manageable in this manner, additional support will be needed.

One of the more difficult decisions is determining what constitutes an emergency where more help is needed. Clearly an international educator may be the professional who knows the student best, but your skills may be limited in assessing just how urgent it is for the student to receive psychological services. EMTs and police personnel have clearer professional experience and guidelines in situations requiring further assessment at a psychiatric facility or emergency room. A call for further assistance certainly would be made in the event that the student is destroying property or threatening to harm himself or anyone else.

The advantage that the international educator brings to the situation is a clear understanding of the organization of the institution and what is likely to transpire as the crisis unfolds. Very likely what may be most frightening to an international student is fear of the unknown and the concern that public shame will result from seeking out help, particularly as additional help is called in to manage the crisis. Reassurance to the student that she will not be left in the hands of strangers can be very comforting.

Depending on the emotional state of the student, she needs to know that the helping professionals who join you will ask a series of questions to assess her grasp on reality and whether she is excitable, depressed, or aggressive. Throughout this experience, the international educator will need to determine whether information about this procedure will be upsetting or calming. Manic, excitable, angry, or aggressive behavior may escalate when the student hears about this procedure. Depressed students may benefit from an explanation of what procedures are to follow. Frightened students may be comforted by the explanation, but each individual is different, and it is not uncommon for the reaction to be one of panic.

An international educator can assume the unique role of a "cultural informant," or guide for the student in emotional crisis. Evidence that the student is a threat will lead to a decision to have the student taken to an emergency room or psychiatric facility.

Some students may feel that they are out of control, and may be waiting for a therapist to articulate this for them. The therapist always needs to be working from a developmental model: When will the patient be ready to take a given step? Can the student be led to the obvious conclusion: hospitalization or return to the homeland?

Understand that uniformed EMTs and security personnel may be an emotional trigger for international students. Furthermore, depending on the protocol on the campus and in the community, once an ambulance is called, there may be a concurrent response from local police, a sheriff, or state troopers. It may be important for the international educator to serve as an intermediary for the group of "helpers" arriving on the scene. If the EMTs and security personnel know and respect the educator, the educator will have a better chance to influence how things will proceed. However, the personnel may not have much time to stand by until the student tries to regain composure. Keep in mind that students in psychological distress need to be assessed for their ability to take care of themselves. The acid test of a decision to release or admit for additional observation and care will be based on the student's potential for hurting himself or others. Will postponement of care now create a more difficult crisis later? The mental health providers need to help the international educator assess the need for immediate hospital care versus some less urgent form of support.

As in situations where the police ask a student to cooperate, here too, a student's refusal can lead to a forced hospitalization. The international educator needs to discuss this possibility with the student. How he or she goes may be negotiable. The international educator's skill at negotiating such an interaction between the student and the emergency personnel may be required to maintain calm and avoiding an even more traumatic event.

If indeed the situation requires a trip to a mental health facility the distressed student will be interviewed to assess the type and seriousness of the problem. Know that there are some clear cultural biases in this type of assessment. There is an excellent role for the international educator to play as informant and advocate. For instance, besides asking the student's name, the date, and current location, some versions of this exam ask the patient to identify the hospital and county name. Patients are asked to do simple math problems, and may be asked to interpret proverbs. A good clinician with cross-cultural sensitivity should interpret the results of this exam with consideration for the international student's cultural and language differences. Here, too, it is important for the international educator to be able to speak with mental health professionals and discuss the student's way of functioning prior to being depressed, as well as the student's level of acculturation and English language proficiency.

Diagnosis is a key step in the treatment process of persons suffering from psychological difficulties. Generally, a psychiatrist or psychologist will provide a tentative diagnosis after completing an intake interview. Decisions about the diagnosis will be made based on the Mini Mental Status Examination and information that the examiner gathers about behavior and symptoms described by the patient, family members, and close friends. In arriving at a diagnosis, the psychiatrist or psychologist will almost always use the *Diagnostic and Statistical Manual of Mental Disorders,* most current edition. This reference tool, a compendium of psychological maladies, contains a glossary of culture-bound syndromes that could prove helpful to international educators as basic reading in understanding cross-cultural mental health issues. It should be in university counseling centers or college libraries.

This manual can help you understand and learn more about the six major diagnostic classes. However, it becomes clear as one reads through the descriptions of such diagnoses as social phobia or agoraphobia that it is difficult to distinguish between culturally-sanctioned behavior such as quiet, passiveness that may seem psychopathological in the host culture. Also, it should be noted that an international student's tendency to avoid embarrassing situations where someone asks questions in public may be a coping mechanism if she struggles with English seemingly every waking moment.

Psychotropic medications may be prescribed for students in crisis. Responses to such drugs can be quite varied from person to person. Good therapy requires that medication be one of several supports for the student in crisis, including psychotherapy. The student's attitude toward the medication needs to be assessed so that she can be provided whatever information is available to make her feel more comfortable taking the medication.

Psychotropic medicines come in four broad groups, and each medication has a generic name that is universal and a trade name that can vary from country to country. So as to avoid confusion when helping a student, you should ask the student to present the medication vials so that you can copy the information directly from the label.

Many of the psychotropic medications take several weeks or more to alleviate depression or other problems. Working with these medications requires patience, and perhaps changes, if results are not seen after several months. The medications do not cure psychological problems; they simply manage them. A qualified medical professional needs to explain to the patient and caring parties the risk of long-term side effects, that can include sexual dysfunction, weight gain, or purposeless and sometimes irreversible motor activity.

Admission to a psychiatric facility can be a frightening experience for anyone. Some patients are insulted by the apparent assumption that they are unable to function outside the hospital. For other patients, admission to the hospital may be a relief. The distressed student may feel that she no longer has to try to hide her difficulties. Admission can also be considered a postponement of the feared trip home that will bring even more shame and embarrassment. As difficult as the admission may be, it leaves room for the student to hope that she can return to the campus, rather than face being sent home.

All international educators should have fundamental training in the area of cross-cultural counseling, especially to make educated decisions about international students who are in psychological distress. See Appendix C for an abbreviated reading list to supplement your training and experience.

When Eating Becomes A Crisis

Scenario 1

Hae Sook is a 35-year-old Korean graduate student who has been a secret binge-purge eater for 15 years. She discovered the practice in Korea as a means of weight control. When she came to the United States for graduate study three years ago, Hae Sook discovered that her practice was part of a well known syndrome, bulimia. Prior to that, she believed she was "the only one in the world doing this shameful practice." Coming for help at the student health center started to relieve Hae Sook of some of her guilt and shame, but her eating practices continued as a stress coping mechanism. Being a foreign graduate student with limited English skills at a competitive institution added to her stress. Hae Sook was placed in a multi-disciplinary holistic program involving therapy, medical review, nutritional guidance, and weekly monitoring by a primary care nurse. She was also sent to a dentist who had expertise in working with bulimic patients, whose repeated vomiting destroys tooth enamel. After a brief "honeymoon" period with a psychotherapist, Hae Sook refused to go anymore, stating the therapist did not understand Korean culture. With some effort, a Korean therapist was found who agreed to take her case. After two years of treatment, Hae Sook reduced her binge-ing-purging from two to three times a day to two to three times a week. She returned to Korea after completing her degree and at last contact, was maintaining two binge-purge cycles a week. Although she had improved, Hae Sook was not "cured" and may continue in this chronic disease state for years to come.

Scenario 2

Anna is an African-American anorexic undergraduate student majoring in language who has been in treatment for one year and has yet to maintain her "goal weight." She is now applying to study abroad in Spain. She is informed that she will not be approved for the program unless she can exceed and maintain her weight at two pounds above her "goal weight." The open anger this requirement elicits in Anna indicates that she is not yet vested in her recovery. She is also informed that she will be required to have a weekly weigh-in in Spain if she does make the program, and that she will be sent home if her weight drops below the goal for two consecutive weeks. Anna is not selected for the study abroad program, drops below her "danger" point weight, and has to be hospitalized before the end of the semester.

Eating disorders cover three broad categories: anorexia nervosa, bulimia, and a third category that functions as a "catch-all" for practices like binge eating without purging. Attempts have been made to sub-group these categories, but there tends to be a lot of crossover among individuals with eating disorders in behavior patterns ascribed to one category or another.

Bulimia

Bulimia is binge eating that is out of control. Behavior associated with bulimia includes vomiting, laxative abuse, fasting, over-exercise to prevent weight gain, and extreme concern with body shape and size. The currently accepted diagnostic criteria for bulimia are bingeing at least twice a week for a period of more than three months. The repeated vomiting can cause the individual's glands to swell, resulting in swollen cheeks that can exacerbate the belief that s/he needs to lose weight. During a binge, the bulimic individual is out of control with regard to how much and what type of food s/he will eat.

Both anorexia and bulimia have been classified as psychological illnesses in the U.S. Anorexia tends to occur at earlier ages than bulimia, often at puberty while bulimia tends to develop between the ages of 16–20, with college years being a prime time. Bulimia may be more difficult to identify and diagnose, as these individuals may start out overweight and through the bulimia, arrive at and maintain what could be considered a "healthy" weight and attractive figure. Obsessive-compulsive behavior is common among bulimics and when interfered with, the individual will exhibit undue anxiety.

Someone who is bulimic may show signs of the condition through her behavioral patterns, such as going to the bathroom immediately following meals, eating in secret, or being preoccupied with food. The eating binges may be planned or spontaneous, they are usually done alone and often at night. A bulimic may have tooth decay or a sore throat. A bulimic student may start experiencing financial problems, as she will often buy a large amount of food that she later purges, only to repeat the cycle, ever hungry.

Anorexia

Although the term anorexia nervosa is part of the modern lexicon, it is not a new disease. It has been identified in medical literature dating back to the 19th century in London and Paris. Outside the United States, eating disorders have been identified and treated in growing numbers in Belgium, Canada, France, Germany, Italy, Japan, Russia, South Africa, Switzerland and the United Kingdom. Current research is redefining eating disorders as a continuum, for which those at the "mild" end may never receive treatment. It is hard to say at this time whether there is an actual increase in incidents or whether there is better reporting of eating disorders.

The National Association of Anorexia Nervosa and Associated Disorders reports that "The mortality rate for anorexia is higher than for any other psychiatric disorder. In fact, it is the number one cause of death in young women. Five to 10 percent of anorexics die within 10 years of its onset, 18—20 percent within 20 years, and only 50 percent ever report being cured." Symptoms of anorexia nervosa include significant weight loss (at least 15 percent of the normal body weight), refusal to maintain normal body weight, fear of weight gain although already underweight, and interruptions to menstrual cycles. Anorexics often are not overweight when the disease begins. Anorexia can start with dietary changes that may be viewed as healthy, such as omitting certain types of foods, for example, adopting a vegetarian diet.

What types of behavior might one see in an anorexic individual? She may experience cracks at the corners of her mouth, dry skin, and feelings of being cold. She may have scalp hair loss and in the body's effort to conserve heat, she may develop very fine baby hair on the extremities, called lanugo. This is an important clue and may be noted on the forearms when talking to someone suspected of having anorexia. She may dress in layers, show fears of food, or strange eating patterns. She may give signs of low self-esteem, depression, irritability, withdrawal from others, and denial of any problem if questioned about her behavior. An anorexic often will not eat in a group setting; for example, she may not go to the campus cafeteria with friends. It is not unusual, however, that she will cook large amounts of food and insist on others eating.

Here is a journal excerpt from a young U.S. woman who documents the initial treatment of her anorexia and how this affected her self-perception. "After setting up sessions with numerous psychiatrists, nutritionists, and personal trainers, I began my journey. I knew that I would have to start eating more and the thought of gaining weight scared me. I was so used to my by now 80 pound frame, that any new pound seemed like a hundred. Starvation not only makes you weak, it also messes with your head. It distorts your vision. I was 25 pounds below average weight for my height, and I thought I was fat."

Manners of Treatment

There is no agreed upon treatment for eating disorders, in fact, there is disagreement as to their cause. Basically, the three schools of thought are that the disorders are biological, psychological, or cultural in origin. Each of these taken individually fails to explain eating disorders in their entirety. Common questions about eating disorders include: Why are they predominantly found in women? Why are some women in a given country affected with an eating disorder and others are not? Are they found in every country in the world or only those with the mass media influence to be thin? How are their historical roots explained if they are so enmeshed with today's media?

Given that the cause of eating disorders is still not known, it is not surprising that treatments differ. The treatment models are evolving as more research is being done. The first decision must be medically determined—how seriously does the eating disorder threaten the student's life? Does the student need to be hospitalized as an inpatient? There are day treatment programs that are highly structured but do not involve 24-hour hospitalization. They are often part of the discharge plan for a hospitalized individual and are used for those whose condition, while serious, does not require hospitalization. There are also residential programs for the physically and mentally stable eating disorder patient, that usually require a commitment to treatment, possibly for four to six weeks, and they are usually expensive. There are also halfway houses that have less structured programs, and may work better with students who are vested in their recovery.

The majority of successful programs involve behavioral, cognitive, and family therapy combinations. If the weight loss in an anorexic is so extreme, she often cannot be in counseling until the body is released from the "starvation mode" and the person is once again capable of more rational thinking. The international student/study abroad adviser should make it clear to the student, in a friendly caring way, that the adviser will be in weekly contact with the care provider and must obtain written permission from the student to receive information from the care provider. The more closely the adviser works with the health care provider and the student, the less chance there is that the student will manipulate the system to her ultimate detriment.

"Cures" are seldom, if ever, 100 percent. The bulimic is often more open to admitting there is "something wrong" but the resistance to behavioral change is just as profound as it is with the anorexic. As hard as it may be for the over-achieving anorexic to admit, life is truly "progress not perfection" a principle of the 12-step program "Overeaters Anonymous (OA)." OA is a lay-directed support group derived from Alcoholic Anonymous principles. OA has meetings where individuals offer each other support and an open forum for discussing overeating, binge eating, purging, and some restrictive eating. These meetings seem to have more success with the bulimic than the anorexic, but some restricted eaters have found the "right" group and have been helped. Antidepressants are also being used with some success in treating bulimic individuals.

Family or friends may not treat an individual with an eating disorder in a sympathetic manner. Sufferers may often get "common sense" advice about their condition, since food is something that all of us are familiar with and have developed patterns around. It is important to understand that whatever the origins, eating disorders are illnesses that can be life-threatening. In fact, as anorexics starve themselves, their ability to reason becomes more fragmented, so bestowing "common sense" advice may be a waste of interventionist energy.

Here are some final thoughts from one anorexic woman's journal: "I never knew how hard it was going to be to overcome this disorder. I thought I'd just start eating again. Yeah right. Try telling an anorexic to 'just eat' when the whole disorder is about not eating. And it didn't make things easier when people at my school started to joke about it. I guess they thought that making fun of the amount of food I ate or how skinny I was allowed them to deal with it lightheartedly. Sometimes I would laugh too, just so they'd leave me alone. . . . they just don't realize that what they are saying goes beyond a little joke and that behind the laughter I am crying inside." (Thanks to Kathryn Tarr. We appreciate her bravery and generosity in sharing excerpts in this chapter with readers.)

The good news is that there are more treatment models and resources for eating disorders than ever before. There are many eating disorder clinics in the United States, whose staffs include psychologists, social workers, internists, general practitioners, and nutritionists. These clinics are not limited to the United States, but can be found in a number of countries. As with any crisis management strategy, pro-active partnering with the appropriate resources, in this case the student health and counseling centers, will make the challenge of an actual occurrence much easier to manage.

What's a Foreign Student Adviser to Do?

An Interview with Donna Boguslav, R.N., B.S.N, C.E.N. Donna was a professional dancer and "successful" functioning anorexic for years; cognitive therapy helped in her recovery. As a "late career" choice Donna went into nursing and graduated summa cum laude from Hunter-Bellevue School of Nursing with a B.S.N., and a concentrated interest in eating disorders.

Q: I've worked with students for two years and haven't run across anyone with an eating disorder. Is it really something I need to worry about?

A: On any college campus in the industrialized world, you will find a surprisingly large number of students somewhere on the continuum of disordered eating. This can be anywhere from what is seen as "normal" dieting— post holiday visit home followed by a one-two week calorie restricted diet — to pathologically significant eating disorders.

Q: So should I be actively looking for students with eating disorders?

A: It probably should not be your mission to do "case-finding." Problems and concerns will be brought to you by professors, roommates, friends, and even the student him/herself.

Q: What can I do to prepare myself for the time when I do encounter someone with this condition?

A: I strongly recommend that you have a good understanding of your institution's stance on eating disorders. Is there a written statement of policy specifically for suspected and diagnosed eating disorders? How does your institution handle other health-related crises? Some institutions view eating disorders as potentially contagious states. That is not far off the mark, since there have been cases where whole sororities have lived in an anorexic competitive environment. Further, you should work closely with your student health center. What is the diagnostic criteria, their intervention criteria, their treatment philosophies? Who is your primary contact at the center?

Q: Can you suggest any institutions that have a policy statement on eating disorders that I might use as a model?

A: The University of Arizona, Penn State, and Yale all have well written, well considered policy statements which they are willing to share, as well as the University of Minnesota and University of Kansas. I would contact the "Eating Disorder Program" through the Student Health Services

Q: What would you recommend I do if I suspect a student has an eating disorder and there is no student health center on our campus or overseas program site?

A: If an eating disorder (ED) is "suspected" it is important to gather as much information as possible without compromising the student's privacy. What are the grounds for suspicion? Has the student demonstrated "high risk" behavior—e.g. refusing to eat with others, eating "only salad," extreme obvious loss of weight, disappearing to the bathroom after eating, compulsive exercise patterns, fainting, hostility when questioned about eating patterns, very rigid and restrictive eating patterns or ingestion of large amounts of food at one time, repetitive purchasing of large amount of junk foods, laxative usage, among other behaviors? Who besides you has voiced suspicion of an ED? If abroad, is it possible to contact the institutional health center in the United States? If on a campus without a health center, is there any primary care practitioner in town who works with closely with your college?

It is important to remember that denial is part of the ED pattern, particularly with anorexics. Express your concerns in a nonconfrontational manner, but be prepared for anger and hostility and do not argue with the student. Have a complete assessment/intervention team and plan in place if possible. Try to locate knowledgeable medical personnel who would be able to do a physical assessment. Tell the student that his or her weight may indeed be normal and part of their heredity, but it would be reassuring to all to get some validation of "good health status." The student may or may not cooperate, but concern has been expressed and documented. Reassure the student that the concern will continue on your part. The student may well view this as a threat. You can quietly express that the college or university holds itself responsible to intervene if a student is perceived to be a threat to themselves or others. You may just have to play the quiet observer, but the student will know she or he is being watched.

Q: Is there a diplomatic way to ask someone if they have an eating disorder?

A: There are ED "questionnaires" available, but they should be administered by a health care professional. Frankly, I question their value in the lay world. A group of health care providers at NYU self-administered one of these questionnaires and we all came up with EDs; we then retook the questionnaire with the role- playing mindset of being an anorexic. . . . to assume that an anorexic is going to answer the questions honestly is naive. The diplomacy in asking if someone has an eating disorder is in truly expressing concern...it must never be confrontational or a control issue.

Q: Are eating disorders limited to middle-class white young women in the United States?

A: No. The statistics have been skewed here somewhat in that it is diagnosed predominantly in the white, middle class female, but this is a population that has easy health care access. We are definitely diagnosing males, and EDs are being diagnosed in all ethnic groups, but the incidence does seem to be higher among the industrialized nations. There are physicians specializing in eating disorders in Japan, Korea, and Taiwan.

Q: I have heard that young men with eating disorders feel a great deal of shame because it is a "female" disease. Is that true?

A: Many young men with anorexia have sexual orientation issues, so the "female" or gender-related shame concerns regarding anorexia are really not the locus of the "shame." Bulimia is more often found among male athletes who are trying to "spot" a specific weight for competition, e.g., wrestlers or boxers. The "shame" felt here might be due to feeling morally "weak" in not being in full control of appetite and weight. Such "weakness" may be interpreted as "female."

Q: If a study abroad adviser knows a student has an eating disorder, wouldn't it be best to advise him or her not to travel?

A: Probably it would be best for the student if she or he is being actively treated for ED not to travel. The ED patterns are very often reinforced during times of stress, and study abroad will have stress inherent in the experience. If the person is in the "recovery" phase, a complete medical clearance should be obtained prior to departure along with a contract with the student stating weight to be maintained, etc. Such a contract will be harder to construct with the bulimic student, but it can be done.

Q: What if a foreign student denies having an eating disorder and states that her body size and eating habits are culturally based?

A: Get a factual reference base here. The Asian female particularly likes to hide behind this claim. A medical practitioner can obtain the standard weights of a given country. Then, she or he can discuss with the student the "small bone" and percentage of body fat for the age group and assure the student that these are universal.

Q: Is it possible to maintain a "low-level" eating disorder for several years?

A: Not only possible, but quite prevalent. A non-life threatening ED that does not interfere with the person's activity of daily living frequently becomes a "chronic" state. The longer ED patterns are maintained, the more difficult complete recovery becomes.

Q: Could living in the United States trigger an eating disorder in a foreign student?

A: This is a possibility, especially if the student comes from a culture that does not value thinness. We are particularly seeing an increased incidence of ED in females from the Eastern European countries; and their parents are totally bewildered by their daughter's desire to "look sick" as one appalled Russian father stated to me.

Q: Do you have any suggestions for how to explain to the family of a foreign student what an eating disorder is, especially if it is not common in their country?

A: Get or prepare with the collaboration of your Health Services or Health Education Department, a simple brochure. The family of a foreign student must be given something in writing. Ask them to read the material and to come back to discuss the situation. They are too "ashamed," "confused," or "angry" to really hear you the first time around. Many times the first response is that the family is just going to take the student home and feed her. That will not work, needless to say, and the family dynamics will quickly deteriorate from strained to possibly dangerous. You do not want a suicide attempt!

Q: My institution is in a small town and we don't have counselors from different ethnic backgrounds the way that New York City or other large cities do. What can I do?

A: As an advocate for the student, it is important for you to work with the health care providers that are available to assure a level of cultural sensitivity. Offer to present cross-cultural sensitivity workshops for staff. Offer to share articles and books on this topic.

What to Do When a Student Is Missing

Scenario

The scenario is frightening. An undergraduate Nigerian student who has been suffering from psychological problems all semester agrees to return home at the beginning of the Christmas holiday. The Office of International Services adviser accompanies him to the airport and sees him off, fearful of the New York City to Nigeria transfer, but unable to do any more than see him off from the campus town. The student seems ready to maneuver the layovers in both New York and Europe. His parents are prepared to meet him at the airport in Lagos when he arrives. You breathe a sigh of relief as the plane departs, but anxiously await news of his arrival as Christmas Day approaches.

Christmas Day in Nigeria arrives on your Christmas Eve. The phone rings at home. The student has not arrived, and has not called his parents. Anxious parents plead with you to "find our son!"

The New York City Police are not very interested in this case. They suggest phone calls to all hospitals and shelters. Transit authorities at Kennedy Airport take a report and promise to "keep a lookout" for the student in the airport terminal. Anyone who has ever been in the JFK Terminal can understand the futility of this effort. You call a contact at the Nigerian Consulate in New York City, but of course, on the holiday, no one answers. A call to the personal residence of the Educational Attaché of the Nigerian Embassy in Washington, D.C.—the value of networks!—yields a mild interest, and a promise to investigate when the work week begins again in three days. Calls to all the homeless shelters in New York City that can be found yield very little. Thankfully, hospital emergency rooms can offer no reports that would lead one to think that this student had been brought to a hospital.

The mixed relief of no bad news, combined with no good news, must be conveyed to the anxious parents. They accept the report better than expected, and you promise to contact them immediately with any news.

Continued phone calls and legal efforts over the next week prove fruitless. Some written reports come in and are shared with the parents. The airline confirms that the student never made the New York to Germany connection, so you can only assume that the student is either roaming New York City in some delusional state, or has been accosted and met some bad end, which will eventually be known. Both sides just wait.

You receive a phone call at your office on New Year's Eve morning. The student walked into his parent's courtyard in Lagos at 11:45 p.m. New Year's Eve in Nigeria, just as they were departing for midnight mass, a Nigerian Catholic custom on New Year's Eve. He seemed unfazed by the long absence, and relatively well. The long story, as it unfolded, was amazing, and frustrating at the same time.

The student had not been allowed to board the Germany flight, because he did not have a transit visa to enter Germany! Nigerians need such a visa. Since it was Christmas Eve when he arrived in New York City, the German Consulate was already closed, and he had to wait until Monday to go into the city and obtain this visa. He found himself with four days with nothing to do. An attempt to call the university OIS collect was refused by the operator! The psychologically frail student decided to sit in the JFK terminal, doling out his limited funds to last four days. A friendly JFK terminal worker took pity on him, and took him home for the holiday, and helped him obtain the visa the next week. However, by that time his ticket was invalid, and it took several more days to arrange a new ticket, all by himself, with limited psychic and emotional strength. He never thought to call home, since his first effort to obtain help by calling the international office had failed.

The summary: All ended well, but so much anxiety and potential for disaster could have been averted if....

Thinking Ahead to Prevent a Crisis

A student missing is a crisis no one in international education wants to face, but prevention techniques can help. Thorough investigation of all possibilities is the only procedural guideline that can be provided. Advice to the adviser involved is: maintain a calm, broad perspective. Remember: this individual has already managed to travel thousands of miles from his home country to study in the United States. The "umbilical cord" to authority, and even to parents, may be much less attached in this student's cultural context. The student, his friends, and family may not recognize your need to know where the student has chosen to travel, or "hide out." Experience has taught many concerned advisers that the worst-case scenario in the case of a missing student—abduction, death, hostage-taking, amnesia, etc.—rarely develops. It is much more often a case of missed flights, changed plans, and blissful unawareness that people are concerned about his absence, and occasionally, purposeful abandonment of student status in the United States. Cultural components of the missing student scenario weigh heavily into the guidelines for action.

International students in the United States are unaware of the *in loco parentis* principle, which characterized the relationship between a university and its students for many generations. Although no longer operative in a legal sense, the philosophical posture that a university, its staff, and its structure, are "responsible" for a student is part of the culture of the United States. In these days, the phenomenon of binge drinking and deaths from alcohol overdose on campuses have brought this issue into the news vis-à-vis U.S. nationals. Each time a new crisis occurs of that kind, the outcry is, "Why didn't the university control the activities of its students?"

This concept is quite alien to students who come from countries where even attendance at university classes is unnoticed, unexpected, and completely optional. As one student from Finland explained, "It is our education. If we want to attend the classes, we attend. The professors offer the material, and we can study at home or attend class; either option is acceptable." With this casual position, is it any surprise then that a student would find it unusual that his whereabouts over a three-day holiday period would be a cause for concern to a university administrator?

To prevent unexplained absences from campus, an orientation program and a student handbook should discuss "missing person reports," and the legal activity which could ensue. Students should be advised always to let someone know where they are and where they could be reached. Scenarios that make this real to the student should be included, such as: "In the case a parent calls about an emergency at home, if they cannot reach you at your residence, the international office is usually the next place to be contacted. We need to have a contact here in the United States who will know where you are!"

At check-in, and then once a year thereafter, students should update their personal files in the international office with the name, address, and phone number of an emergency contact in the United States. When asked "Why? When would such a person be contacted by the international office?"

the adequate response is "If you were sick, in the hospital, or missing." It seems to satisfy the need to know why, and those emergency contacts have been priceless in times of crisis.

Preparation also includes a well-established network within the ethnic communities on your campus. Know the president, executive officers, faculty adviser, and local leaders in that community. Be familiar with the religious organization(s) and affiliations with which the students worship and socialize. Participate in their national holiday celebrations and festivals so that you are a known entity, and a trusted figure to them. Invite them to activities on campus where their own prestige can be recognized. Let your students see that you have a connection with their community both on campus and off. Be aware of the social and political trends that activate the various communities. Offer to help when the occasion arises. (For example, a local community did an outreach within their ethnic group for a possible bone marrow donor for a three-year-old with leukemia. The international student population from that ethnic group responded, at the initiation of the international student adviser, and showed their support of the community in that way.) Then, when you need the community to help you find a missing student, or face a worse crisis, they will be there for you.

First Notification

Quite often, the first notice of a possible missing student is cautionary, tentative, and hesitant. The information that comes to the adviser or authority figure is generally anecdotal and incomplete, and the conveyer of the information is motivated by fear and anxiety. It is essential to obtain as much factual information as possible from the first moment. The following checklist may be helpful to keep by the phone:

❑ Name (full spelling of all names used by the student)

❑ Address, both local and home country

❑ E-mail and phone number(s) of the student

❑ When and where last seen and by whom

❑ Expressed intentions of the student at that time (e.g. flying home, visiting friends, going to the library, etc.)

❑ What did the student have with him/her at the time? (e.g. passport, money, ATM and/or charge cards, books, extra clothing, luggage, backpack)

❑ Had the student had any mood changes or reasons to be unhappy?

❑ Was the student ill or recovering from any illness, hospitalization, or accident?

❑ Are the roommates, parents, and close friends aware that the student is missing?

❑ Does the student have any known social problems, such as drinking, drugs, sexual behavioral patterns such as visiting prostitutes or sex "chat" rooms on-line, or gambling?

❑ Has the student been recruited in any way by religious groups, which practice cult-like behavior? If so, where, when, and who was involved?

❑ Has the student been attending classes regularly? Does the faculty know the student?

Answers to these questions can give you, investigators, relatives, and interested friends some direction as you move ahead to locate the student.

First Actions

So, when one receives a report about a missing person, the first, most important thing to ascertain is if, indeed, the person is actually missing! Answers to the above questions will help with that search. A search can then be conducted, incorporating the guidance and leadership of the campus public safety office, the dean of students, the leader of the ethnic group, and any other appropriate campus official who has a logical connection (i.e. the director of residence if the student lives on-campus, the academic adviser if the student is close to his academic department, as in the case of a research assistant, for example). Very often the public safety office will take the lead role, investigating:

- Last class attendance

- Last bank activity

- Residence activity, such as presence or absence of luggage, personal hygiene items, any signs of forced departure or criminal activity, and whether the bed has been slept in recently

- Mail delivery and mail returned

- Telephone and computer e-mail activity

- Contact with friends, roommates, classmates, and faculty.

Keep in mind that the public safety officers will operate from their own U.S.-based cultural perspective. Interviews with roommates or friends who come from a different culture may not yield any real information, if privacy is an issue. Asian students may feel that "saving face" for the missing student is more important than providing information to a public safety or police officer. Students who come from a very independent-oriented culture, even as similar as Western Europe, may find our investigation efforts intrusive and an infringement on the independence of their friend or colleague. With this in mind, the clarification of concerns by the international student adviser will facilitate and ease the investigation.

Prolonged Investigation

Cultural components of a missing student situation are complex and require the experience and knowledge of a person very attuned to that culture. The investigation should include a private conversation with the most respected leader of that ethnic group in the community, if possible, or at least with representatives from the community. Issues to look for include:

- Political instability or activity in the home country: would there be motivation for a student to go underground, or apply for political asylum in the United States?

- Financial urgency: does the student need to find money, either for personal or family needs, or to fund some activity in the home country or ethnic group?

- Marriage: is an arranged marriage on the horizon, and could the student be avoiding this future?

- Divorce or abuse: is the person involved in a domestic situation that cannot be changed? Escaping may be perceived as a possible solution.

- Unexpected pregnancy: is the student "missing" to avoid dealing with an unexpected/ unwanted/impossible pregnancy? Would the community help in this case? Would the student be ostracized or face extreme criticism for a decision to keep the baby?

- Religious affiliation: does the student have a strong religious affiliation, or could a cult-like group have influenced him? Have cults been operating within this ethnic community?

- Trends from that ethnic group of immigration into the U.S., both legal and illegal.

- Business or investment ventures that may have targeted or attracted the student.

Resolution

The missing international student will remain missing until such time as the university, local community, or family is informed as to his or her whereabouts. An active investigation can only be conducted for a limited time period. After that, the leads become old information, and new concerns take precedence in the life of the public safety officers. The international community needs to be kept informed as to the status of the "missing student" on a regular basis. They need to know what has been done, and what remains to be uncovered or explained. A group meeting is helpful if the missing status carries on for more than a week or so.

The cooperation of the university public relations office should be obtained so that published reports keep the cross-cultural sensitivity aspect of the case in mind. Cultural taboos should be respected if at all possible, such as not mentioning a pregnancy if one is involved—discussing an unborn child is a curse in some cultures, and an intimacy that is offensive in other cultures. Assumptions of political or financial causes based upon current problems in the home country should also be avoided as the public connection of an individual with political sides in his home country could have negative, even disastrous, repercussions upon family members at home (e.g., a hypothetical news release in a local paper: "Lin Shu, known to be a leading dissident in China, has not reported to his academic department at XYZ University since the recent arrest of his former teacher, Yan Wan, in ABC city, China").

Repeated questioning of friends and community members will often yield more information in the future, as they become more assured of your trustfulness. They may also need to be assured of the safety of their friend or colleague before they will reveal any information to you. Parents can also be a source of information. Remembering that the U.S. is still seen as the land of opportunity for many, some parents give their approval to the abandonment of studies, even scholarship and academic success, for the possibility that their son or daughter might obtain the prized green card in the United States through whatever means available. Citizens of countries where corruption and "beating the government" is a way of life do not necessarily view "going underground" as illegal. The ends justify the means, and if that is a better case than returning home to fight in a war, or face poverty and unemployment, lack of opportunity and a dismal future, they would prefer the student to find his or her own way here, at whatever the cost. If the student must deceive authorities to accomplish that goal, it may be viewed as a price worth paying.

There are times when resolution of a missing person case takes direct action on the part of interested and committed parties, most often the international student adviser. Removing someone from a religious cult is such a resolution. Campus safety and local police are not going to take on that role. Family members from abroad only want the student safe and back home. But how to accomplish that task is difficult, to say the least. Campus religious leaders can provide support, and help find "deprogramming" experts to assist in this cause. The help of U.S.-educated friends may also be instrumental in winning over the trust of the student in order to bring him back to campus or home. Relatives may have to come to the States to accomplish this task, but convincing them of this may be the role of the adviser. Who else has the knowledge and the commitment to this student?

The "right to privacy" in the United States is one encumbrance to finding a missing person. If someone is hospitalized, either for a physical or a mental condition, it can be the case that no one knows about it for the entire duration of the hospitalization. This is a situation where good networks with the insurance carrier, and the hospital social workers can be and enormous help. Even when all leads have ceased, a constant check-in with emergency rooms, insurance carriers, and psychiatric facilities might yield new information. After all, a student missing for a prolonged time might not be practicing a healthy lifestyle, either physically or mentally. Even if the student was not in the hospital at the first stage of the investigation, continued check-ins might find her receiving care at a later stage.

Campus police should also bring the FBI into the investigation. Be aware that information contained in the files in the international office might be helpful in this investigation. Passport and visa information, at the very least, will facilitate a review of border crossings. Copies of the I-94 and I-20 could also help verify entry into the United States, or exit from the country. When was the I-20 last signed for travel? Has the student ever been associated with any terrorist activity in the United States?

Summary

The "missing student" scenario is difficult because of its ambiguity. In other crises, one has a visceral reaction to the news—whether grief, anxiety, fear, terror, or other emotional responses. In the case of a missing student, one simply doesn't know whether to be angry at the student for taking a vacation without telling anyone, disabused because the student has flaunted all rules and regulations of the U.S. Immigration and Naturalization Service by abandoning student visa status and going "underground," or fearful because of the possible disasters that may have befallen the student. One must command respect and authority in the face of uncertainty and potential tragedy. A prescribed plan will help, and the support of others who are committed to the well-being of your student also will help. Successful resolution of these cases often is possible.

Chapter 5

Racism, Relationship Violence, Sexual Harassment, and Rape

Ellen H. Badger, Patricia A. Burak, Sidney (Skip) Greenblatt,
Stephen Marcoux Nelson, and Deirdre Colby Sato

International students in the United States can be as susceptible to social and relationship violence as students anywhere. As in any society, stresses and strains occur in personal relationships and can increase in a new environment that challenges individuals' comfort levels; a certain segment of our society disdains the same cultural differences that others of us see as enriching; and as everywhere in the world, sexual violence will occur if victims do not seek assistance early and sometimes even if they do.

What can make highly sensitive and serious situations of personal safety all the more complicated, however, are the differences in cultural beliefs, acceptances, and morés that our international students bring with them to the United States. Sensitivity and insight into these cultural differences is crucial before the victimized or offending students can be helped, making the role of the international educator key.

International Students as Targets or Purveyors of Racism

Scenario 1

One warm April night, following a party, a group of six students, most of them Japanese, went to a restaurant for an early morning snack. Despite repeated requests to be seated, late arriving patrons were shown to the tables while they were left standing, and when one of their number protested, the on-duty staff called security guards to "escort" the students out the

91

front door. While protesting their treatment outside, a group of young white males emerged from inside the restaurant and attacked the internationals. They struck out at both men and women, and when others, who were not a part of the international group, sought help from the security guards, they refused to intervene. It wasn't until police backup arrived that the fighting stopped.

The security officers, off-duty police, described the internationals as drunk and hysterical. When the victims of the attack brought suit through the Asian-American Defense League, the district attorney sided with their assailants. Student-led demonstrations and protests continued in the months that followed the incident, and the case is still under litigation.

Scenario 2

Xianfa had read about black people and their struggle against racism in text books going all the way back to his high school days. He read Uncle Tom's Cabin in Chinese, and learned about the struggle of black people in many countries against racism, imperialism, and colonialism. He knew it was a major, unresolved issue in the United States.

One day, he left home to come to school and found his car blocked by another vehicle in the driveway. He blew his horn several times until the apparent owner, a black man, came out of the house next door. The man swore at Xianfa, called him names, and told him to "Go to hell!" He banged his fist on Xianfa's car and threatened to beat him up. In spite of what may have been his best instincts, Xianfa began to suspect that this one, angry man represented other black people.

The Complexities of Racism

Racism, including reverse racism, is a difficult topic to address. American notions about race relations among our own citizens are subject to intense, emotional discourse, which can carry over to international students who enter the realm of American society and culture. They become both the subjects and the objects of American discourse on race, and of the institutional imperatives and ambiguities governing campus discourse and conduct. When racism toward international students reaches a crisis, its sources can usually be traced to American roots even though, as the scenario noted at the beginning of this essay suggests, the stereotypes that inform expressions of racism, resonate in countries beyond our own.

International students have been the objects of racist remarks, discriminatory treatment, harassment, and tragically, assault, rape, and murder. Since the range of racist behavior and attitudes is so broad, any of the palliatives, strategies, and resources used in response must reflect this breadth.

Teaching About Intolerance

A good place to begin discussing racism in the United States is with preregistration orientation for new arrivals. Advisers should consider sessions on racial intolerance and discrimination essential elements in orientation programming. International students, particularly the visible minorities among them, need to be made aware that they may become the targets of slurs, and that racial slurs are a product of ignorance and insensitivity. Anger and shock are therefore appropriate responses. Advisers need to make it clear that they are available to provide support and understanding when incidents occur. They should also discuss appropriate responses when a victim becomes angry and frustrated. Physical actions against a perpetrator must be characterized as completely inappropriate.

The Hostile Campus

Students should be required to read and become familiar with campus codes of student conduct. Most campus regulations ban targeting groups by race and penalize the use of campus facilities including e-mail and the Internet toward racist ends. Students should learn how to access the student judicial system to initiate action against peers who violate the code of conduct, and they should be aware of both the strengths and weaknesses of the campus judicial system.

The search for remedial action is more complicated when the offending parties are not peers but faculty and administrative officers of the university, people to whom most of our students defer. Racism and discriminatory behavior, in this case, is all too often protected by a veil of silence that descends on students who, for obvious reasons, are reluctant to bring charges against the very authority figures who govern their careers. Access to faculty governance units (e.g., the Senate Committee on Tenure, Academic Freedom, and Professional Ethics), and to superior officers of the university, is often essential to the successful pursuit of a remedy. Students need also to be made aware of the limits of lawsuits. It is usually the better part of wisdom to let the hierarchy of academic authority run its course before turning to legal intervention.

Internationals enter the campus community where the stakes for others and the channels of communication, support and advocacy are already established. As graduate assistants they compete for scarce resources that are also in demand for domestic students including domestic minorities. They fall into the organizational bailiwick of the international office on campus, an institution whose personnel have followed a different career trajectory, and whose constituencies are distinctly different from those who serve domestic students, particularly domestic minorities. This double, sometimes triple form of organizational tracking may serve the special needs of enclaves within the community very well, but fails to integrate their varied constituencies in any meaningful way. Intergroup relationships hardly exist, and stereotypy flourishes in the empty spaces between groups.

International offices need to do their part to detoxify the campus environment and close the community gap in order to benefit from the diversity to which everyone lays separate claim.

How successfully they do so is a measure of an individual campus's likelihood to experience a racial crisis. There are several dimensions to inclusiveness:

- Representation of both international students (or former internationals) and domestic minorities in staff and student employee ranks;

- Recruitment of domestic minorities into leadership roles for language and support group programs, orientation sessions, workshops and special events for students, faculty and staff;

- Joint programming with minority cultural affairs offices on and off campus, including sensitivity training; and

- Encouragement of faculty to draw upon the backgrounds and interests of both international students and domestic minority students in courses where self and social identifications are featured aspects of disciplinary learning.

There are natural allies in these endeavors on every campus, and they typically include anthropology, sociology, social work, psychology, education, and political science and related sub-fields and specialties.

But the search for allies should not be limited to the social and behavioral sciences since, in this regard, it is concern with community that identifies who one's allies are. The most important bridges are often the most difficult to cross, namely the bridges between international offices and the minority affairs administrative systems on campuses. Joint programs serve as incentives to become more directly and formally involved with one another.

Racism As a Universal Problem

As the second scenario implies, the noxious effects of prejudice are not confined to Americans. They are echoed abroad in the xenophobic literature of colonialism and nationalism, picked up through transitions into this society mediated by prejudiced people, and they emerge out of the social context of intergroup conflict in the United States. Few offices of international services are equipped either to assess the extent of such prejudice or to address it. Yet it undermines the meaning of "diversity" and "community," reinforces racial enclaves, and encourages the scourge of discriminatory behavior.

Here again, workshops and dialogues that bring prejudice to the surface are critical aids to community building. Programs such as the President's Dialogue on Race convened on and off campus offers one such approach. The dramatization of racial conflict in film and on the stage serves college audiences well. The 1992 film "The Color of Fear," serves as one example. The object, however, is to involve international students in these events because they do not sell themselves to international audiences, building them into orientation programming or drawing on the commitments of international student group leaders may be essential to their success.

Community Conflict and Violence

Whether international students come to harm by being caught in the middle of communal riots or by because they are specifically targeted by hate groups and their minions, the international office has to be prepared to deal with violence and its repercussions. In such cases, the targets may be individuals, but the impact cuts across the entire campus community and often reaches far, far beyond it.

Death, assault, rape, and battery caused by racial hatred are among the least explicable acts of inhumanity. They send a traumatizing chill through targeted groups on and off campus, in and beyond one's own community as far and as fast as e-mail and the Internet broadcast incidents to the world at-large. Emergency protocols intended to deal with trauma in the campus community also apply in this instance. But, because of the horrendous and willful nature of such crimes and the implication of culpability, it is of the utmost importance that university officials make a public commitment to protect endangered students, relieve the trauma, and bring perpetrators to justice at the earliest possible date.

Making Public Commitments. Whatever the protocol, the international office should have some role in the review of public statements since the audiences for them include internationals and allied communities on campus and off, in this country and abroad. Messages crafted in Syracuse (concerning the Denny's incident) were received in Tokyo, and that is a matter of international protocol within the bailiwick of the international student office. Hence, there should be either direct or indirect linkages between that office and the university's principal officers for public relations.

Protecting Endangered Students. Incidents on campus fall within the on-campus crisis protocol and should trigger immediate liaison between campus security officers and the international student office. The purpose of that liaison is to identify the individuals and/or groups targeted by the attack, and the potential threat to other members of the community. Then, it is necessary to insure that other potential victims are alerted to the threat, and are provided means of protection through enhanced police and security patrols, emergency telephone connection to security and, if necessary, temporary safe haven. Many of these measures require collaboration between campus security and local police, and/ or FBI investigators.

Off-campus incidents are more difficult to handle, but require, at the least, the closest possible liaison between campus security and police as well as the collaboration of other investigative offices including the FBI, the district attorney's office, and where appropriate, local, regional, or state human rights organizations. At every level, it has to be the function of the office of international services to point out the international and intercultural dimensions of the incident to all parties involved at the earliest possible juncture. Soon enough, that role may be overtaken by political gestures, reaction and demonstrations, investigation, and legal suit.

Relieving Trauma. Survivors of attacks are most urgently in need of relief, and most offices of international services are poorly prepared to provide it. Counseling offices, familiar with trauma, may have much more difficulty coming to grips with the fears and anxieties of internationals who are not now at home in their own cultures of origin, and are now at the mercy of the most terrifying aspects of the host culture where they are living. Relief, in this instance, means a commitment to providing a full panoply of counseling resources, with the aid of the international office, on a continuing rather than intermittent basis. The resources called upon must include experienced faculty and staff, rape counselors, cross-cultural counselors, and health service professionals.

Members of targeted groups and their allies and sympathizers are the second most needful category. The chill caused by unreasoned attack spills over into the community as a whole. That, in itself, can produce traumatic responses. Students are unable to participate in classes, fearful of being left alone in the laboratory or in their apartments; they become distraught, stop eating, cry uncontrollably. Both survivors and those who are chilled by such events report that parents and siblings at home fail to understand the sources of their anxieties. Parents may say that their son or daughter chose the university they are attending; therefore the problem is theirs. At the very least, the traumatized need sympathetic listeners. The most sympathetic listeners tend to be located in small, intimate, and mutually dependent groups, and they, in turn, need sustenance from the staff of the international office.

Bringing Perpetrators To Justice

The wheels of justice often turn extremely slowly, all the more so when community interests are allied against outsiders, when institutions seek to minimize liability, and activists protest while evidence is being gathered and trauma sinks in. Survivors often feel as though they are being sullied by everyone. Litigation may provide one route toward justice, but it also tends to undermine the solidarity of the small groups of mutual dependency that survivors need as they transit from crisis to something approaching normalcy.

International offices should be prepared to deal with these dilemmas and provide support to survivors, even when the institutions they are part of are forced to move in low gear until evidence is sifted, and the perpetrators are legally sanctioned. They will need to bring a broad range of referral services and learning systems to bear. A short list of several organizations that have proved useful are included in Appendix D.

Relationship Violence

Scenario

An FSA relates her experience working with a woman from the People's Republic of China whose husband had battered her. He had slammed her up against the wall and throttled her. He had grabbed their television and had thrown it against the wall. The woman was eight months pregnant at the time. The next day she took a bus and went to the campus police. The incident happened in Iowa, a state with a mandatory arrest law for this kind of behavior, so he was arrested and jailed. When she later tried to have the charges dismissed, she learned that only the county district attorney could dismiss the charges and since there was evidence of assault, it was impossible.

The Chinese community immediately turned against her, ostracized her, and gossiped about her. She tried to stay in a shelter, but since her English was poor, she didn't understand the counselors and was embarrassed by the questions they asked her. She also found that the kitchen had no soy sauce, no cooking knife, and everyone thought her food needs were strange. She was bothered by the smells that emanated from the foods the others cooked.

When she tried to explain that her problems began when she changed from a J-2 visa status, which allowed employment, to the F-2 visa status, which did not, the counselors had no basis for understanding. Their standard line of counseling and advising focused on independence, both psychological and financial, and this meant that she was to take the initiative and get a job.

The foreign student adviser tried to explain to other Chinese that the woman had done the right thing, and that her husband had no right to physically abuse her no matter what he felt were the justifying reasons. She tried to work with the shelter counselors, explaining immigration laws and restrictions. She met with the husband, who begged and pleaded with her to "return his wife" since he was a respectable, serious student who deserved to have his wife at his side.

The wife eventually went back to the husband, and they have remained together. There was no mention of the incident in any subsequent meetings with the foreign student adviser.

This scenario highlights some of the legal, social, cultural, and personal issues involved in managing a crisis involving domestic violence, or at least, what is perceived to be domestic violence in the United States. Not all cultures consider similar behaviors as reprehensible, much less criminal. An international student adviser in Texas reported that "one international family we worked with at the Children's Protective Services was totally shocked and humiliated that the law would interfere with things they considered to be family matters only."

A New York Times article (February 24, 1991) on Ugandan women reported: "In many places, women treat wife-beating as an accepted practice. The Uganda Women's 'Lawyers Association recently embarked on a campaign to convince women that wife-battering is not a sign of a man's love."

The very fact that this initiative was started by Ugandan women lawyers indicates that wife-beating was not a fully accepted practice. A United Nations study on domestic violence concluded that "violence against women is a function of the belief, fostered in all cultures, that men are superior and that the women they live with are their possessions or chattels, which they may treat as they wish and as they consider appropriate." It goes on to cite "certain customary practices and some aspects of tradition are often the cause of violence against women.... female genital mutilation...foot binding, male preference, early marriage, virginity tests, dowry deaths, sati, female infanticide and malnutrition are among the many practices which violate a woman's human rights." An old proverb affirms this thinking: "A wife married is like a pony bought. I will ride her and whip her as I like." The Los Angeles Times in December 1997 ran a feature story on "Russia's Ugly Little Secret: Misogyny." The subtitle reads: "Underneath gallantry and sentiment, a widespread contempt for women often ends in black eyes, broken bones, and worse. And activists say the violence is increasing." From these cultures come our students and their spouses. Is it any wonder, then, that what we have come to recognize and treat as domestic violence erupts among international populations?

The work of the adviser, counselor (program supervisor if the incident takes place abroad), faculty, or community member who chooses to get involved, must go beyond the actual physical or psychological abuse at hand. A primer for action follows to help guide those who dare to stand up for and help a victim of relationship abuse, whether it is recognized as such or not.

First Actions

When an incident of abuse is reported, the adviser has an obligation to act. That obligation is defined by both professional and moral codes that may be articulated in procedural manuals, or learned through socialization within the cultural environment of the United States. The adviser should have ready reference to both legal and institutional resources to call upon in such cases. A listing of these resources appears at the end of the chapter.

Depending upon professional limitations, the adviser may choose to undertake many of these actions him/herself, or may call on others to act. That choice is the adviser's to make, with the understanding that such choices have major significance for the successful resolution of the crisis.

Ascertain facts as thoroughly as possible before initiating action. Try to speak with both parties—all parties, if children are also involved. Be conscious of the possible need for an impartial interpreter. If the abuse or violence is reported by neighbors, check with other neighbors as well. If the abuse is reported by fellow countrymen or women, discuss it with the leader of the national group or other closely aligned ethnic group. Be aware that this exposure to the national group, leader or otherwise, may bring with it risks for the parties involved.

Have a frank discussion with the victim if possible. Understand her/his perception of the situation before you present options for action.

Be authoritative and confident in presenting options to the victim. Your indecision or uncertainty will negatively influence the victim's resolution to act. Interpret U.S. law and customary practice, from your informed vantage point, and freely present your past experience with the issues at hand. Reassure the victim that she is not the only one who has ever had to react to such circumstances.

Be present for and emotionally responsive to the victim. A phone call is not enough. If you cannot be physically present, arrange for another appropriate authority figure to represent you. Your experience, authority, and knowledge are needed in such times of crisis.

Second Steps

If the victim has been taken to a shelter, ascertain the rules of the shelter. What duration of stay is allowed? Who determines the time of departure? Are visitors allowed? What kind of transportation system exists to allow her to continue her studies, or employment, or to take her children to school and appointments, etc.?

Are the physical needs of the victim met? Is there a need to bring clothing, medicines, personal hygiene items, ethnic food staples, books, etc.? Does the victim need his/her personal phone and address directory to be in touch with friends and relatives? Does the victim need/have access to email? Does the victim have spending money to purchase newspapers, coins for the telephone, a phone card for long distance calls, postage?

How long can she remain in the shelter? Will she incur any costs? Who can visit her and does she want visitors? Whom does she want to see? Do her language skills warrant that an interpreter will be needed?

Sustained Support

Ascertain if a support network exists for the victim. If so, activate it. If not, assist in the creation of such a network. Call upon fellow countrymen or women; members of the same religious group; neighbors; parents of the friends of the family children; an international wives organization; or a faculty spouses club, if such organizations exist.

If the victim is reconciling with a spouse or partner who was the abuser, arrange an appointment with the perpetrator. Discuss the legal implications of the behavior, and the possible impact upon his immigration status. Let him know that you, as an authority figure, know about the situation, and that you will be available to support the victim if such behavior occurs again.

Counsel the victim about alternatives the next time the behavior occurs. Provide written options, such as names and phone numbers of shelters, and how to reach them. Provide written information with phone numbers about police protection, and instructions on filing an order of protection. Provide names and phone numbers of possible legal counsel, and if possible, inform the legal counsel in advance, to prepare the way for a future call. Provide names and phone numbers for medical assistance on a 24-hour basis, with information as to how to access this help (e.g. ambulance, campus safety, dialing 911).

Provide a safety net where the victim could easily turn if the need should arise. Be reassuring to the victim, clarifying that if a decision to return to the abusive situation is made, support will still be available immediately and unconditionally.

Advising Victims of Relationship Violence

Do not be judgmental, although you may feel compelled to give your evaluation and advice since the life of the victim could be at risk.

Encourage full disclosure, with no recriminations, but work with what you are given. Be aware that a great deal might not be revealed to you, initially, until you establish a trusting relationship. Even then, full disclosure is rare until you have contributed something to the relationship, such as securing a safe place for the victim to stay.

Be aware that immigration regulations do not support an F-2 or J-2 victim leaving the primary visa holder for safe harbor reasons. The legal status is interwoven with the F-1 or J-1 student or scholar status of the primary alien. Once a divorce becomes final, the non-immigrant dependent spouse must change status or lose all legal status in the United States.

Legal Recourse Available to Victims

An "Order of Protection" can be obtained through family or criminal court for victims of domestic abuse. The victim must file the request, detailing the threatening behavior. Depending upon the determination of the court, an "order of protection" can make it an illegal action for the perpetrator to talk with the victim, enter the house in which she is living, call her on the phone, or send her letters. The length of the order's validity depends on the court. Important: Immigration legislation (IIRAIRA) enacted in September 1996, addresses "Offenses of Domestic Violence and Stalking as Grounds for Deportation (Section 350)." This section adds crimes of domestic violence, stalking, child abuse, child neglect, or child abandonment as grounds of deportability. It also adds violation of a protective order as a ground of deportability. The language applies to convictions or violations of court orders occurring after September 30, 1996."

By law, in instances of domestic violence, if one is related to the abuser by blood or marriage, has a child in common, or is divorced from the abuser, one may pursue her case in family court, criminal court, or both. However, if the victim has never been married and does not share a child in common with the alleged abuser, she cannot go to family court and can only proceed in criminal court.

Both criminal court and family court proceedings seek to stop the violence and provide protection. A proceeding in criminal court allows for the prosecution of the offender and can result in a criminal conviction. In family court one has the right to an attorney. If it is determined that the victim cannot afford an attorney, one must be appointed to represent the victim without cost. If a victim has a case in criminal court, the district attorney will represent the person.

Custody issues and requests for temporary support are separate from the abuse and can be taken to Family court, even if a case is already in criminal court. When such help is needed, contact local police and/or the office of the district attorney.

General Advice

Once legal action has been taken, the victim should request a copy of any incident report (at no cost) from the law enforcement agency.

If children are involved, and the victim takes the children from the abuser, the Court can require payment of temporary child support while a couple is not living together. The victim should seek temporary custody of any children.

As in the incident detailed at the beginning of this chapter, be aware that the community may not support the victim. In fact, the victim may be ostracized and shunned by other members of the community, especially by male members if the victim is female. In these cases, other support groups should be found to substitute for national group support. Some examples might be: religious groups, university spouses or women's clubs, single, female graduate students from that ethnic group, or female members of the community who have been victims of relationship violence.

Summary

All cases of relationship violence within the international student and scholar population should be brought to the attention of the program adviser, foreign student adviser, faculty mentor, or resident adviser. Cross-cultural issues must be addressed from the onset in order for any remedial action to be effective. Age, gender, social status, marital status, and educational background of the person "assigned" to help the situation must be assessed for appropriateness. Getting the victim and any children into a safe environment takes priority. Interpreting the options that are truly viable for the victim is an absolute necessity from the start. Understanding the community and religious framework in which decisions must be made is essential.

However, all these matters considered, international educators must be careful not to be blinded by cultural sensitivity to the serious consequences of spousal abuse. As an assistant dean of student affairs-international student adviser at the New England College reported: "The young man, a student from the Middle East who had been charged with sexual assault, did not understand why we were taking issue with his behavior. In his culture, men have all the authority as to if, when, and how intimate relations would be conducted. We held him to our level of expectations. His separation from the college included his ability to return if he underwent counseling to address sexual assault and gender issues, particularly from a western view." The high road is to be commended and perhaps emulated, but it is important to read the final comment from the assistant dean: "I am not sure how successful I was in this attempt. He has not followed through, and I do not see him returning to NEC."

Ameliorative efforts can include going to the community when the perpetrator is from a "culture of shame," as is true for some Indians, Pakistanis, Middle Easterners, and Asians. Threatening exposure is sometimes the best deterrent. Carole Cumps, foreign student adviser at the University of Massachusetts tells a story of an African wife, who learned in the United States that the regular pattern of beating inflicted upon both herself and her children by her husband was wrong by watching television! A series of ads on television for a local shelter explained that the children could be taken away from their mother if the mother "allowed" the beatings! The woman then pressed charges against her husband, but said that if it had not been for the exposure on television, she never would have known that U.S. laws existed for protection as well as for punishment.

Finding a way for the F-2 or J-2 spouse victim to earn admission to the college or university with financial support is often a dream come true for these victims. Immigration is generally accepting of a change of visa application under such circumstances, provided that the situation is well-explained and documented and that there is adequate financial support for the student to-be and any dependent children. This new status can enable the victim to prepare for eventual return to home country newly empowered. If staying in the United States is the most viable alternative under the circumstances, very careful counseling about legal status should be pursued. If the program adviser is unable to provide such legal advice, the services of an immigration attorney should be obtained. In cases where divorce is the necessary recourse, a divorce lawyer who understands the implications of the ensuing immigration status issues should be retained.

In whatever form you may provide help, rest assured that it will be appreciated, needed, and effective. The emotional, physical, and psychological damage inflicted upon victims of domestic violence demands informed and concerned response. Often, you may be the individual who can make a tremendous difference.

Rape and Abortion

Scenarios

Aminah didn't want to tell the story, but she needed help; she needed a listening ear. She needed reassurance that she hadn't been to blame. After all, Roy was her teaching assistant, and held in high esteem in the department. The evening wasn't supposed to have turned out the way it did.

Anna had already made her decision when she came into the office. Although she was married, her husband refused to even consider the possibility of a child at this time. The pregnancy was unexpected, unwanted, and would have to be terminated. Anna had only been in the United States three months. She didn't have a penny, and her husband refused to pay for any medical care. The pregnancy was "her problem," in his opinion, and she "had better take care of it" immediately.

Carina, at 42, had already heard and felt the biological clock of motherhood. With no serious relationships on the horizon, perhaps it was something instinctive that allowed her to be lulled into such a passive state that an acquaintance rape took place; or was it drugged wine that made her unable to protest? In any case, she confided in you that she was pregnant and uncertain as to whether or not to have the baby. Two months of indecision turned into a joyful acceptance of her condition, until the amniocentesis revealed Downes Syndrome. She immediately decided to terminate the pregnancy, which required hospitalization, at this late date. Only she could know the immensity of the loss.

Rape is one of the most invasive and violent crimes a human being can experience and it happens all too often. Statistics show that 50 percent of all rapes in the United States occur in a person's own home; 75 percent are premeditated. Most of the time, but not always, men victimize women, rather than the reverse. Though sexual behavior varies from country to country, in most cases violent sex crimes are not tolerated, though verbal and physical abuse of a less extreme type may be accepted. Helping international students avoid embarrassment and worse, foreign student and study abroad advisers need to educate in order to prevent such situations from occurring. Preventive measures are critical. International students are often unclear about the norms of social interactions in American college social life. Orientation or discussion sessions can enlighten international students to the many styles of dating and relationships acceptable in the United States.

Awareness of typical patterns leading up to sex crimes, and particularly date rape, the most common type of rape among college students, can be enhanced through presentations by security or campus police, the campus women's centers, the health center, School of Nursing, and Division of Student Affairs staff.

Sexual harassment, which runs the gamut from verbal abuse to unwanted physical advances, is sometimes viewed very differently in other parts of the world, so it is important to help international students understand the American definition and consequences. Many universities have written policies on sexual harassment, so being familiar with them, as well as the procedures for filing and processing grievances in your institution, is key to being prepared to advise international students and scholars.

If your student is a victim of rape in any of its forms, it is important that you have a general idea about your state's legal definition of rape and the medical and legal services available to your student. Are comprehensive services for survivors of rape offered at an area hospital? Which ones have trained volunteers or counselors on call 24 hours a day? Has your police department and security staff had training in rape sensitivity? Are there female police officers available if the rape survivor is female? Is there a victims' services hotline available in your city? Will they pay for transportation, clothing, and medical expenses? How is it administered? What are the eligibility criteria, if any? Is there a religious center on campus or nearby where the student might find comfort? Is the counseling center sensitive to the issues that exist with rape, and are they sensitive to the cultural values of the student concerning this issue?

How will the student feel about pressing charges if she/he can identify the rapist? Even among the U.S. domestic population, the rate of prosecution is low, particularly when the rapist is an acquaintance. It is critical for you to help your student understand the legal process in your state from arraignment to sentencing and the levels of sex offense charges or other charges, if any, so that the student can make an informed decision. Helping the student understand his or her role as a defendant in a court hearing? How will the student feel about communicable disease testing? About evidence collection from clothes, body and the scene of the rape? These are all part of building a case and protecting the survivor, but can be very traumatic for anyone. Is there a group of fellow students who can be relied on to be supportive to this student during this phase and after? Rape is a very personal and shame evoking crime, so in the interest of confidentiality and being non-invasive, it is important to consult the student as you move ahead with the proceedings.

Incest is less often found among international college students, because they are usually living apart from their families. However, it is important to bear in mind that the psychological and physiological effects of any type of sexual assault, termed rape trauma syndrome, can be long-lived. After an initial phase of shock, instability and disorientation, a survivor may resume her normal activity and outwardly appear to have dealt with the experience. However, the effects of the rape can again emerge many years after the incident occurred, after the survivor blocks them out as a coping mechanism, sometimes for years. Sensitive counseling becomes critical on the part of the international student adviser as well as the counseling center.

Rape affects the whole family and, in the case of female survivors, may be particularly upsetting to sexual partners and male family members. Men involved may display proprietary indignation, thoughts of retribution and rage, and depression, or may have confusing emotional reactions toward the victim. The situation is made more complex by the addition of cultural values and beliefs from the home country that heighten the importance of culturally-sensitive, ongoing counseling for the whole family.

Pregnancy

Pregnancy, especially when unexpected, can cause a great deal of turmoil in the life of an international student or scholar. Not only will it cause immediate and long-term lifestyle changes, but it may also cause financial strain.

Planning ahead whenever possible is key. It is important for university advisers to have an idea of what the health center can offer as well as what off-campus services are available. A suggested list of resources to have readily available appears in Appendix D.

Knowledge of insurance policy options for your university is critical and the extent of coverage for prenatal and postpartum care must be clearly understood. Policies for adult dependents may differ from that of the student. In addition, coverage for the baby should be anticipated and, if not automatically covered by the student's policy, paid for. In cases of no insurance coverage, what is available to the student in your state or through area hospital systems? A prior awareness of this information is helpful when a crisis presents itself.

Clear approval policies and procedures must be developed by the international student adviser for F-1 and J-1 students may carry a lighter course load, or don't attend school at all during the pregnancy, childbirth, and after. Both partners need to assess the advantages and disadvantages of having the baby in the woman's home country versus the United States. Consideration should be given to the mother's nationality and wishes, as well as the father's. Understanding the implications of being married or unmarried when a baby arrives in the culture of the mother-to-be might be helpful for university advisers. Cultural informants, or the student herself, might provide insight.

Many students do not expect to have morning sickness or medical complications during pregnancy, but the unexpected can always happen. Attitudes about pregnancy can also vary across cultures, sometimes equated with harmony or the balance of mind and body, for example. These concepts may be very foreign to the adviser, but sensitivity to the student's feelings is critical. Advisers should articulate U.S. cultural expectations and norms, as well as university requirements. Information about delivery in the United Sates need to be discussed. Is the woman comfortable with a doctor (male or female), or is she familiar with the services of midwives? Is she aware of the use of medical monitoring during labor and the frequency of cesarean sections in the United States? Does she want her mate to be present for the birth, perhaps a very uncommon or even unacceptable practice in some parts of the world? Or is another companion available for assistance, or coaching, during labor?

In addition, researching resources for secondhand baby equipment and clothing and inexpensive diapers and formula can be greatly assist students.

University daycare services or women's centers can be helpful. Assistance for the mother after the birth via family members, friends, spouse, or child care services should be discussed, particularly if the student intends to return to the university right after the birth.

Abortion

A key issue for advisers in dealing with abortion is putting aside personal opinion on the subject and allowing the woman to make her own decision. This is a volatile issue in the United States, but it is critical for advisers to be aware of the fact that abortion is a very common form of birth control in other parts of the world, sometimes the most common because chemical or other options (except abstinence) are unavailable. Attitudes about the issue may be very different from our own. It is therefore essential that open conversation and discussion of all issues take place before action commences.

As a preventative measure, enlightenment about alternative forms of birth control is important. For some students this will be a whole new area of information. Though promiscuity should not be encouraged, an awareness of the fact that young people may become sexually active while at your university is important. Written information on birth control for both men and women should be made available at the health center, as well as in other easily accessible locations around campus.

An awareness of laws and restrictions on abortion in your state is critical. In some cases, a student may have to travel to obtain services. State laws on privacy, waiting periods, or permission and the male partner's role, vary widely. Your health center or area women's centers may be good resources for information. The important issue is for the student to find the reputable and safe services she needs, should she decide to have an abortion. Because of the political climate in the United States, this can be challenging. Adoption is a very foreign concept in some cultures, though quite common in the United States. Helping the student understand this option by thoughtfully and impartially answering of questions or researching information will be greatly appreciated.

Awareness that there may be residual psychological or physiological issues for the student after an abortion is important. Making sure that there is a support network including medical and counseling professions sympathetic to the woman's decision is critical.

Sexual Harassment

Allegations of harassment by one student against another may require varied official campus responses, depending upon the preferences of the victim, the nature of the alleged harassment, the response of the alleged harasser, and whether or not the harassment takes place on or off campus. The following two cases highlight these issues.

Case Study—Stalking and Aggravated Harassment On Campus: A Male International Graduate Student as the Alleged Aggressor

A male Chinese graduate student confided in a professor of his, who was also Chinese, that he (the student) was feeling very lonely. The professor suggested that the student find himself an American girlfriend. The student decided to focus his attentions on the American ESL TA, who was very outgoing and friendly. Despite the fact that he was married, the student made repeated phone calls to the woman, sent her e-mail messages and a lengthy letter proclaiming his love and admiration for her, presented her with small gifts, and made repeated visits to her on-campus apartment.

The undergraduate student wrote a letter back to the international student, rejecting his advances. He telephoned her, and she told him that she did not want to have any further contact with him. He then appeared at her apartment door with another gift for her. She telephoned the university police, who spoke with the international student and told him to leave. The female student did not wish to press charges at that time.

The undergraduate student met with the director of the ESL Program to express her concerns about the international student's behavior, as well as her own concern for her personal safety. The director of ESL in turn called the director of international student and scholar services, who referred the student to both the university police and the office of judicial affairs. When the victim filed a report with the university police, she was offered the options of campus judicial action, arrest, or both, and she chose campus judicial action. She also had her telephone number changed, and was issued a two-way radio by the university police so that she could summon officers to her aid on campus, if the international student approached her.

The dean of students, after receiving a copy of the police report, phoned the director of international student and scholar services, and requested that the director contact the international student, ask that he come in to meet with her, and explain to him the serious nature of his behavior and that it must stop.

The director of international student and scholar services contacted the international student and asked him to make separate appointments to meet with both her and the director of judicial affairs, and he readily did so. After interviewing the student, the director of judicial affairs issued him two letters. The first letter formally charged him with harassment through the campus judicial process. The second letter informed the male student that any further contact with the female student would subject him to further judicial action and possibly arrest. In both his meetings with the director of international student and scholar services and the director of judicial affairs, the male student continued to express his obsession with and admiration for the female student.

The harassing behaviors continued. In an attempt to get the female student to drop the campus judicial charges, the male student requested that his friends call her to plead his case, and he attempted to plead his case with her housemates. These events were subsequently reported by the undergraduate student to both the director of international student and scholar services and the director of judicial affairs.

The director of international student and scholar services consulted with the director of the university counseling center for advice; the director of counseling expressed his willingness to provide Counseling Center services to both students.

At the request of the director of international student and scholar services, the international student came in to discuss the matter further. He promised that he would not contact the female student again. He declared that this relationship was "over." He claimed not to understand why gifts he delivered to the female student's apartment that she had rejected had not been returned to him, not understanding that she did not want to provide any opportunity for additional contact. The director informed him that his behavior must stop, that he was jeopardizing his status as a student at the university, and that several campus offices were aware of his behavior and would take whatever steps were necessary to make sure that the female student was protected. She then told him that his behavior was inappropriate, and why. She offered him the services of the university Counseling Center, and he responded that going there might help him understand Americans better, although he did not follow up on this idea.

Meanwhile, the female student's boyfriend threatened to take physical action and requested the international student's telephone number, which the female student declined to release. There was further discussion between the director of international student and scholar services with the international student. The student advised the director that the problem wasn't that the female student didn't like him, she just didn't like the fact that he was married to someone else. However, at least for the time being, all contact between the international student and the undergraduate student seemed to stop.

Six weeks later, the female student received an e-mail message from the male student, but originating from another student's e-mail account. She contacted the university police and pressed criminal charges. The male student was arrested and charged with aggravated harassment, a misdemeanor. He claimed that he sent the female student an e-mail message because she had smiled at him a few days earlier when their paths crossed on campus. He interpreted the smile to mean a renewal of her affections towards him. He signed a sworn statement that he sent the e-mail message and that he would have no further contact with the female student. The male student's campus e-mail privileges were suspended and both the director of international student and scholar services and the director of judicial affairs advised him to find an attorney to assist him with the criminal charges, which he did. He contacted a professor who knew him, and asked the professor for her advice regarding whether he should telephone the female student and ask her to drop the charges. She advised him not to do so. After consulting with the director of judicial affairs, he agreed to accept sanctions from the university in lieu of a judicial board hearing. He also indicated that his wife and child were scheduled to arrive from China the following week.

There were no further incidents, and at the end of the semester, the female student graduated and departed the university. The male student had his court appearance one month later. His case was adjourned in contemplation of dismissal. The male student saw the director of international student and scholar services again and seemed very bitter. He complained that he no longer had access to campus e-mail, and that if the female student ever attempted to contact him, HE would call the police. He referred to her as "crazy." He graduated the following semester.

As a result of this incident, the director of ESL decided to add a new component to her ESL TA training that discusses how American openness and friendliness might be misinterpreted by some individuals from other countries, and emphasizes that messages must be clear and unambiguous.

This case did not have a fully positive outcome in that the male student persisted in his behavior long after it had been identified as morally and culturally inappropriate, and did not alter his understanding of the point of view of the female student. However, it did involve the interaction of multiple university offices working together. The victim was empowered to choose how she wanted the case handled and understood that the university was deeply concerned. This case does show the difficulty of dealing with an alleged harasser, who cannot let go of his obsession, yet is willing to talk freely about it to any university official and sees nothing wrong with his behavior. The student continued to maintain contact with the director of international student and scholar services, seeking advice on a variety of immigration regulatory issues, for nearly a year after this incident. However, he never mentioned it or the female student again.

Case Study—Aggravated Harassment Off Campus: Female International Graduate Student As Victim

A male, single graduate student from Korea and a female, single graduate student from Japan in different academic departments met in the university's main library while standing in line to use a photocopier. They had what she regarded as a casual, meaningless conversation, the sort of conversation you might have with a stranger to make the time pass more quickly. She then received a letter from him in her campus mailbox, which she read and returned to him after photocopying it and writing "please do not bother and contact me any more and in any future" on the envelope. He made repeated phone calls to her off-campus apartment from his off-campus apartment. Although she told him that she was not interested in him and asked that he stop calling, the calls persisted.

The female student's friends suggested that she contact the director of international student and scholar services. The female student sent an e-mail message to the director seeking assistance, and a meeting on the weekend when the most recent phone call incident took place. The director replied by e-mail to the female student urging her to come in the next day. The director then checked with the university police to determine jurisdiction since the calls were off-campus and to confirm the best way to handle any additional calls from the male student. She followed up with a telephone call to the female student, expressing her concern and suggesting how the student and the student's house mates might handle any additional calls from the male student (the advice was to just hang up if he called again). An appointment was scheduled for them to meet.

The director consulted with the director of judicial affairs and learned that the telephone calls, which all occurred off campus, were outside of campus judicial and university police jurisdiction. However, the letter from the male student, which was sent via campus mail, did open an avenue for campus judicial intervention. The female student met with the director of international student and scholar services, and provided a written chronology of the male student's interactions with her as well as a photocopy of the letter he had sent to her. The female student was reminded to hang up if he should call again, and was encouraged to meet next with the director of judicial affairs.

She did so, and was given judicial options, limited as they were because most of the alleged behaviors took place off campus. The female student was also given legal options that would have involved local police authorities arresting the male student. She chose to have the director of judicial affairs write a letter to the male student telling him to cease and desist all attempts to contact the female student by any means, for as long as he was a student at the university. In the letter, the male student was warned that should there be any further contact, campus disciplinary action and even criminal arrest against him might occur. The letter was sent with copies to the female student, the dean of students, the chief of the university police, and the director of international student and scholar services. The letter had the desired effect, and there was no further contact between the two students. The female student was very pleased with the timely and effective university response and that her allegations were deemed to be serious and important. The director of international student and scholar services was not asked to contact the male student regarding this case, and did not do so. However, had there been any evidence of continued or escalating inappropriate behavior, the director's response would certainly have been to take further action.

This was a case that did have a completely successful outcome. It began with the female student's friends recommending that she contact the director of international student and scholar services for help. From the student's perspective, the director responded quickly, regarded the student's concerns as serious ones, helped prepare the student for her meeting with the director of judicial affairs, and by doing so, turned the case over to the office in the best position to provide an appropriate response. The director followed up with the student after the case had been resolved. The student was left with the sense that her friends' recommendation had been a very appropriate one, that the University had responded promptly and correctly to her concerns, and that she, the student, played a critical role in guiding the University's response.

Practical Considerations

If one or more international students are involved in situations of alleged harassment, the director of international student and scholar services may become involved, although not necessarily in all instances. It is important for such incidents to be treated in a manner consistent with standard university disciplinary procedures in effect for all students. It is equally important for the director to establish through his or her interactions with the students involved in these cases, especially with the alleged harasser, that the issue is the student's behavior, not the director's personal feelings towards him or her. This allows for the advising relationship with the student to continue, so that there will be the potential for future consultations on other matters that may have immigration regulatory consequences.

The preceding cases highlight the different ways a campus might officially respond to alleged student harassment based on jurisdictional issues, and how important it is for the director of international student and scholar services to have an already established network of campus contacts for obtaining "expert" advice on issues involving student behavior. By having a close working relationship with key university offices, an understanding of the kinds of assistance each office might provide, and working within a well established "chain of command," the director can respond quickly and efficiently if he is the first contact, and be part of a coordinated response if he is not. An understanding of and sensitivity to cultural differences that might affect student behavior is an important and useful skill. However, it is equally important to be sure that clear, unambiguous messages are being conveyed to all parties involved about what behaviors are and are not appropriate.

Chapter 6

Crimes and Misdemeanors

Adapted by Patricia A. Burak from several sources

["Counseling Foreign Students Accused of a Crime," *NAFSA Newsletter,* Summer 1978, Peter Levitov, Associate Dean of International Affairs, University of Nebraska-Lincoln; *Crisis Management in a Cross-Cultural Setting,* Patricia A. Burak, NAFSA, 1987; and "Crimes and Misdemeanors: International Students in Trouble with the Law," session chaired by Danielle Guichard-Ashbrook, Assistant Dean of International Students, Massachusetts Institute of Technology, at the NAFSA 1999 National Conference in Denver, Colorado.]

Scenario

It is the third Monday in January, the federal holiday celebrating Martin Luther King, Jr.'s birthday. Your campus is officially closed, but the international office is open, to welcome new students who have arrived over the weekend. The phone rings. One of your "old" students has been arrested for disturbing the peace and assault. He appears to be intoxicated, is now in the custody of city police, and will be imprisoned overnight. You try to contact the university legal services and the bondsman, to get the student released pending arraignment the next morning. The legal holiday makes that impossible. You frantically try to find legal counsel to meet with him before his arraignment. Finally, you go to the jail to see him yourself. How do you proceed from here?

Resolution

In this crisis, the student's academic adviser is able to convince her personal attorney to come to accompany her to the jail. Efforts to call for an emergency hearing before a judge fail because it is a federal holiday, so the student remains in jail overnight. The adviser and international student adviser is allowed to see the student, and the attorney is allowed to consult with him. The student is assessed by a mental health professional as psychologically disturbed, a judgment both the international student adviser and academic adviser made at the outset, when they heard how out of character the student's behavior had been. The

International Student Office arranges medical evacuation, after the student is hospitalized and stabilized.

The international student adviser occasionally counsels students facing criminal charges ranging from simple speeding offenses to felonies. Your involvement in these situations is complex and delicate, and there are many considerations.

Some international students accused of crimes will not share circumstances of the alleged crimes with their advisers. They may feel shame at their situation, whether or not they are culpable. Loss of face is intensified by their relationship with the advisers, whom they often view as respected counselors, authority figures, school officials, and mentors. In fact, the students' diminished self-image may result in an avoidance of almost everyone with whom contact is not absolutely necessary.

Many students may perceive the adviser as an agent of an institution with awesome power over international student status on campus and, ultimately, in the United States. This is particularly evident at public institutions, where the international student adviser sits as a functionary of the state. On the other hand, if the student introduces the subject of criminal activity or charges in a conversation with the adviser, it is a sign of trust.

Be aware, however, that legislation requires you to report such information to the public safety division of your institution. The "Jeanne Clery Disclosure of Campus Security Police and Campus Crime Statistics Act" (originally known as the "Campus Security Act") was enacted in 1990, and amended in 1992 and 1998. This law requiring public disclosure of criminal activity applies to all institutions of higher education, both public and private that participate in any federal student aid programs. The 1998 amendments impose additional reporting obligations upon university staff who might advise and counsel students, but are not protected by professional codes as are clergy or professional counselors. For more information, contact the web site for the Jeanne Clery Act, www.securityoncampus.org, and/or your own campus public safety office, to understand your liability.

To be able to counsel in such matters, you should broadly comprehend criminal law of your jurisdiction. This includes substantive law (larceny, rape, assault) and procedural law (arrest, charge, indictment, arraignment, plea, bail, discover, trial, pre-sentence investigation, and sentencing). Be familiar with the rules of evidence to know what statements between a counselor and client are privileged in the legal sense—that is, are protected as confidential. Furthermore, understand the ramifications of a guilty plea and conviction on the student's non-immigrant status in the United States.

As a student adviser, supplement this information with knowledge of local resources that can be called upon for further advice and/or representation. These resources may include the public defender's office (legal aid handles civil matters exclusively), private defense counsel, private immigration law specialists, and campus legal services attorneys. While locating resource people or organizations, the adviser has a unique opportunity to educate them in culture specifics and certain aspects of cross-cultural communication. These resource people—the police, prosecuting attorneys, and the sheriff—might see themselves in adversarial relationships with international students. As you learn about the policies and practices of these enforcement agencies, you establish credibility that can prove valuable at a later time when you may be called upon to act in the role of student's advocate. It may be productive to visit with members of the local press, to make them aware of the way that their headlines, choice of language, layout, and photographs are perceived by foreign students, and how the reporting surrounding a particular incident may influence public opinion regarding foreigners in general.

Advising, Not Practicing Law

The distinction between giving advice and practicing law without a license should be clear, explained at the outset of the counseling relationship, so that the student has realistic expectations of the adviser.

In addition to providing emotional support, you must assist the student in developing an intellectual framework that integrates past, present and future events precipitated by the charges. If possible, explain the pertinent laws and procedures. At the same time, guard against giving the student a false sense of security by predicting outcomes or evaluating the cause for concern. You may help the student focus on the charges by discussing the lawfulness of certain behaviors in different societies (for example: the differences between legitimate parental discipline and child abuse; between borrowing and stealing; between promising to pay by a certain time and being legally obligated to meet payment schedules). When students participate in these discussions, they are likely to feel less tense and more involved in the counseling process.

On some occasions, the international student adviser may be asked for confidential information supporting the student's interests. One example would be the disclosure of high grades and proximity to graduation, might be persuasive to a judge determining whether someone should be released or detained prior to the filing of formal charges or pending trial. However, the student must grant permission before such information can be released. To do otherwise is to violate both the trust conferred upon adviser and requirements of privacy laws (e.g. FERPA, the Family Educational Right to Privacy Act, also known as the "Buckley Amendment"). When seeking the release, reassure the student that you will vigilantly safeguard shared confidences during contacts with the police, the Immigration and Naturalization Service, prosecuting attorney, the embassy or consulate, host family, relatives, friends, and others.

Whether discussing the charges during a visit to the jail or over coffee in the student union, the adviser should treat the situation seriously. Students might joke about the charge as an avoidance technique, but this should not give you fiat to deal with it lightly. Through sensitive counseling, including long periods of silence at times, you can help the students redevelop a positive self-concept, continue their academic work to the extent it is compatible with their emotional condition, maintain supportive social relationships, and feel comfortable about seeking continual counsel from the you without guilt or reservation.

The adviser may serve as an intermediary between the student and defense counsel, between student and prosecuting attorney and between defense counsel and prosecutor. In fact, you can be very helpful in the negotiation of a dismissal, a reduction of bond, or a release from detention. While these negotiations are neither initiated nor conducted independently of the students or their legal representatives you can participate effectively in these discussions.

Dismissal of criminal charges or an acquittal may not comfort the student. If, in fact, the student was not involved in the criminal event, anger and hostility toward the accuser, the prosecutor, and the system of justice and the United States likely will be aired, and almost certainly will be felt. On the other hand, remember that the student has suffered humiliation, continually reinforced by the knowledge that the indelibility of public records in the U.S. will mean the incident cannot be forgotten easily. Counseling, therefore, may continue long after the student is exonerated.

A guilty plea or conviction creates additional anxieties. There will be a pre-sentence investigation during which time the students may be remanded to jail. Deportation may be ordered with official notification to diplomatic representatives and a return home under less than favorable conditions. Under these circumstances, the dimensions of counseling may extend to a resumption of coursework and research projects after a considerable lapse of time, a rebuilding of status with the immigration authorities and, possibly, a re-entry and transition to society at home, fraught with all the overtones of readjustment.

The responsibility attached to counseling foreign students accused of crimes can be overwhelming. It is up to the adviser to be aware of the complexities of each situation and to marshal all resources, personal and external, to extend the quality of service that best serves the interests of the student.

See Appendix K: Criminal Classes of Deportable Students and Scholars

Chapter 7

Coping with the Death of a Student

Gary Althen, David Austell, Jane Howard, Peter Maramaldi, Lynn Reilly, and Michael B. Smithee

A nyone in student services work on a college campus knows that there is hardly a more difficult and troubling occurrence than the death of a student. The trauma that so deeply affects the student's immediate family and home community also profoundly affects the adopted community—your campus and surrounding communities, the various faculty and staff members who have come to know the student, and the service structure of the institution itself.

The trauma intensifies with the death of an international student. When the special experience of study abroad is abruptly ended by a student's death, the distant family must be notified. Language differences may be among the first hurdles to overcome. Cultural norms involving the death of an international student require special sensitivity in addition to that called for in deaths involving domestic students.

It is very often the case that foreign student advisers (FSAs) become the institutional vanguard when a foreign student dies. FSAs will help fill in the gap when family members are far away, will serve as communication links between the institution's various departments and the family, and will be the institutional guides in dealing with cultural issues that may not occur to others. Repatriation, or the sending of the remains of the deceased to the home country will become a primary concern. FSAs often are the ones who manage repatriation, with all of its attending technical complexities.

Death in international education is, happily, not an everyday event. But as with any student population, it does happen, and having a response plan can greatly ease the devastating effects of the tragedy for family and all of the campus. The following scenarios describe several colleagues' experiences coping with death on their campuses. Their responses are similar in many ways, but also different—tailored to their own campus and departmental crisis management plans, and personalized for their individual communities. The causes of death described here vary as well, and include death from an accident, a murder, and a suicide. A final section deals with the very important task of repatriation of remains back to the homeland, something that, in large part, usually becomes work for the international educator.

Accidental Death

Scenario

The phone rang at 4:20 a.m. on the last day of classes before final exams early in December. The dean of students was at the other end of the line, saying an automobile accident had happened after the soccer team's celebration. A local police sergeant had reported two students killed, possibly international students. During the seven-minute drive to the college, my mind cleared enough to begin to work through the steps I might have to follow once the students were identified. The names the police sergeant gave me indeed belonged to two of our international students, one British, the other Irish. The details, arrangements, and logistics would soon begin to confound us, but not until after we made the crucial and difficult long distance calls to family.

The driver of the car in which the students died was an American member of the soccer team who was seriously injured and also arrested for driving while under the influence of alcohol. Accountability for the accident, as well as the student's physical and emotional well-being, heightened the crisis.

I was six weeks into my new position as director of International Student Affairs at Mount Ida College, a small, private college in suburban Boston. There was almost no "game plan" for me as a newcomer to both the institution and the field. I had been exposed to accidental death of an international student when a high school exchange student was killed in an automobile accident a few years before, but had no experience, concrete information, or advice as a basis for current actions and decisions. My institution was small—under 1,800 total enrollment—and as the only part-time international administrator, much of the burden was mine.

The Response

Identify the Body. Identifying the bodies became the responsibility of the soccer coach, who had recruited the boys, knew them well, and had met their families.

Inform the Family. In all cases, it is important to think out the process and its variables before making the telephone call. Language issues, cultural traditions, time zones, and choosing the best person to inform the family, are all considerations with this type of tragedy. If the institution has the name of an emergency contact in the United States, a staff member may want to contact that person first and consult them about the best way to notify the family. Absent a local contact person, and if the institution is not familiar with the culture or is concerned that nobody in the family may speak fluent English, the consulate can serve as a valuable resource. In our particular situation, the soccer coach who knew the boys again was our choice. He contacted the local police departments in each of the communities and requested that a trained professional personally inform the families of their sons' deaths. When no willing party responded, the coach made the phone calls.

Notify the Consulate. Calls were placed to both the Irish and British Consulates, where personnel were extremely helpful and supportive, and made themselves available to us without restriction. The students were English speaking, Roman Catholic, and Anglican Church members from western cultures we knew well. Had the students been from cultures unfamiliar to anyone at the school, we would have relied heavily on advice from the consulates and other resources in the area.

Assemble an Administrative Committee. Within hours an Administrative Committee was assembled that included the college president, executive vice president, academic vice president, vice president for student development, dean of the college, dean of students, college chaplain, and directors of international students, counseling, residence life, student activities, public relations, and athletics, the soccer coaches, several faculty members, counselors, and support staff. The director of our School for Death Education, the New England Institute, coordinated our committee, a resource clearly not available to every institution.

- Identify a point person who has the ability to make decisions. The committee coordinator became the point person. He had the authority to make decisions and was the one to whom each member reported. He made sure that they were not working at cross- purposes nor overlapping efforts.

- Name a liaison to the family. The soccer coach became the liaison to both families. He kept them informed and advised them about decisions they needed to make. He was available to them at all times and always ready to respond to their questions and concerns.

- Name a logistics coordinator. The director of international student affairs assumed responsibility for the logistics.

- Identify those responsible for helping the community deal with grief. The chaplain and director of counseling assumed the responsibility for helping the student body deal with the deaths and the grieving process. The director of athletics assumed the responsibility of supporting the soccer team, and serving as a liaison between them and the professional services of the Counseling Center personnel.

- Appoint a public relations person. The director of public relations, working with the president, was named liaison to the public. Speaking with one voice was essential. Rumors needed to be quelled.

Any number of these activities were carried out simultaneously.

- Repatriation. Allow the family to make decisions. One of the first decisions the families had to make was whether to repatriate the bodies or cremate them in the United States and return the ashes. In both cases, the families chose repatriation.

- Work with a knowledgeable funeral home. The college has a funeral service program, and through that, an affiliation with one of the largest funeral homes in the greater Boston area. They are knowledgeable of the rules and regulations that govern shipping bodies across borders, which vary from country to country. The families selected a funeral home recommended to them to handle their arrangements. The personnel were not only knowledgeable, they advised us how to arrange transportation with the airlines.

• Work with the airlines. Both British Air and Aer Lingus, the airlines of the countries involved were contacted. A request was made to both to fly the bodies home at no cost to the families, particularly since both students were at the college on full athletic scholarships, and family funds were very limited. British Air was very cooperative and not only made space available, agreed fairly quickly to fly the body to England at no charge. Aer Lingus, a much smaller airline, found it difficult to offer space or to cover costs. A call made to the Irish Consulate helped resolve these problems within hours. Both airlines arranged for space within three days of the accident. (See the section on "Repatriation of Remains," further along in this chapter, for discussion of this topic.)

• Dispose of personal belongings. The students' personal belongings had to be packed, shipped home, or otherwise disposed of by the school. The soccer coaches and team members assumed that responsibility. (Note: Some insurance policies have an "accidental death" added benefit that may cover moving company expenses to pack and ship all belongings.)

Counseling and Support Services. Since many students had already traveled home for winter vacation, campus counseling and support services were not accessible to many of them. The Administrative Committee requested the college president to send a letter to the parents of every student explaining what had happened and sharing our concern that the students may need some extra support dealing with this crisis (See Appendix N.) For many students, this was their first experience with the death of friends.

The Counseling Center offered support services for those who remained on campus. Advised to be on alert to students in need, many faculty and staff members simply opened their doors and were available to any student who wanted to talk about the situation. It was felt that the Residence Life Staff needed to be particularly alert to troubled students and make sure that referrals were made as needed.

Clearly many international students were troubled by the deaths, and felt they easily could have been the victims. Reassurance and rationality were what they needed and what they received. Different backgrounds brought forth different perspectives. One Irish student said the deaths were God's will: if the students had not died in an automobile accident that day, they would have died another way. Those offering support learned a great deal that weekend.

Had classes been in session, we would have offered a place where students could go to discuss their feelings and perhaps even write notes to the families to help them feel that they were doing something. In similar cases, a notebook or "memory book" could be started for each of the deceased, and given to the families when all friends and faculty members had recorded their messages. The Counseling Center staff could logically help carry out this service.

The parishioners at a local Catholic Church wanted to celebrate a Mass for both boys even though one of them was not a Roman Catholic. After the boys' families voiced approval, the church priests worked with some of the soccer team members, the coaches, and the brother of one of the boys who had been killed, to prepare a very moving service. The church was filled to overflowing with students, faculty, staff, and local parishioners, and all of this contributed to a very appropriate tribute to the boys.

Memorial Service: Consider the Campus and Community. Plans were made for a memorial service on campus after winter break. Many groups were called upon to participate, in what would be a cross-cultural, ecumenical, yet spiritual and positive service. While a distinct challenge with all the varied input, the service proved to be very successful. (See copy of service program in Appendix M1). The soccer team had a large role; classes were canceled during the afternoon for the service.

- Involve the family. Both families had been invited, as guests of the college, to come to the United States for the memorial service. The British family chose to participate, and the soccer coach and the international student director assumed the responsibility of serving as hosts to the family. Although hosting is an everyday experience for most international educators, it is impossible to prepare for the stresses and strains of this experience. The emotion of grief, the complex psychological issue of a child dying before the parents, plus the fact that the family had never visit-

ADVANCE CRISIS PLANNING CAN EASE THE STRESS

Although one never knows when or how a death may occur, advance planning can make the nightmare of it all easier to handle. There are several important steps to take:

✓ Formulate an administrative committee to handle crises of this nature. This committee might only be convened when needed;

✓ Find and maintain a list of appropriate funeral homes, ones that have the expertise to handle repatriation; introduce yourself to the directors, and establish a rapport in advance of a crisis situation;

✓ Maintain a list of all consulates with addresses and telephone numbers. Knowing the personnel at the consulates would be an added benefit where the school's geographic location makes this possible.

✓ Meet your institutional personnel responsible for institutional policies. Consult with insurance companies and link them up with responsible personnel at your school if necessary. Know and understand what is covered in the students' policies and understand how to facilitate payments, complete forms, etc.

✓ Maintain a current address list of all students. Include their local telephone numbers, a contact in the United States to be called in case of emergency, and the students' addresses and telephone numbers in their home countries. If a telephone call must be placed to a non-English speaking country, it is important to have an interpreter available.

✓ It can be important to have appropriate legal counsel available to advise the college and the community members.

✓ Know where to find resources. There is no way that one could maintain a database of all of the people one might need in a crisis, but you can maintain an extensive list of sources of information.

✓ Attend memorial services and funerals when appropriate and possible to learn about other religious, cultural, and social traditions in such settings. Save the printed programs for adaptation when you need to develop a service for one of your students.

✓ Read and save obituaries of all students or visiting scholars who have died. You can adapt them when your time of need arises again.

✓ Be visible on your campus. If a crisis does arise, you will be regarded as an established, responsible professional, known in the community. ●

ed the campus nor met their son's friends, and the very nature of the automobile accident made it extremely difficult for the family. Although the international student director was not involved in the budget decisions, it was important to allot as much money as the college felt it could to afford a warm welcome to the family.

The Irish family visited campus in the spring, when an appropriate luncheon and campus visit was scheduled for them. Great sadness accompanied their visit, but the stresses, strains, and initial pain surrounding the loss had somewhat subsided since the deaths.

Follow-Up

Express Appreciation to Everyone. Once the initial activities surrounding the crisis ended, the director of international students sent thank you notes to everyone who had played even the smallest role in helping to deal with the crisis. Clearly coping had proven to be a group effort.

Assign a Person to Monitor Bills and Payments. For months following the death, the paperwork ebbed and flowed. Bills from the ambulance company, the hospital, and the funeral home were regularly delivered to the International Student Office. As long as it took to sort out, it was positive that the bills were not sent to the boys' families abroad. It was important for a university official to be able to speak with the billing agencies, intercept these bills, and forward them to the appropriate insurance companies. Coverage by the students' medical insurance and other coverage by the driver's auto insurance required a great deal of sorting out, as well as the application of some pressure to make certain that the bills were paid.

Provide Continued Support. The Counseling Center, the Residence Life staff, and the athletic department continued to monitor students dealing with the deaths. It took some students much longer than others to come to terms with the death of their friends, as is the case with the grieving process. Support was available for them as long as it was needed. The Catholic Church that held the original Mass for the boys, continues to hold an anniversary Mass annually. Former students as well as former and current faculty and staff attend each year.

Create an Appropriate Memorial. Six years after the accident, a convocation was held where a memorial plaque was unveiled honoring the two boys.

While it was too delayed for those directly involved to benefit while still on campus, the memorial is in place and serves as a proper tribute to the two students. It is hoped that it also serves as a reminder that students are not impervious to accidents or crises.

Maintain Contact With the Family. Communication with the families continues. Both the soccer coach and the director of international students have maintained contact with the families with at least an annual letter that is appreciated. It helps the families know that their sons are remembered still.

Conclusion

The horrific car accident on the sad stretch of Interstate 75 had left two of his friends dead and another maimed, but the young Indian student felt happy to be alive. He felt called upon by a higher power in the Hindu godhead to live for some, as yet unknown reason, not shared with his slain friends. He had broken legs and collapsed lungs, and broken facial bones, but he was alive and healing from the scars of body and heart. He saw delight in his father's eyes when he was able to walk again unaided by cane, crutch, or arm. He knew that he would not return home as his young friends had, cold and alone, but strong and purposeful, the delight of his proud family.

When an International Student Is Murdered

Scenario

You are on the staff of an international student office. It is midnight on the eve of your departure for an annual conference where you will present at two sessions. You are watching a late night talk program and enjoying the revelry. Your phone rings. A university public safety officer asks if you can confirm the identity of an "oriental female" who has been found dead in her own apartment. From police reports, it was probably murder. You agree to meet a university security officer accompanied by a city police officer at your office within 15 minutes.

Once at your office, your heart sinks as you locate a folder with the name provided by police. In it is a photo that verifies you know her. She had begun the fall semester two months earlier as a transfer student from another U.S. institution; you had met her a few times during the semester. In the presence of the city police you gain additional verification that she had been murdered in her own apartment in a particularly violent way, and, that an alleged assailant has already been apprehended and is being held without bail.

Components of the Crisis

In the case of a violent death of an international student, the International Student Office should be prepared play a major role in resolving the crisis. The ISO plays the role of guide, support, resource, and consultant. These roles can be assumed by the ISO, but can also be requested, or assigned by other individuals, authorities, or organizations in the university or community.

Circumstances must be personalized to the particular crisis. The context and setting of the incident helps determine how to proceed, as well as the role of the ISO. Players and resources will guide how many tasks need to be completed. The murder described here came at a time when more than five rapes and one other murder had been reported on the campus in the previous two months. Although there was no evidence that rape occurred in this incident, the fact that a violent crime had been committed in the midst of other violence certainly resulted in a heightened sense of vulnerability and anger among the females on campus. The family of the deceased had to travel from afar to attend to the necessary details.

The Incident

Notification of the Incident. Ideally, those who are first aware of the incident will notify the campus Public Safety Office, who will work with local police. They will contact the ISO to verify that the victim is an international student. The ISO begins to assess and develop its role.

Verify Status of the Incident and Student. An officer of the ISO should assist the authorities (campus security, local, state, and national) in their investigation by reviewing records to determine the student's status at the university, what emergency contacts are listed, family details and contact information, likely language capability, and insurance coverage. If local or state police are not able to converse with the family in their native language, then the ISO should offer to provide interpreters to assist in notifying the next of kin. Often, authorities will notify the embassy directly, where an officer will be designated to handle details. In this case the ISO should establish close contact with the embassy. In addition, the ISO should offer resources and services to local authorities, as well as provide a source of support for the next of kin, and the campus members of the national group. It helps if a friend of the deceased or someone from their home country is available to help cushion the shock of the event. At this time the ISO officer will gather basic information on the incident for dissemination to the crisis team.

Initiate Appropriate Crisis Management Procedures. Upon verifying that the incident involves an international student, the ISO officer will begin the establishment of the following crisis management procedures. It is helpful if other offices in the university know about and understand the CMP involving an international student. Here are some initial steps:

- Identify and notify the crisis management team.

- Establish lines of communication, contact times, and methods.

- Establish responsibility for components of the crisis both within the team and within the ISO.

- Assist in identification of the body as needed.

- Identify and maintain culturally sensitive issues and traditions related to the deceased.

- Keep a log of events and people contacted or involved in the crisis.

- Establish a phone reference list for use during the crisis management.

- Coordinate and redistribute ISO staff workload.

Set Up a Crisis Team. The death of an international student is normally of a magnitude that brings many individuals together to resolve the crisis. A crisis team is responsible for managing various components of the crisis. The team functions vertically and horizontally in the organization, and represents key support areas. Although the team may never meet as a group, the functions and responsibilities are agreed upon via coordination by the ISO, and assistance from the appropriate university officer. The members of the crisis team might include some of the people listed in the box on page 134.

- The university response to the crisis will depend upon (a) knowledge about the incident and the needs of others external and internal to the university. In some cases parents may learn of the incident prior to official notification, or the media may seek a response or interviews prior to an official identification of the student; and (b) members of the crisis team available when needed.

> **POSSIBLE MEMBERS OF A CRISIS TEAM**
>
> ✓ ISO designated officers;
> ✓ University CEO, or representative;
> ✓ Campus Security Office;
> ✓ Press/media representative;
> ✓ Nationality consultants;
> ✓ Dean, school or college;
> ✓ Director or representative, Counseling Services;
> ✓ Dean, or head chaplain;
> ✓ Psychiatric social worker;
> ✓ Embassy official;
> ✓ Others as needed.

- University statements. The first statement developed and made should be to the next of kin, after the official notification of death. The highest university officer available or the individual representing the chancellor or president should deliver this statement. This statement should only be made after positive identification of the student by the county medical examiner. The second statement should be developed for the media, and is best coordinated by the university relations officer. The crisis team assisted by the nationality consultant should decide on the amount of information to be given to the media, and who will give it.

- Make contact with the embassy of the deceased. If positive identity has not been made, simply alert the embassy to the possibility of the crisis. Once positive identification is made, seek the name of an embassy officer who will assist with the crisis, information regarding embassy procedures, and whether the embassy prefers to notify the family. Coordination with the embassy is very important. This type of situation is one that requires the embassy and the ISO to help each other.

- Contact with the family or next of kin. After the family has been notified, the university should officially make a call of condolence. A university officer should make this call, with assistance from interpreters and the ISO. At the same time, lines of communication with the family should be established in order to determine the family's wishes for disposition of the body, and who among the family or friends is the family's designated spokesperson. This person will become another key contact for the ISO in managing the crisis. You will also need to determine whether the family will travel to the United States to accompany the body home, or to take care of the deceased student's affairs.

- Contact with other key people. In the course of responding to the nature of the incident, many other people will be brought into the management of the crisis. Care should be taken to follow the crisis team guidelines.

- If the family decides to travel to the United States, then preparations should be taken to receive and host them during their stay.

The Family/Sponsor/Representative

Pre-Arrival. Establish who will arrive when, and via what transportation. The university should establish who will be billed for what and then make arrangements for:

- lodging and food;

- local transportation

- interpreters, as needed; and

- development of a daily schedule.

Arrival. A delegation should be formed to meet the family at the airport. If an official car with driver can be obtained, the better. Be sure to verify the arrival of the flight before leaving for the airport. Establish liaison with airport security (through Campus Security or city police investigators). Arrange for a private room to meet with the family as they arrive. At this time condolences can be offered, a brief overview of the situation can be given to the family, and the immediate wishes of the family can be determined. Friends or volunteers can collect baggage while the family is being briefed. Care should be taken to preserve the family's privacy.

Post-Arrival. Developing a daily schedule will depend upon the wishes of the family, the cultural issues involved, the help of nationality consultants, and the family's desire for assistance by the university and the ethnic community. If the family is to be registered at a hotel, it is recommended that the room be reserved in the name of someone other than the family. Media and well-meaning community members often impose themselves on the family.

Non-Arrival. Should the family or kin not wish to visit, then the ISO or other representative will establish liaison with the family and or embassy for disposition of the deceased body and estate.

The Community

National Group Population. Students from the deceased student's national group should be invited immediately to participate as part of the crisis team. The ISO should coordinate a meeting with the national group leaders to review the impact of the death on their community. The meeting need not be long but should cover:

- facts of the incident as known;

- safety issues;

- where counseling and advising are available;

- what the family's wishes are, if known; and

- when a memorial service will be held.

NOTE: In the case of a violent death, there will be many questions and concerns about violence in the United States. Public safety officers, investigators, and others should be invited to speak about these issues. Alert the speakers to be direct and simple in their language, but to avoid bluntness and slang. It is important that the ISO staff listen closely to what is being said and how it is being said. While the language may be clear to Americans and even to students from the nationality group, the intent and the rationale behind the statements may not. ISO staff should be prepared to interpret these statements as needed.

Other International Students. When a crisis of this magnitude occurs, a letter should be sent to all international students, explaining the circumstances of the crisis, and offering assistance and counsel.

Other Students on Campus. The campus media should be requested to provide as much information as possible regarding the crisis, without compromising the privacy of the family or those working to resolve the crisis.

Counseling/Advising. Arrangements should be made and information disseminated about counseling and advising services available to the campus community. Once the information has been disseminated, attention should be paid to maintaining a communication and support network throughout the crisis.

Local Officials. In a crisis such as murder, it is important to establish and maintain contact with local officials. The relationship between the local officials and the crisis management team, more specifically those who are coordinating resolution of the crisis, is one of mutual help. The local officials rely on the ISO for interpreters, access to the family, and information of a cultural nature. The ISO relies on the officials to provide information to the family, and to assist with certain aspects of the crisis, i.e., airport arrival, and contact with the media.

The Deceased. The following issues often require the ISO to play a crucial role.

- Funeral arrangements and repatriation. Suggest and contact a funeral home, assist the family with the discussion of funeral arrangements, and help the funeral director and the family understand the cultural differences regarding funerals. The Cremation Association of North America's (CANA) web site features very good information about cremation: http://www.cremationassociation.org. Repatriation is usually conducted by a funeral home knowledgeable about the process (see the section on "Repatriation of Remains" later in this chapter). An ISO officer may need to assist, plan, or make such arrangements.

- Victim's belongings. Contact a reputable moving company, provided funds or insurance coverage exist and help the family negotiate the arrangements, making suggestions to the family regarding items they do not wish to ship, or pack and ship items when a moving company is unaffordable.

- Memorial service. A memorial service is important in resolving the crisis. It provides the campus, community, and the family with an opportunity to pay respects to the deceased. It also allows friends and others to begin to resolve their feelings. The family may at first reject the idea of a memorial service. They need to know that in our culture, a memorial service is a sign of respect and honor, not an event to draw unwarranted attention to the deceased. The dean of the chapel is best suited to coordinate a service, which should help the campus community come to terms with its grief. The funeral is a more intimate setting where farewells are expressed.

- Insurance coverage. Early in the crisis the foreign student adviser will determine the extent of insurance coverage and share that information with the family. There may be a need for the ISO staff to intercede on behalf of the family. The steps, procedures, forms, and terminology are all very difficult—even for Americans—to understand and address. A good funeral home often can also help.

- Judicial procedures. Countries have different judicial procedures, and those of one country may not make sense to those of another country. Regardless, attempt to apprise the family about the process of bringing a murderer to justice. The ISO should ask the district attorney in charge of the crime to meet with the family.

- Civil action. The family may wish to discuss with a lawyer: the process of civil action in the United States, what constitutes a good civil case, and what the advantages and disadvantages are in initiating a civil suit. Prior to seeing the lawyer, the ISO officer should see that the lawyer has some information about the case.

- Disposition of assets and liabilities. The deceased will probably have bank accounts, phone, utility and other bills, and may have an automobile. Rules and procedures differ from state to state regarding the disposition of such property. Normally a death certificate is required along with proof that whomever disposes is a family member. The presence of a member of the ISO helps to speed along such business because the language involved is sometimes complex.

- Confirm change in university status. The registrar and other faculty need to be notified that the deceased student's name should be immediately removed from current lists to avoid embarrassing correspondence being sent to the family.

The University Crisis Team. The crisis team serves as a support structure for the resolution of the crisis. The university's effectiveness in resolving the crisis will depend on the willingness of crisis team members to support the individual or office most on the firing line.

Departure of the Family. Arrangements for departure should be made according to family wishes. An ISO representative should offer to accompany the family to the airport.

Follow-Up. After the family has departed, the coordinators may need to continue dealing with such issues as liabilities—phone bills, letters to magazine and other such subscriptions, etc. Thank you notes should be written to all those who helped with the crisis. Finally, there may be certain commemorative items that could be sent to the family: letters from students, newspaper articles, comments from the memorial service, poems, etc., could all be collected and nicely bound for the family.

Suicide: What to Do When an International Student Loses Hope

Scenario

Jai, a gregarious and brilliant 26-year-old international student with a promising future, has been talking to friends about his thoughts of suicide after "failing" a course with a B+. Several of his friends call to tell you that he is scaring everybody with this talk of killing himself.

You immediately talk with Jai and ask questions to assess the situation. At the end of your conversation you feel relatively confident that Jai is depressed, but not likely to kill himself. Your consulting mental health professional agrees, based upon what Jai told you, that he would benefit from some counseling, but that he appears to be in no immediate danger.

On Friday evening at 5:30 p.m., as you are preparing to leave for the weekend, you receive a call from a psychiatry resident at the local hospital. Jai is in the emergency room. He has not slept for days and appears disoriented with an overwhelming sense of hopelessness and despair. Earlier in the day he tried to hang himself in the shower, but the fixture from which he was dangling snapped off the wall. Then he cut his wrists with a kitchen knife leaving deep scratches in each arm. Finally he went to the train station near school and stood on the edge of the platform debating whether to throw himself in front of an oncoming train. Fortunately, an alert police officer intervened and brought Jai to the emergency room.

Although it is often not discussed openly, suicidal ideation—thinking about suicide as a solution—is commonplace in large segments of any given population. Years of counseling convince me to expect suicidal ideation in students. In fact, suicidal ideation is more the norm than most people think. In some cases it almost can be seen as adaptive and perhaps even as a sign of misdirected resilience. Educators should expect suicide ideation to be part of their students' standard coping repertoire.

Statistics usually indicate that suicide is one of the leading causes of death for people in the United States in age ranges typical for undergraduate and graduate students. These statistics, however, may underreport suicide for a variety of reasons. There is a stigma attached to suicide in the West, which may influence reporting. In addition, accidents, the leading cause of death for college-age people in the United States, may be attributable in part to unknown or underreported suicides. If this is true, suicide in fact may be the leading cause of death for people in their late teens and early twenties in the United States.

Warning Signs of Suicide

It would be impossible to provide a comprehensive list of warning signs. Often, the general warning signs of suicide must be interpreted in the context of the individual experience. The student's stage of development, life history, recent stressors, and adaptation to the host environment and academic culture all should be considered.

Sometimes there are no warning signs and a student tragically is found dead. This, in turn, places surviving students at higher risk for suicide. However, in most cases there are indicators of suicidal intent from a student, noticed by a third party, friend, or acquaintance. For international or study abroad students, the synergistic effects of a series of stressful or painful life events, combined with the pressures of being away from home in a new country, must be considered in the context of known warning signs of suicide.

Verbal Statements, and Behavioral and Environmental Clues

The range of verbal statements can run from explicit statements of suicidal intent, such as "I want to die," to "Soon it won't matter anymore," to more subtle or ambiguous expressions like "I'm tired," or references to someone else who committed suicide. Situational clues often include preparations for death. In closing out, people often settle accounts, return borrowed things, write letters, say their goodbyes to significant others, and so on. Behavioral clues also may include imprudent or reckless acts such as self-injurious or abusive behavior, high-risk sexual practices, accident proneness, failure to comply with medical regimens, drug or alcohol abuse, and other acts that lend to the demise of self. Suicidal individuals often have a history of previous attempts. They may have developed a plan or timetable for their suicide. This is why two of the most important questions to ask suicidal individuals are how and when they plan to kill themselves. Environmental clues include the nature of the suicidal person's real or imagined relationships with other individuals, organizations, and groups. When elements of the individual's environment become the source of overwhelming discomfort or pain, they can be seen as warning signs.

Common Characteristics

The single word that would most likely describe a suicidal individual's emotional state would be "pain." Life is so difficult to the suicidal person that she perceives death as the most efficacious way out of the overwhelming pain that has taken over her existence. This is why it is important to remind the suicidal person that with some professional help, things can get better. Suicidal students commonly express a deep sense of hopelessness, worthlessness, and powerlessness. They are exhausted, feel terrible about themselves, and feel completely incapable of changing their situations. They sometimes experience changes in eating, sleeping, and other regular habits. Their interest may decline in activities that they previously enjoyed, and they may exhibit signs of self-neglect, such as self-starvation or violation of medical regimens. Sometimes suicidal students experience deep sadness, withdraw from people and activities, or experience bouts of anxiety. They also

SAMPLE QUESTIONS TO ASK A STUDENT YOU BELIEVE IS SUICIDAL

Q: Are you thinking about killing or hurting yourself? Tell me about it ... lets talk about it. This is where you must be objective and open to hear what the student says. If you don't understand what they are saying, ask them to clarify in the same manner you would during any other conversation or interview. Be honest and sincere in your reaction, but do not judge. Ask the student to help you to understand their situation.

Q: How will you do it? Do you have a plan? Again, listen carefully, use your interview skills, and listen carefully for the lethality of the plan. Probe and clarify. If they say they are going to jump off the roof, ask them if they know what roof and when. If they say they will overdose on drugs, ask if they have these drugs on hand and when they plan to do it. The idea is to gently get as much detailed information as possible without badgering.

Q: How often do you have these thoughts of dying? This question provides insights into the student's inner struggle. It helps you determine if this is a pervasive overriding chronic drive to die (high lethality) or a feeling that comes and goes.

Q: How long do these suicidal thoughts stay with you? This provides insights into the chronic or acute nature of the current episode. If a student has these thoughts all day long the lethality is higher than if the impulses come and go. However, it is important that you follow up with the next questions the intensity of the suicidal impulse must be considered during these feelings. Low intensity feelings all day may be less lethal than infrequent episodes of higher intensity.

Q: How much do you want to live or die? This may provide some insight into intensity of the death wish and the lethality of the suicidal intent. The problem is that the inherent ambiguity associated with suicide may distort the response depending upon when you ask the question. In addition, the response may be influenced by the cyclical nature of suicidal impulses.

Q: Do you know anyone who committed or tried to commit suicide? Tell me about it. Listen carefully to how the suicidal student relates to the person who died. You may even ask them what is different about them and that person. This also opens the door to anniversary dates. Survivors of suicide and other forms of loss often have difficulty during the time of year that their significant other died. They are also considered to have a higher risk for suicide.

Q: Have you ever felt this way or attempted suicide before? (if yes) What happened then? If the person has a past history of suicide attempts they are at a high risk. A past history of suicidal ideation indicates a lesser, but increased risk as well. Information about past interventions is critical.

Q: Is there anything or anyone to stop you from hurting yourself?
This provides information about resources available to the suicidal individual.

Q: What happened to make life so painful?
Listen carefully to the student's perception of her/his world. Try to understand their experience through their perspective rather than your own.

Q: What keeps you from hurting yourself so far?
This will give you an idea of resources— people, beliefs, or goals and aspirations— that are available to this student.

Q: What is in the future for you?
The less the person is able to project into the future, the higher the suicide risk and visa-versa. In addition, the student's response may identify some sort of an overwhelming and painful obstacle that torments them on their path. This is also a way to understand the kinds of goals the person has/had set for themselves.

Q: If you could have anything or be anywhere, what or where would that be?
This type of question gives you an idea of what the person values. The degree to which they are unable to attain these desires may result in frustration. The response also offers insights into possible reasons for the person to live.

Q: Have you taken any medication, drug, or alcohol within the last 24 hours?
The medication question may indicate that the person is under the care of a physician for medical or psychiatric conditions.

Compliance with the medical regimen also offers insights into the student's state of mind. Drug or alcohol consumption increases acute risk as it may impair judgement. They may also have interactive effects with any prescribed or illicit substances that have been consumed, necessitating immediate medical attention.

Q: Has anyone done anything to hurt you?
Listen carefully for insights into the student's frustration or disappointments that have made life so bad that death seems the best alternative. The student may be using suicide as an opportunity to save face, to cope with victimization, or to escape an intolerable relationship.

Q: Have you talked about this with anyone else?
If they say no, ask with whom they would want to talk. This provides insights into the students support network and their ability or willingness to activate it. It may also provide critical information for the intervention.

Q: How much do you want to die?
This is a direct self-assessment of the student's suicidal intent. It also forces any ambivalence to the surface of your discussion.

Q: Will you promise to talk to (name of resource person including yourself) and explain what you are planning to do before you take any action to hurt yourself?

may show increased temper as they find it difficult to tolerate the stressors in their environments.

Recognize, React, and Refer

The primary action to take when concerned about a student is to ask questions. In providing psychological first aid, it is critical to assure the student that there are ways other than suicide to get out of the pain. Try to frame it as being similar to physical distress: Just as one would see a doctor for a broken bone or a high fever, one must see a mental health professional for the type of painful emotional distress preceding suicidal ideation or thoughts. The mere fact that the student is able to talk to someone openly about suicidal intent may be helpful in of itself.

Recognize. The first thing to do is to recognize a student's suicidal ideation. People often have a hunch, a gut feeling, or an impression that a student may be thinking about suicide. Resist the temptation to deny the possibility that a student is suicidal and acknowledge warning signs.

React. The next step is to ask the student, "Are you thinking about suicide?" The word "suicide" may be an uncomfortable word to say to a student, so practice it or ask the question in a different way. Questions should be objective, and reactions to responses should be nonjudgmental. Questions should be designed to assess the lethality of the case, and provide the student with a safe place to speak his mind. Examples are provided at the end of this subchapter. A standard technique in suicide work, called contracting, sometimes can be employed at this time, if appropriate. The theory behind contracting is that the suicidal individual enters into an agreement not to take any self-destructive action without activating a resource. The problem is that suicidal people often invent loopholes and break contracts. Contracts do, however, provide the suicidal person with an interpersonal connection and a face-saving means to reach out for help in the future.

Refer. Finally, if the student is thinking about suicide, the matter must be referred to a mental health professional. The manner in which the referral is made is based upon the lethality of the suicidal plan. Certainly, the lethality of a case in which a student threatens to jump from the nearest roof is far greater than that of someone who has had repeated thoughts of suicide with no specific plan. In the case of the jumper, emergency procedures for life threatening situations should be implemented immediately. These will be institution-specific and may include campus security, local police, and emergency medical services. In cases with lower levels of lethality, contact a mental health professional immediately. The mental health professional will help decide the appropriate level of response. In the absence of a suicide plan that includes consultation with mental health professionals on- or off-campus, call the local hospital emergency room, speak with a triage nurse, or better yet, speak with a psychiatric resident, and ask for guidance.

Identify and Activate Resources

Suicide is a life-or-death matter. A suicide protocol should be in place before a crisis event. Educators and administrators with direct student contact should be aware of the protocols, and be familiar with the available mental health resources and student counseling programs. Such a proactive stand will help minimize exposure to the tragedy of suicide and help protect students, institutions, and institutional staff alike.

Suicide protocols are specific to institutions and their mental health resources. They will vary by country, state, and region. Consult with mental health professionals. Planning can be facilitated through professional contacts to ascertain what systems colleagues have in place. Protocols should include contingencies for weekends and holidays. In suicide cases with very acute lethality, logistics become crucial: Know how the student will get from the institution to the hospital emergency room.

After a Suicide: What to Do

The tragedy and shock associated with suicide will leave many second-guessing themselves, their actions, and their competency. Others will be reminded of past life events of great pain and heartache. Most will have difficulty carrying out their daily activities. Investigations by local and institutional authorities may put people off, but must occur. Arrangements for the identification, transport, and burial of the victim's remains must be carried out with relative expediency. To prevent an escalating tragedy after a suicide, a postvention plan for the student community should be developed in consultation with mental health professionals.

Every student who is aware of the suicide will be affected on some level. Mental health professionals can assist in the development of a postvention response, specific to the situation and the institution to help survivors pushed into high suicide risk. Typically, counselors speak with groups of students, facilitate discussion groups, and are available to meet individually at the students' request. By these means, at-risk students usually are identified, helped, and returned to previous levels of productivity in their studies. Finally, institutional staff also should be included in postvention services. The impact of the tragedy is not limited to the student's family, friends, and student body. Staff may need to see a counselor in order to put the entire event in order, and cope with lingering feelings of guilt or other persistent disturbances.

Training

Training builds confidence and competence. The deeper the understanding and familiarity with suicide dynamics and procedures, the more likely suicidal students on campus can and will be helped. Counseling components to health services are valuable resources and may be able to provide institutional staff with necessary and life-saving training programs. In the absence of school counseling, mental health providers in the community may provide assistance.

Students, too, should receive training on the subject of suicide. Student orientation materials are appropriate media for communicating this important message. They should include public health material about preventive steps in physical and mental health.

Encourage students and staff to report warning signs of suicide to a confidential and nonjudgmental resource. Silence is tantamount to being held hostage. I always give the example of five roommates who are held hostage by a sixth who made an unsuccessful attempt to suicide by overdose. The five agree not to report the event after the suicidal roommate promises that he is fine and pleads that informing others may get him kicked out of school. Months pass as the five keep a watchful eye over the sixth. All seems fine. Then, tragically, the suicidal impulse returns, and the student dies following an overdose. How many people die that day? Six. The suicide victim, and a piece of each of the five roommates who will spend the rest of their lives regretting not taking action. In fact, they are at higher risk for suicide after that tragic event. Even if the sixth roommate had lost a semester or was forced to leave the school, it would have been better than the final injury count: one dead and five scarred.

Repatriation of Remains

EPIGRAM

My mind is not reconciling to the fact. My mind is still searching for my son. Perhaps this search is eternal, maybe until my own death embraces me. Every fraction of a second reminds me of him, and he is always in my eyes. His voice is ringing in my ears. And my heart is heavy and aches all the time. I persuaded him to go to Tampa to learn and in turn to see the world and enjoy. His amusement gave me lots of pleasure and satisfaction. This abrupt end has shocked me. For me, the world has come to an end. I wish to leave this body and go in search of him. Once again, dear friends, please pray God to relieve me.

—*From a mother's letter after the death of her son.*

Scenario

It is an early winter Friday morning—you cannot forget the timing—when the weather in southwest Florida was not yet beyond the sultriness of summer. Staff persons of International Student and Scholar Services arriving on campus are immediately confronted with their worst professional nightmare. About six hours before, an extremely intoxicated man driving at high speed on the local section of an interstate highway, collided head-on with a car carrying three international graduate students and a companion visiting from Arizona. The impact was catastrophic and brutal, strewing wreckage over a large expanse of highway while trapping the young men, all Indian nationals, in the twisted remains of their rental car. The intoxicated driver of the southbound car died instantly, apparently never having attempted to apply his brakes. Two students died outright, and a third student 20 minutes later, hemorrhaging but conscious until the moment of his death. A fourth student is seriously injured, as is the friend from Arizona. State highway patrol officers and rescue personnel are amazed that anyone survived the accident. The final toll: three students dead and two critically injured.

Key Elements of Repatriation

In trauma situations of this sort, the work of the professional staff begins with the realization that this is not indeed a bad dream, but rather a stark fact involving the irretrievable loss of admired, respected, and loved members of the international community. There is hard work ahead for these staffers, and international educators are well advised to make sure that a crisis protocol is in place, as the framework for the institutional response to the trauma. Key elements of an organized response follow.

Alerting Staff and Institutional Officials. Local police often automatically contact the dean of students after the death of a student. The dean would then contact the director of the International Office. Some institutions may decide to have a direct communication link between the International Office and the local police in situations involving international students. The key requirement is information flow from the community to the institution, and then from the initial institutional contact to institutional departments that will supply the hands-on trauma support services to the students as needed.

After the director of the International Office has been notified, the director or delegated staff person must notify other key members of the institution immediately. The Counseling Center, Student Health Services, the office of the legal counsel, the student's academic adviser, the student's department chair, and the dean of students office (if the dean has not been previously notified) top the list. Other important areas to communicate with include: the director's immediate supervisor, the office of the provost, the office of the vice president for student affairs, and the office of the president.

Alerting the Campus Police. It is often wise to contact and stay in touch with the local campus police, usually the agency having police jurisdiction over the institution. If there are associated security concerns, the campus police will be of key assistance. Second, communication with off-campus police agencies (city and county police, for example) can also be extremely useful, but should be handled with privacy concerns in mind. If these police agencies are already aware of the crisis, then the agencies might be a rich source of information regarding the circumstances of the student's death.

Notifying the Family. The initial telephone call notifying the next of kin of the death of a loved one will be the foreign student adviser's most difficult moment. Many key skills are necessary for this communication to be effective and compassionate. Cultural sensitivity, diplomacy, and kindness are all required. No FSA can be totally aware of the cultural nuances of every nationality present at the institution. It may be important for an FSA to enlist the assistance of a trusted person in the campus or surrounding community who is known to the family in crisis—a member of the extended family or close friend, for example. This action may help the FSA determine the best way to approach the family with the dire news.

Often it is the director of the International Office (or designee) who makes this call, unless there is another established procedure at the institution. Along with compassion, direct and clear communication of whatever details of the death are known is important. The family should clearly understand that the institution intends to assist in any appropriate way and that the family will not face this crisis alone. Make sure that the family understands that a follow-up call to them will be made within a short period of time, perhaps in 24 hours, so that additional instructions about the body can be given to the FSA from the family. After the initial notification call is completed, follow-up calls may be necessary to additional family members or close friends of the family as requested.

Foreign student advisers should use the skills of discretion and circumspection in discussing details of the crisis. This is especially true related to release of information to the general public, including members of the press. It will be useful for FSAs to discuss with the institution's legal counsel the implications of the Family Education Rights and Privacy Act as it is interpreted at the institution relative to release of information about a deceased student. During the notification, the caller will want to secure verbal permission from a parent, if possible, to communicate with whatever persons are needed to assist with the repatriation process. Such persons might include the selected funeral home's mortician or representatives of the covering insurance company. This permission should be documented in the student's file. Written release can be obtained later.

The Role of the Office of the Medical Examiner. The Medical Examiner's Office, usually a county governmental agency having jurisdiction over the place where the death occurred, will be a good source of information regarding the circumstances of death. Depending on the requirements of the state government, a letter certifying that there are no contagious diseases present in the deceased may be required. This letter is typically issued by the MEO after inspection and testing of the remains, and generally will accompany the body to the funeral home. The MEO must order copies of the official death certificate. You may want to order as many as five copies of the death certificate: one copy for the insurance company, one copy for the deceased student's file, two copies two accompany the remains during repatriation, and one copy for the family if requested.

Autopsies. Many state governments require both that the body of the deceased be placed in the custody of the Medical Examiner's Office (MEO) and that an official autopsy be performed by the MEO on the remains in cases where the deceased died under suspicious circumstances (where foul play or substance abuse, for example, might be present); or where the deceased died unattended and alone. An autopsy is a surgical examination of the remains undertaken to determine the cause of death in cases where this is not clearly understood otherwise. The thoracic cavity of the body is opened and examined as is the brain pan and its delicate contents. Multiple tests are run on body fluids including blood chemistry. Extensive photographing of the remains—or drawings rendered by a medical artist—are often made and included in the final report. Copies of the autopsy report may be requested by the FSA, and it is generally advisable to have two copies of the report on hand. Autopsies performed in the United States are often perceived, especially by persons from non-western cultures, as unnecessary, barbaric, and disrespectful to the deceased and to the family. Foreign Student Advisers should be prepared for inquiries and perhaps resistance from the family. Funeral home personnel can be very helpful in acquiring this information.

The Role of the Funeral Home. Help select a funeral home carefully. It is important that the funeral home is culturally sensitive and willing to work with families of various cultural, social, and religious backgrounds. A funeral home experienced and knowledgeable in repatriation cases is most helpful. Cultural awareness on the part of the FSA as well as the staff of the funeral home is essential to explain the western practice of embalming, including the application of mortuary cosmetics, alien and potentially offensive practices to some cultures. It may be necessary for the FSA to mediate between the family and the funeral home, since repatriation normally cannot proceed unless body preparation, including embalming, has been completed. As a general rule, the experienced funeral home can be essentially helpful in guiding the family (and the FSA) through the repatriation process, in communicating with the embassy, and in communicating with the family overseas. Most of the official repatriation documentation will typically be handled by the funeral home staff. It is, nevertheless, important for the FSA to check behind the staff of the funeral home in order to make sure that no details have been overlooked, and to insure that communications are open between the funeral home and the institution. Flight arrangements, for example, should be checked and double-checked thoroughly to insure that the passage of the remains is not delayed along the route home.

When a memorial service is desired as it commonly is, the funeral home can arrange it. The FSA should be prepared for requests to have the remains of the deceased displayed even if the bodies have been severely damaged or degraded. In many cultures, such display is considered a vital part of "leave-taking" and paying final respects to the deceased. The funeral home will also arrange for an automobile procession to the airport cargo area if this is requested. Before the body leaves the funeral home for the airport, the FSA should make sure that the appropriate documents are attached to the zinc-lined shipping caskets according to the requirements of the country where the remains are being repatriated. At the airport, the FSA should make sure that the air waybill is in order (for example, the exact weight of the casket and shipping container and the amount to be billed to the insurance company), and that the destination is correct on the air waybill.

Insurance. Insurance policies purchased by international students and scholars often cover repatriation and medical evacuation. The FSA may want to communicate immediately with the health insurance company in order to enlist assistance from the company for repatriation. In notifying the insurance company, the FSA is officially communicating information about the death so that appropriate billing and payment of repatriation expenses can go forward with a minimum amount of additional stress to the family. The FSA can assist the family in applying for whatever benefits are available under the insurance policy, and can facilitate communications between the family and insurance company. Insurance issues related to accidental death are intensely complex, so there may be a need for the family to have legal counsel to assist.

Religious Concerns. By being sensitive to the religious beliefs of members of the family, the FSA is showing respect to the family, to the specific faith community, and to the deceased. This in turn helps to create bond between the FSA and the family, which enhances trust and goodwill in the midst of traumatic crisis. In addition, sensitivity to religious beliefs can assist everyone involved in the crisis in making proper decisions about funeral or memorial service arrangements, the repatriation process itself, and specific needs of the family related to the deceased. For example, the family's beliefs may require that specialized cloths for washing the deceased's body be used exclusively in preparation for burial. In certain faiths, families may prefer the body to be buried before sundown, and in others, that the body be cremated after ceremonial washing. Certain religious practice downplays expressions of grief, while others emphasize this aspect of the crisis. Not every funeral home is prepared for these types of religious requirements, and the FSA's knowledge of and sensitivity to such details can be extremely helpful, especially to the family.

Stress Points. The death of a member of the international student and scholar community is arguably the most stressful experience possible for a foreign student adviser. It is an undeniably harsh and grinding experience for family and friends of the deceased. Therefore, it is wise to be aware of the negative effects of the crisis not only to the family, but to the staff, the faculty, and the community as well. Resources should be utilized within the institution to counteract the effects of grief and loss. The institution's Counseling Center, for example, can be a key resource to the campus community in times of crisis. Also, campus chaplains can be of great assistance and comfort to the bereaved. The FSA will be wise to self-assess his personal mental and emotional state and take decisive action to keep these healthy.

Summary of Repatriation Issues

- Alert institutional faculty and staff of the death.

- Notify the immediate family of the death.

- Seek assistance from extended family members or friends in communicating with the family.

- Show cultural sensitivity, compassion, and understanding in dealing with the bereaved family.

- Contact the health insurance company to make sure that the repatriation billing process is handled properly.

- Communicate with the appropriate embassy.

- Contact the Medical Examiner's Office.

- Make appropriate arrangements with the funeral home.

- Have counseling services available for friends and family.

- Check to make sure that life insurance benefits have been properly requested.

- Insure that the shipment of the remains is properly managed in conjunction with the funeral home.

- Request that the deceased student be posthumously conferred with an honorary degree as a courtesy to the family.

- Request that the family be reimbursed for tuition and fees for the semester during which the student died.

- Hold a memorial service for the deceased as appropriate and approved by family.

PART III.

*Crises Involving U.S. Students
Studying Abroad*

Introduction

Doug Brown, James Buschman, Barbara Lindeman, Melissa Martin, Lester McCabe, Beth Rascoe, Gary Rhodes, Brenda Robinson, Skye Stephenson, and JoAnn DeArmas Wallace

C rises affecting foreign students studying in the United States usually occur on or near the U.S. campus, although their impact can of course spread overseas. The cross-culturally sensitive response they demand can involve anything as basic as one-on-one counseling provided by a foreign student adviser to a crisis management team made up of a spectrum of campus and community members. The team typically works with a broader group, including diplomatic personnel, overseas parents, and next-of-kin. In contrast, the crises that affect U.S. students by definition always originate far from the U.S. home campus and U.S. campus-based international educators. The crisis response plan for overseas emergencies may involve many of the same U.S. offices and personnel who respond to foreign student crises, depending on campus structure. However, since the American student is far away, what the home campus can do immediately to alleviate or resolve the crisis may be extremely limited, especially in the short run. It can and must of course put itself on high-alert and be ready to spring into further action. Exactly how the home campus winds up participating often depends on the level of its planning, forethought, and communication with overseas locations, and vice versa.

An overwhelming majority of foreign students are living and learning in the U.S. as individuals, and are in the U.S. to earn an undergraduate or graduate degree—the exception being those on short-term language or other training programs, or those on quid pro quo exchanges. They are hence are long-term visitors. Most have carefully prepared themselves for this extended sojourn and adjusted to American and campus life. In contrast, only a small minority of U.S. study abroad students—just under 10 percent, according to the latest Institution of International Education (IIE) data—remain overseas for an academic year; over half are abroad for less than an academic semester. They are thus truly short-term visitors. Much of what they do is circumscribed by this transience and by the study program or foreign institution that sponsors their stay. While American students sometimes court their new-found independence and often strike out boldly on their own, they remain U.S. students and their links with their home campus are undeniable, something that emerges emphatically when things go awry.

No matter where they are in the world, how long they are away, or how immersed they are in the foreign culture, American students can and occasionally do run into severe difficulties that bring about a crisis situation for them, for their overseas program or host institution, and ultimately for their home campuses and parents. Crises often emerge complicated by the cultural "baggage" students bring with them; by their short-term status; and by living and learning in a new environment they seldom fully enter. Nevertheless, American students abroad have the same visitor status of other international students, which can be an advantage or disadvantage, depending on a lot of variables: the country, the program, etc. The overseas crisis response may leave little for the home campus to do in the short run, and depending on the circumstances, may leave everything to be attended to from the distant home base.

Logistical obstacles, caused by the distances involved and the vagaries of long-distance communication with U.S. constituencies can be daunting and frustrating. It is nearly impossible for you, as U.S. campus advisers and administrators, to know all the local logistics and potential assistance that pertain in the many locations, and on the many programs that host American students. This lack of detailed on-site information can make it more difficult for you to get an accurate or immediate read on the details and severity of the situation, and what to do about it. Other complicating factors are the foreign cultural setting and prevailing indigenous circumstances, customs and habits often quite unlike those familiar to Americans. The kinds of support and assistance available an emergency may be unclear and unfamiliar, heightening the sense of crisis.

Lines of administrative, and perhaps moral, responsibility between the home campus and the overseas program are complex and seldom easy to define, especially in the midst of a trauma situation. About 73 percent of U.S. students studying abroad, according to recent IIE data, are enrolled in programs "sponsored by" their home campus. But "sponsorship" can mean anything from direct program ownership and oversight to affiliation with— or sometimes just "approval" of—programs owned and run by other U.S., or overseas, educational institutions, agencies, and consortia. In the first instance, direct communication links between overseas sites and the home campus should be in place, although they often aren't. In the second instance, effective communications links are less likely to exist. Without plenty of forethought and planning, having multiple parties involved can complicate action and make lines of responsibility unclear.

The whereabouts of the other 27 percent of U.S. students studying abroad without home-institutional "sponsorship" may not be known to the home campus, especially if the students are considered to be on leave. These students may be directly enrolled in foreign universities or be participating in programs hosted by other U.S or foreign-institutions, and may be out of reach with the home campus. Nevertheless, when disaster strikes overseas, the home campus likely will be expected to respond in some way. A lack of institutional administrative responsibility does not necessarily release a college or university from identification with students in distress. In these ambiguous circumstances, however, there is great potential for confusion and faltering actions.

To complicate matters, the state of modern telecommunications often means that when crises erupt overseas, on-site personnel—whether U.S. faculty or staff with the group, or program directors and advisers resident abroad—may not even be the first to know about it. Individuals in charge of the program may not be informed immediately, or may not have complete information, especially in the case of an individual crisis, or if students are separated from each other, missing in transit, or reluctant or unable to come forth. Telephone calling cards and e-mail allow program participants to contact their family or friends first. Those individuals, in turn, contact the home campus, perhaps before the program director is even aware that a problem, or the perception of one, exists.

In the case of a more general threat to a group of students, CNN or other media broadcast reports, can sometimes hit the home front with early accounts of a "hot-spot" well before overseas staff hear about it. In many instances, such media coverage is sensationalistic or misinformed, or at least not directly applicable to American students or programs. These media reports can set off varying degrees of domestic concern, even panic, and must be countered both on-site and at home with more accurate or at least current information. The point in mentioning these many variables is to recognize fully that crises affecting U.S. students abroad require a response on at least two fronts: where they erupt overseas, in their foreign cultural milieu, and in the U.S., on the home campus, often in conjunction with other programs, sponsors, and with parents.

If overseas staff are informed immediately about an emergency, if they work in foreign universities or in large U.S. sponsored "branch campuses" or agency programs, in at least semi-permanent positions, they may know precisely what to do, from good training, previous experience, or both. In this case, like foreign student advisers on American campuses, overseas program directors or foreign student advisers are often able to call upon immediate colleagues and coworkers for counsel and support. They may or may not need guidance from the U.S., and they may or may not be in a position to seek it.

Usually, front-line overseas personnel tend to be American faculty or staff members, in residence with an American group only for an academic semester or year, or traveling with a group of students on some sort of short-term program. Such solitary leaders often have to function entirely on their own, under stress, in an environment not fully familiar to them. Especially in the latter situation, it is imperative that they have received thorough pre-departure training in crisis management, and that highly dependable communications systems and crisis protocols have been set up in advance. That way, immediate contact can be made with the affected students' home campus and the program sponsor, which may not be the home campus.

Crises originating overseas require understanding and quick response, taking into full account the geographical and cultural distances involved between the student and home. Differing administrative responsibilities, priorities, and procedures between overseas units and the home campus also must be considered. Planning for crises therefore needs to be done with program staff who will be in the home country and overseas. Dealing with crises far from American shores and the home campus can be substantially more complicated than dealing with the very same emergencies at home.

Colleagues in the field of international education have convened to discuss how to minimize the potential for crises occurring, and how to lessen the impact when they do happen.

Chapter 8

Crises Prevention

Guidelines for the Promotion of Health and Safety on Overseas Programs

Statistics are in short supply, but most study abroad professional conclude from their professional experiences that study in a foreign country usually is no more dangerous than study in the United States. Nevertheless, maximizing the safety of all program participants and staff is a prime concern to all parties involved in institutionally-sponsored and approved study abroad ventures: participants, their families, advisers, student's home institutions, host institutions, and the staff of all organizations that operate programs. When incidents occur, the impact on participants and their families can be more profound because the program participants are in unfamiliar settings, often far away from the comforts and conveniences of home.

It is essential that the home campus do everything possible to avert the potential for crises in the program planning and participation approval stages. The Inter-Organization Task Force on Safety and Responsibility in Study Abroad formed in May, 1997 to develop health and safety guidelines for study abroad, sponsored by the Association of International Education Administrators (AIEA), NAFSA: Association of International Educators, and the Council on International Educational Exchange. The guidelines were developed based on initiatives taken earlier by each of these organizations, and by many others in international education concerned about safety issues.

Health And Safety Guidelines

Statement Of Purpose: Because the health and safety of study abroad participants are primary concerns, these guidelines have been developed to provide useful practical guidance to institutions, participants, and parents/guardians/families. The guidelines are intended to be aspirational in nature. Although no set of guidelines can guarantee the health and safety needs of each individual involved in a study abroad program, these guidelines address issues that merit attention and thoughtful judgment. Although they address general considerations, they cannot possibly account for all the inevitable variations in actual cases that arise. Therefore, as specific situations arise, those involved must also rely upon their collective experience and judgment while considering the unique circumstances of each situation.

Guidelines for Program Sponsors

To the extent reasonably possible, all program sponsors should endeavor to implement these guidelines as applicable. At the same time, it must be noted that the structure of study abroad programs varies widely and that study abroad is usually a cooperative venture that can involve multiple sponsors. The term "sponsors" refers to all the entities that together develop, offer, and administer study abroad programs. Sponsors include sending institutions, host institutions, program administrators, and placement organizations. The role of an organization in a study abroad program varies considerably from case to case, and it is not possible to specify a division of efforts that will be applicable to all cases. All entities should apply the guidelines in ways consistent with their respective roles.

In general, guidelines that relate to obtaining information and assessing circumstances apply to all parties involved. Much of the information called for by these guidelines is readily available and can be conveyed to participants by distributing it and referring them to, or utilizing materials from recognized central sources. Guidelines that refer to the provision of information and the preparation of participants refer to parties that advise, refer, nominate, admit, enroll, or place students. Guidelines that suggest operating procedures on site apply to the entities that are directly involved in the operation of the overseas program.

In addition, program sponsors that rely heavily on the collaboration of overseas institutions may exercise less direct control over specific program components. In such cases, sponsors are urged to work with their overseas partners to develop plans and procedures for operating consistently with these guidelines

Program sponsors should

* *Conduct periodic assessments of health and safety conditions for the program, and develop and maintain emergency preparedness processes and a crisis response plan.*
* *Provide health and safety information for prospective participants so that they and their parents/guardians/families can make informed decisions concerning preparation, participation and behavior while on the program.*
* *Provide clear information concerning aspects of home campus services and conditions that cannot be replicated at overseas locations.*
* *Provide orientation to participants prior to the program and as needed on site, which includes information on safety, health, legal, environmental, political, cultural, and religious conditions in the host country, dealing with health and safety issues, potential health and safety risks, and appropriate emergency response measures.*
* *Consider health and safety issues in evaluating the appropriateness of an individual's participation in a study abroad program.*
* *Either provide appropriate health and travel accident (emergency evacuation, repatriation) insurance to participants, or provide information about how to obtain appropriate coverage. Require participants to show evidence of appropriate coverage.*
* *Conduct appropriate inquiry regarding the potential health and safety risks of the local environment of the program, including program-sponsored accommodation, events, excursions and other activities, on an ongoing basis and provide information and assistance to participants and their parents /guardians/families as needed.*

* *Conduct appropriate inquiry regarding available medical and professional services, provide information for participants and their parents /guardians/families, and help participants obtain the services they may need.*
* *Provide appropriate and ongoing health and safety training for program directors and staff, including guidelines with respect to intervention and referral, and working within the limitations of their own competencies.*
* *Communicate applicable codes of conduct and the consequences of noncompliance to participants. Take appropriate action when aware that participants are in violation.*
* *Obtain current and reliable information concerning heath and safety risks, and provide that information to program administrators and participants.*
* *In cases of serious health problems, injury, or other significant health and safety circumstances, maintain good communication among all program sponsors and others who need to know.*
* *In the participant screening process, consider factors, such as disciplinary history, that may impact on the safety of the individual or the group.*
* *Provide information for participants and their parents/guardians /families regarding when and where the sponsor's responsibility ends, and the range of aspects of participants' overseas experiences that are beyond the sponsor's control.*

In particular, program sponsors generally
* *Cannot guarantee or assure the safety of participants or eliminate all risks from the study abroad environments.*
* *Cannot monitor or control all of the daily personal decisions, choices, and activities of individual participants.*
* *Cannot prevent participants from engaging in illegal, dangerous, or unwise activities.*
* *Cannot assure that U.S. standards of due process apply in overseas legal proceedings or provide or pay for legal representation for participants.*
* *Cannot assume responsibility for the actions of persons not employed or otherwise engaged by the program sponsor, for*

events that are not part of the program, or that are beyond the control of the sponsor and its subcontractors, or for situations that may arise due to the failure of a participant to disclose pertinent information.

* *Cannot assure that home-country cultural values and norms will apply in the host country.*

Responsibilities of Participants

In Study Abroad, as in other settings, participants can have a major impact on their own health and safety abroad through the decisions they make before and during the program and by their day-to-day choices and behaviors.

Participants should:

* *Read and carefully consider all materials issued by the sponsor that relate to safety, health, legal, environmental, political, cultural, and religious conditions in host countries.*

* *Consider their health and other personal circumstances when applying for or accepting a place in a program.*

* *Make available to the sponsor accurate and complete physical and mental health information and any other personal data that is necessary in planning for a safe and healthy study abroad experience.*

* *Assume responsibility for all the elements necessary for their personal preparation for the program and participate fully in orientations.*

* *Obtain and maintain appropriate insurance coverage and abide by any conditions imposed by the carriers.*

* *Inform parents/guardians/families, and any others who may need to know, about their participation in the study abroad program, provide them with emergency contact information, and keep them informed on an ongoing basis.*

* *Understand and comply with the terms of participation, codes of conduct, and emergency procedures of the program, and obey host-country laws.*

* *Be aware of local conditions and customs that may present health or safety risks when making daily choices and decisions.*

*Promptly express any health or safety concerns to the program
staff or other appropriate individuals.*

* *Behave in a manner that is respectful of the rights and well-
being of others, and encourage others to behave in a similar
manner.*

* *Accept responsibility for their own decisions and actions.*

* *Become familiar with the procedures for obtaining emergency
health and law enforcement services in the host country.*

* *Follow the program policies for keeping program staff informed
of their whereabouts and well-being.*

Recommendations to Parents/Guardians/Families

*In Study Abroad as in other settings, parents, guardians, and families
can play an important role in the health and safety of participants by
helping them make decisions and by influencing their behavior
overseas.*

When appropriate, parents/guardians/families should:

* *Obtain and carefully evaluate health and safety information
related to the program, as provided by the sponsor and other
sources.*

* *Be involved in the decision of the participant to enroll in a particular program.*

* *Engage the participant in a thorough discussion of safety and
behavior issues, insurance needs, and emergency procedures
related to living abroad.*

* *Be responsive to requests from the program sponsor for information regarding the participant.*

* *Keep in touch with the participant.*

* *Be aware that some information may most appropriately be
provided by the participant rather than the program.*

Planning Safe Programs

Program sponsors can reduce the risks of crises overseas by developing a
comprehensive "safety profile" and even a "legal audit" for every program
enrolling students from your institution, beginning with any programs that
your own campus has developed and sponsored exclusively. This task is

something best accomplished during the program development process, but it can also be completed as part of your ongoing program review process. The profile should be revised annually by administrative officials charged with decisions on institutional risk, in response to any significant in-country developments that unfold.

You also can investigate and assign risk factors to different aspects of programs sponsored by other institutions, an exercise that will require extensive collaboration with other campuses, sponsoring agencies, and over-seas institutions. Reputable campus-, agency-, or consortium-based pro-grams should be very open and willing to discussing with anyone—campus advisers, students, parents—any risks inherent in program participation, and what preventative measures they have undertaken to maximize student and staff safety and security. They should also be willing to share their crisis management planning and how similar planning can be coordinated at your own campus. An institution's inability or unwillingness to articulate a crisis management plan is good reason to reconsider enrolling your students in its program.

Along with program safety profiling, institutional legal counsel may choose to conduct a "legal audit" of all programs, to identify areas of high exposure for students and staff, and potential liability for the institution. If legal counsel identifies areas of exposure and concern from among a pro-gram's activities—planned excursions for students that involve extensive travel over risky terrain, for example—you will have to decide whether to retain or eliminate these program features.

The same careful institutional policy planning applied to on-campus programs should be completed for study abroad. Parents and others often conclude that campuses have heightened levels of responsibility for students participating in study abroad programs, and assume that students will be "taken care of" when studying abroad, even if *in loco parentis* expectations on domestic campuses is no longer an expectation. Legal experts generally agree, and advise often, that institutions have a duty to effectively support students who participate on study abroad programs at "a reasonable stan-dard or level of care."

It is important to consider whether a risk of harm is foreseeable and unreasonable. American law in this area is not entirely clear, but legal precedent exists. One such opinion concerns acceptable risk: "In determin-ing whether a duty exists, the court may consider whether the harm that befell the individual was foreseeable." For example, in *Kleinknecht v. Gettysburg College,* the court noted that the specific event need not be foreseeable, but that the risk of harm must be both foreseeable and unreasonable. In analyzing the standard of care required, the court noted that the potential for life-threatening injuries occurring during practice or an athletic event was clearly foreseeable, and thus the college's failure to provide facilities for emergency medical attention was unreasonable (Kaplin W. & Lee, B. (1997), *The Law of Higher Education,* Jossey-Bass, San Francisco, p. 94).

This interpretation of the institutional responsibility to "foresee risks" and take "reasonable and prudent" actions is not universally accepted, but it suggests that there is a special relationship between the institution and the student participating in study abroad. Each campus needs to investigate this relationship and apply it to its own programs and policies.

Other lawyers use a "dependency" approach to determining when a special relationship exists: "Under this approach, a student who can be said to be dependent on the institution for his or her safety has a special relationship with the institution. As an example, contrast the cases of a graduate student crossing a street on campus with the case of toddlers enrolled in the campus day care center crossing the same street. The toddlers are dependent on the supervision of the college's employees. The graduate student is not. The toddlers, therefore, stand in a special relationship with the college. The graduate student does not. A court using this analysis might well find that a student who was clearly not dependent on her college while on its United States campus, would be dependent on it, while enrolled in at a foreign campus in, say, Africa." (Burling, P. (1992), *Managing the Risks of Foreign Study Programs,* Foley, Hoag & Eliot, Boston).

The challenge to every institution is to use its legal counsel to balance a sufficient level of care without evoking claims of absolute *in loco parentis* status, or without exercising too much control. The basic principles seem to be to:

- Determine what foreseeable risks exist abroad;

- Provide information about them to staff and students; and

- Provide support services for students that minimize risks and maximize safety.

In the case of an emergency, study abroad program administrators in the United States and abroad may be the only resource available to support students. Parents expect that the institution has a special, heightened role in supporting the student through the crisis. Thus, it is important to be able to confirm that students have been reasonably and prudently informed of pos-

SAFETY PROFILE

Information	Source
Political climate	• U.S. Department of State (*http://travel.state.gov*) travel advisories, links to web pages of American embassies
	• *http://cn.net.au/country.htm* links to other countries' advisory sites
	• CNN, host country newspapers/satellite news
Health, disease risk, prevention	• Center for Disease Control advisories (*http://www.cdc.gov/travel/index.html*) sites for health information from insurance providers.
	• *www.medexassist.com/index.html*
	• *http://www.intsos.com* university health services, travel clinic
Treatment	• medical and psychological services quality, accessibility, language/cultural limitations
Weather/climate	• Weather Channel
Heat/cold	• in-country or local meteorologists
Severe weather	• on-site staff
Highway/travel safety	• Association for Safe International Road Travel (*http://www.asirt.org*)
	• AAA, travel agents
	• safety records of transport providers
Living conditions	• inspection of dorms, hotels, homestays
Security	• student reports
Accessibility, food, variety (vegetarian?)	• visits to providers, restaurants
	• student reports
Safety, emergency response, evacuation routes	• host institution
Safe houses	• local contacts, faculty expertise

sible risks and realities prior to going abroad, about how to act appropriately while abroad, and about how to respond to emergencies, both independently and as a part of the group.

Insurance companies, travel providers, and lawyers each have their own formulas for calculating risk. No one formula can apply to all situations. A program studying tropical medicine in the Amazon may assign a lower risk factor to the presence of cholera in the area than would a program in India studying Buddhist writings. In the same way, a group learning about Celtic literature may give a higher risk factor to political unrest in Belfast than one that is looking at peace and conflict studies. Part of the challenge of developing a safety profile is deciding which risks are acceptable and which ones are not. Different programs' profiles for the same site may vary drastically. Factors such as faculty expertise and contacts, local institutional ties, and potential support systems must be considered in your institution's profiles for each site. The box on the preceding page lists information that can be included in a safety profile.

Program Admissions and the Buckley Amendment

Student behavior, whether simply misguided or intentionally aberrant, takes the lead on a long list of causes of study abroad crises. There is no way to be fully prepared for the foreign environment—a factor that is part of the great appeal of living outside one's national borders. Sometimes the most apparently prepared students, once overseas, have trouble adjusting. For other students, study abroad can be emboldening and liberating, resulting in new-found confidence, maturity, and direction. But, the freedom and new environment sometimes lead students to become overconfident and careless in their habits and actions.

Colleagues at overseas institutions are often puzzled over American university reluctance to say "no" to students with poor academic and behavioral records, even though an excellent academic record may not predict success or adjustment, or lead to model behavior in a different and stressful cultural situation. Crises that result from pre-existing problems, if not always fatal, often represent setbacks for the student, are usually stressful for the group, and frequently damage institutional relationships. Everyone agrees that overseas program directors and host institutions may be ill-equipped to deal, for instance, with the effects of culture shock on recovering alcoholics, students with severe eating disorders, or those using prescription drugs for mental health conditions, to name just a few types of crises that can surface in the face of cultural adaptation.

Ideally, the campus student selection processes for overseas study would include consultation with student affairs and housing personnel who can make recommendations based on candidates' previous health and behavioral records, and can help study abroad offices and affiliated institutions place students in appropriate settings, or support them in saying "no" when necessary. In addition, students should be informed as to all the challenges and expectations presented by program participation, and be given ample opportunity to measure themselves against these challenges and expectations. After all, it is in their own best interest to be admitted only to programs in which there are good prospects for healthy, safe participation.

However, U.S. colleges and universities are institutionally constrained in what they can discover and what they can share vis-a-vis student personnel or academic records. This is because each student has legal privacy rights guaranteed under the Family Educational Rights and Privacy Act (FERPA), also known as the Buckley Amendment, that need to be considered in admissions decisions, in preparation for sending them abroad, and in nearly anything that happens to them while they are overseas. Campus personnel are also restricted from readily sharing private matters with other domestic or overseas colleagues. The U.S. State Department points out the following:

"The provisions of the Privacy Act are designed to protect the privacy and rights of Americans but occasionally complicate efforts to assist U.S. citizens abroad. As a general rule, consular officers may not reveal information regarding an individual American's location, welfare, intentions, or problems to anyone, including family members and Congressional representatives, without the expressed consent of that individual. In all potential cases, consular officials explain the Privacy Act restrictions and requirements so that all individuals involved in a case understand the legal constraints."

Given this law, students occasionally assume they have a personal right to withhold information about anything in their private life, or academic or medical records that they choose to conceal. Home campuses, sponsoring campuses and agencies, and overseas programs can often do little legally to ferret out this hidden information. To release private information to parents, even in crisis situations, is therefore illegal without the permission of the student. There have been instances where students have stopped taking medications, or for other reasons, became psychologically distressed abroad. If asked while unwell, students may tell directors that they do not want family contacted. In other cases, students have been arrested and jailed, and requested family not be contacted. For safety reasons, it may be prudent to involve families and either to consider sending a student home, or bringing family members abroad to assist the student.

What programs *can* do in advance, however, is to have in place a code of behavior that applies overseas; that this code is not only made known to students prior to departure, but that participation in the program is contingent upon their *informed consent.* To document their *informed consent,* all students (and parents for students under 21) should sign one or more "conditions for participation" forms. These forms usually contain the legal language designed to absolve the institution of responsibility for calamities beyond their control (war, pestilence, famine, etc.) and other situations that might be causes for lawsuits. But their main value is in requiring students to confirm that they fully understand and accept the conditions of their enrollment and continuation in overseas programs.

The following is a list of provisions that students could be asked to read and affirm:

- That they have read the information about the challenges and risks of the program and affirm they are ready for them.

- That they will read and further research the place and culture they will be entering, and be respectful of its primacy.

- That they have determined, with or without professional medical and psychological help, they are capable of enduring the rigors of the program.

- That they will adjust their dress and behavior to suit the expectations of the program and the host culture.

- That they grant the providers the right to make changes, deletions, or adjustments to the program in the interest of safety.

- That they grant the director the right to send them home if their academic performance, behavior, or dress is deemed to be detrimental to the program or represents an unacceptable risk to themselves or the group.

Informed consent is one of the cornerstones of risk management. By indicating *in writing* that they understand and accept these provisions, students are morally, institutionally, and to some degree, legally bound by this acceptance. Of course, no one can be forced to surrender their legal rights if they feel they are the victim of negligence. Having the release form at the home institution and with the overseas director, if there is one, the institution is legally free to communicate with parents, guardians, or significant others in the event of any sort of overseas crisis, whether the crisis is caused by student misbehavior or by an accident.

Absent consent forms, institutions, in dire emergencies, might have to do what needs to be done without student permission, taking the chance that these actions will be seen by students and parents as well-intentioned, beneficial and essential. Having this in writing and in advance of departure will definitely speed-up the communication process, saving time, and perhaps a life. There are, of course, no guarantees for programs or institutions against lawsuits, or absolute protections against instances of negligence.

Background on the Buckley Amendment is available at the Department of Education's web site, http://www.ed.gov. Do a simple search for the amendment by name.

Preparing Students for Potential Emergency Situations

Most students know that when they are abroad they might have to learn and act by a new set of social and cultural standards. But they will not, on their own, give much thought about how to avoid potential crises or what to do in an emergency. An unprepared student can exacerbate a situation, escalating something relatively minor into a crisis, or worsening what is already an emergency. Informed students are crucial to successful crisis containment. Campuses and programs do best when they not only educate students about avoiding trouble, but about what their response should be in the event of crises circumstances. Among other things, before departure students need to understand specifically what to do and whom to call if they are injured, sick or in some kind of trouble. They also need to know overseas and domestic emergency numbers to call 24 hours a day, seven days a week, with back-up contact information, as well.

Just as the surgical patient has the right to be told of all possible outcomes of a medical procedure, students embarking on an overseas program should know the challenges and risks that are a part of living, working, or studying in a foreign country and culture. If they are required to dress or behave in a certain way, this needs to be communicated in as much detail as possible. There should be a clear description of consequences for violations of cultural, academic, or behavioral standards.

Information must be made easy for students to remember. Present it in a variety of ways: oral, written, online, and/or written on a wallet-sized card that they can carry with them. Inquirers, applicants, participants, and parents should receive this same information in at least three ways: in the program brochure; in the acceptance materials; and in the written program manual. The information should also be communicated verbally, through telephone contacts or on-campus orientations.

If fear of driving students away leads you to avoid giving full information about the potential dangers of a program or site, reconsider. If a large proportion of students are discouraged from participating when they hear or read complete information about the risks of a program, perhaps that program is too challenging for that population, or presents too large a risk for the sponsoring institution. The wisest course always is to provide honest and prudent counsel, delineate what is and isn't acceptable behavior, and let all parties know what is expected of them in an emergency.

Chapter 9

Planning for Study Abroad Crises

N o matter how conscientious you are and no matter how many risks you avert, sooner or later a crisis may occur, either to an individual or to a group of students. All crises demand an immediate response when, where, and as, they unfold. Close coordination between the student's overseas program site and the home campus is essential. How well the overseas program site and the home campus work together to respond to a crisis depends to a great extent on how well both parties have prepared for the complex demands and often frightening realities that crises inevitably bring.

Campus Preparations: Drawing Up the Crisis Management Plan

Crisis management plans should be both broad and flexible to allow for adaptation to the crisis at hand. Each overseas crisis is unique in its details, and no concrete set of steps applies equally to every campus and every given situation. Yet, there are certain common threads that run through each crisis and certain common approaches that can be adapted to your own experiences.

One of the truths in overseas crises is that the response needs to occur both onsite and back at the home front. The effects of crises that occur overseas will inevitably be felt back home. All crises become linked with the home campus, family, and domestic friends. Whether the cause is fate; conditions, assumptions, and problems that exist uniquely in the overseas environment; or behavior problems that students may have brought with them, an overseas crisis will impact the home campus. Whether the student is participating in a program directly sponsored by your institution, in an affiliated program, in a program with no formal relationship to the home campus, or is directly enrolled in a foreign university, once the student's affiliation with your institution is known, your institution will need to activate its response to the situation.

In developing your plan, you should seek input from all personnel who could be involved in responding to a crisis. Include a protocol that spells out roles and responsibilities; procedures, policies, and priorities, and that outlines the basic response steps to be taken at home, in coordination with overseas on-site staff and program directors.

Agencies and organizations that sponsor programs overseas should have their own crisis management plans in place, and must thoroughly train both domestic and overseas staff for emergency situations. Simultaneously, program sponsors also need to share their plans with U.S. colleges and universities that enroll students in their programs. If sponsoring institutions do not volunteer the information, enrolling colleges should request crisis management plans from the program sponsors. Preparing for a potential emergency must be both proactive and ongoing; waiting until crisis strikes is too late. Having the crisis management plan in place, along with criteria for program cancellation, demonstrates care for the safety and well-being of all participants, and offers solace that proper precautions were taken.

Contacting the overseas institution/organization staff, both home and host governmental agencies, police departments, airlines (or transportation contractors), medical personnel, and consular staff should be among the first steps that the home institution/organization undertakes. If it is something that may affect other programs in the same location, overseas staff might be able to make contact and get such information from their counterparts. Simultaneously, American campus international educators can and should make contact with others via direct calls or via the SECUSS-L listserve, which functions as an emergency information network. Such information will assist your program in responding appropriately.

As contact with all responsible parties is being made, the program staff's first priority is of course attending to the physical and psychological well-

SUMMARY OF STEPS

The first step in facing the realities of any crises is being prepared. All campuses and organizations with students studying abroad should have in place:

✓ A crisis management plan, often based on the existing campus crisis management plan, specifically adapted to the particular realities of overseas crises;

✓ A preselected crisis response team in place, possibly within the program-sponsoring organization, or, at least 6 protocols for assembling an appropriate group for a particular kind of crisis;

✓ A 24-hour answering "system" on the home campus, with a telephone tree or similar plan that spells out simply the sequence of calls, so that rapid response to an overseas crisis can be initiated at any time of the day, every day of the year;

✓ An required orientation program for all staff leading your own programs, prior to departure, that covers what to do in emergency situations involving individual students or the entire group, and includes an emergency action check-list;

✓ Communications procedures for dealing with overseas institutions and other program sponsors/organizations that receive your students, complete with instructions on what to do in the event of an emergency to alert your campus, parents, etc.;

✓ A required orientation program for all participants, prior to departure, specifying potential dangers, expected behaviors, and contingency responses in times of emergencies;

✓ A list of emergency and after-hours government, insurance, Red Cross, overseas institution and organization addresses, phone contact numbers, e-mail addresses, web sites that provide up-to-the-minute information on overseas locations, etc.;

✓ A list of lawyers with expertise in host country law; of faculty with expertise in each program area; and

✓ Emergency evacuation planning and repatriation insurance for all program participants and staff. ●

being of the individual student and the group, in the best possible manner. While home country staff can only assess this situation when it has full information, providing such information should not happen at the expense of on-site assistance and counsel. In extreme situations, back-up plans may be needed and could include finding short-term local assistance for the program staff or even traveling immediately to the site to provide help.

Once all information has been gathered, the home country program staff should assemble its response team and communicate its crisis management action plan for immediate implementation. This team may either be a standing group, specified in the crisis management plan, an ad hoc group assembled for this particular type of crisis, or a combination of standing members and ad hoc appointees added to the team because of their special expertise. Standing groups may include the institution/organization president, chief academic officer, international program staff, student services staff, counselors, health personnel, safety officers, legal staff, and—of high importance—public information officers.

When the crisis has been resolved, the team should conduct a debriefing that includes a review of all information, actions taken, and personnel involved, both overseas and domestically. The team should discuss what worked well, what might have been done differently, and how they might handle a similar crisis at a different time. The team should also consider what psychological counseling may be needed by those involved in responding to the crisis. The bottom line is to have a good plan, to assure that all information provided is consistent, in writing—particularly helpful so that it can be relayed to inquirers over the phone—and reassuring.

Gathering and Coordinating Vital Information

Perhaps the most critical information that needs to be gathered and shared between domestic and overseas staff is the range of skills and services that are available on site. Each country will have a different palette of emergency services, shaped by the culture, the history, the current conditions, and even the geography of the country. Similarly, overseas program staff offer a range of experiences and skills that need to be familiar to the home campus, so it can gain access to them in an emergency. Without this knowledge, U.S. campuses are left waiting for services that never arrive or, worse, struggling to manage a crisis when help is actually close at hand.

It makes sense that, early on, you survey your campus and overseas staff, including faculty to take stock of special skills or talents that may be useful to you. Faculty members can provide translation and legal assistance, render emergency medical attention, and counsel victims of an incident. Doing so is often much faster than involving local authorities, and can also yield a response that is more appropriate to the particular needs of your students and your program.

What you need to know may be drawn from government agencies, non-governmental organizations (NGOs), local citizens, or private companies. Familiarize yourself with the strengths and weaknesses of each contact. Identify what they can do for you, where they can do it, when they are available, and how they operate. Just as the range of possible situations is great, your list of resources needs to be equally comprehensive. Among the contacts that you might consider locating, provided they are available, are:

- The U.S. Embassy or Consulate;

- Local emergency medical services;

- The nearest hospital;

- A western-trained, English-speaking physician;

- The local police;

- The fire department;

- A crisis counselor or psychologist;

- A rape counselor;

- A translator;

- A lawyer familiar with local laws;

- Your landlord, if you have one;

- Your insurance agent;

- Your travel agent or airline;

- Local search and rescue services;

- Local politicians;

- Local weather services;

- A HAM radio operator or Internet resource; and

- Humanitarian relief agencies (The Red Cross or Red Crescent, for example).

At times, you may be best served by calling United States Government resources for additional support. Examples of such avenues of information would include:

- Crisis hotlines;

- Medical specialists;

- Medical evacuation services;

- The U.S. State Department desk for the country in which you are operating;

- The State Department's Citizen's Overseas Emergency Center, 202-647-5225;

- The U.S. Coast Guard, as appropriate; and

- Your Congressperson.

If conditions warrant, you may consider sending a team from the U.S. to provide additional assistance to local authorities, particularly in the case of an ill-equipped local medical system. In any case, have a back-up for each service. During a situation such as the bombing in Kenya in 1998, even well-established support networks like the U.S. Embassy may be unavailable to help you when they are directly involved in the crisis or they are out of contact. Having a secondary plan allows you a work-around solution.

Establishing Emergency Communications Systems

All on-campus education abroad administrators should have a reliable system for round-the-clock, emergency contact coverage. Some programs rely on voice mail, beepers, cell phones, a dedicated study abroad emergency line, or the university emergency switchboard. The method will depend upon the number of students you will have abroad at any given time, your level of involvement with your students' study abroad experience—for instance, does your institution send students on its own programs or those of other schools— the size of your office, and the amount of backup you will have. All players involved must be adequately informed about the emergency communication system, including: home university staff, sponsoring administrators, on-site administrators, students, and parents.

The system you have should meet the following criteria:

- Reach a live person within a reasonable amount of time;

- Have a back-up system in place that considers the primary contact person may be out of touch at times during evenings, weekends, and holidays;

- Have a vacation policy for when the primary contact person is away;

- Take into consideration differences between catastrophic emergencies (fatalities, terrorism/state of war, natural disasters) and more typical emergencies (minor injury, stolen wallet, conflict with host institution);

- The person calling about an emergency should only have to dial one number;

- Students must be able to call collect easily from any place in the world;

- Students may not be calling from the location of their program;

- Emergency calls may come from many different sources: overseas administrators, study abroad students, students' friends, parents, host families, or local authorities, to name several.

Sponsoring institutions and administrators abroad both need to be informed about your institution's emergency communication procedures and be willing to abide by them. In addition, you need to have your contacts' emergency phone numbers so you can reach them after office hours. Keep these numbers both at home and at the office. Finally, you need to feel comfortable that their emergency system overseas is adequate to ensure the health and safety of your students.

As noted previously, students themselves must be well informed about the emergency communication procedures. It should be a part of both their written and spoken preparation and orientation. Again, some programs give students brightly colored, laminated cards with emergency phone numbers and the international AT&T operator number.

Campuses also need to maintain a database of each student's emergency contact person(s). This does not need to be a sophisticated computerized document. For example the College of Staten Island assembles notebooks containing all the students' emergency contact forms, along with other emergency contact information. Remember, you cannot assume that a student's permanent or billing address on the registrar's system is the appropriate contact. Neither can you assume that the appropriate contact is either the mother or father. Remember to keep this list with you outside of work as well as in the office.

Parents/guardians, or other appropriate family members should be part of your alert plan. There is a strong possibility that students in crisis will contact their parents and leave it to them to call you. A parent will quickly lose confidence in a study abroad program if they cannot reach a responsible person in an emergency. During orientation at Northeastern University, students write their family's or guardian's address directly on an envelope, so that staff can mail all written materials and forms, including health, safety, and emergency information, directly to the correct parties.

Having in Place and Knowing How to Utilize Medical and Accident Insurance

There is no national health care system in the United States, so most Americans enroll in private health insurance programs. Typically, students are insured through family health insurance policies, often part of a benefit package offered by employers; others are covered by policies offered or mandated by their home colleges or universities. Despite cost-sharing between employers, employees, institutions, health maintenance organizations, etc., health insurance is expensive in the United States. Furthermore, Americans are accustomed to paying for more than just the health insurance premiums, as domestic insurance policies require patients to pay part of their health care costs.

As the cost of medical care has skyrocketed in the U.S., health insurance companies have become more stringent regarding medical services they will cover—*so it is imperative to make sure that overseas travel is covered.* A list of covered services is normally provided as part of the health insurance policy. Insurance companies may question whether someone actually "needs" certain medical services, even if the services are recommended by the attending doctors. This kind of questioning can cause substantial stress to students and families.

An increasing number of institutions *require* that all students have insurance coverage through their own institution's student health plan or another comprehensive insurance plan that provides coverage while they are overseas. *Help students understand as much as possible that it is the responsibility of each student to understand his/her health insurance policy.* Unless they are covered by a national health insurance plan overseas, country (unusual, but not unheard of) students need to know in advance that they will be asked to pay for all medical expenses up front, ideally, to be reimbursed at a later date for a portion of these expenses (generally 70 percent) by their U.S. health insurance policies. If students have difficulty securing treatment because they do not have enough money with them, they can be instructed to call collect the 24-hour traveler's assistance service that is a benefit of their International Student Identity Card (ISIC), but this is never a good substitute for being financially prepared.

International Student Identity Card (ISIC) Traveler's Insurance

Most students are asked to have supplementary insurance coverage through the International Student Identity Card (ISIC), issued by the International Student Traveler Confederation (www.istc.org). This insurance provides Medical Evacuation or "Medivac" coverage, in the event that a student needs to be transported to another country to obtain medical care. The ISIC policy also provides a 24-hour travelers' assistance number that students can call collect from any country in the world at 713-267-2525. As indicated above, students have been instructed to call this number if they are having difficulty obtaining treatment. In addition to financial assistance, the traveler's assistance line offers help in translation and interpretation.

Assist America Traveler's Insurance

Assist America provides a more deluxe version of the traveler's assistance services offered by the ISIC card (e.g., no monetary limit on the costs of Medivac coverage, 24-hour traveler's assistance number, provision for a family member or friend to visit if a student has a long-term illness, etc.). Assist America is generally offered by multi-national corporations in the U.S., enabling the higher level of service.

Before the Crisis

Most international educators urge that no college or education abroad program should allow a student to travel abroad without sufficient insurance coverage for all possible medical needs, including coverage for medical evacuation and repatriation of remains, and both accident and life insurance. Many institutions can arrange to extend the policy that covers students on campus, sometimes for an extra fee.

Major Medical Coverage. Major medical coverage supports a student's medical needs while abroad, that can range from a broken wrist to sexually transmitted diseases or a pregnancy. It is important to confirm the limitations of insurance policy coverage, and whether students will need to pay in advance and be reimbursed, or if the insurance company will make payments immediately to providers around the world.

Medical Evacuation Coverage. A student's injury or sickness may require emergency evacuation to a medical treatment facility or return to the student's residence or country of residence, the United States, or elsewhere. Generally an emergency evacuation is ordered by medical personnel when local care is considered insufficient. For instance, a student injured on a mountain while skiing might need to be evacuated by helicopter to a local hospital. If a student is seriously injured abroad and the doctor confirms that appropriate care would be best in the United States, it may be necessary to include a charter aircraft with full medical staff from abroad to the United States. This can be very expensive, in extreme cases costing over $50,000. In these cases, having appropriate insurance keeps the focus on how to provide best care, rather than "who will pay."

Repatriation of Remains Coverage. As with any travel experience, the possibility exists that a student could die while taking part in a study abroad program. According to the U.S. State Department publication, The Office of Overseas Citizens Services: "Approximately 6,000 Americans die outside of the U.S. each year. The majority of these are long-term residents of a foreign country. ACS assists with the return of remains for approximately 2,000 Americans annually. When an American dies abroad, a consular officer notifies the next-of-kin about options and costs for the disposition of remains. Costs for preparing and returning a body to the U.S. are high and are the responsibility of the family. Often local laws and procedures make returning a body to the U.S. for burial a lengthy process."

Important Considerations. Many U.S. insurance policies do not provide coverage for overseas travel. Make sure that your students have contacted their health insurance carrier to confirm their continued protection while overseas. Alternately, they may be able to arrange for additional coverage through a temporary traveler's health insurance program. Many institutions require proof of adequate insurance prior to enrollment in study abroad programs. Even with proof, institutions may offer additional emergency evacuation coverage, because even carriers that cover medical expenses abroad may not pay for evacuation home to the United States in the event of a serious injury or illness. In some cases, you may need to consider a special policy if your chosen locations or activities fall outside of standard coverage. In one specialized yet possible example, neither evacuation insurance nor medical insurance will provide for re-compression therapy in the case of a scuba-diving-related accident.

You should assess your organization's insurance needs for its coverage of all program needs. If you are connected with a college or university, you will in most cases be covered by the institution's carrier. If you are not affiliated with an existing organization, you will instead need to investigate general liability coverage, educator's legal insurance, and, perhaps, a policy covering any motor vehicles or property that you own. Unlike medical and evacuation insurance that protect the health of individual participants, these policies are designed to safeguard the program as a whole.

Examine your policies for holes and fill them. Don't skimp on coverage, nor assume that you are ever fully protected from every conceivable incident. Know what you are buying, and what is and what is not covered. Read your policy's fine print. Know how to activate your policies' benefits. At a minimum, you will need the phone number of your carrier, the name of your account representative, and knowledge of any notification requirements that apply. Unfortunately, toll-free phone numbers (800 and 888) don't always work from overseas. Instead, you will need a toll or collect number, together with a calling card and a U.S. access code. You can follow the practice of issuing wallet-sized cards to students and staff members; to be carried at all times, the cards contain all relevant information needed in an emergency. Some programs also ask their participants to wear Medic Alert bracelets or tags indicating special medical information for all to see.

You will also need to know your workers' compensation obligations under the law. If a staff member is injured on the job, what paperwork do you need to file? How long do you have to do so? What information is needed? Because workers' compensation is legally mandated, the rules and regulations governing it are strict, and you may be fined if you fail to fully comply with the law. Having the procedures clearly established in advance will allow you to better meet these obligations.

When preparing for a medical emergency, it is important to note that many foreign medical providers, both doctors and hospitals, require prepayment before providing treatment. Medical providers have substantial experience treating patients who never pay them for services rendered. They may know from experience that it can be difficult or impossible to track down foreign students for payment. As a result, they are wary of all new patients, even students who promise immediate reimbursement. We instruct our students to bring extra funds for basic medical care such as an examination or a needed prescription.

In the event of complex and expensive treatment, family or friends may need to wire funds from home. If time permits, this is a preferred option. Only in the event of a serious injury, where time is critical, might payment be advanced for critical care for students. To be prepared for medical emergencies with your students, we recommend that you contact local physicians and medical centers to clarify their payment policies well in advance of any emergency.

Regardless of prearrangements, you should make it clear to your staff that they are authorized to spend whatever amount is necessary in the event of an emergency to provide for proper victim care.

During the Crisis

Contact insurance carriers immediately with a preliminary report. Some carriers require preauthorization and refuse to honor bills for services that they did not approve and arrange in advance. This information might include the plan name, the policy number, the location, the name of any injured people, and a number where calls can be returned. If preauthorization is required, you may need to make medical and evacuation arrangements through your carrier. Keep them fully informed of developing situations. Notify your property insurers, too, if property damage has occurred in an accident.

To speed treatment, bring any medical or insurance information that you have on file with you to the hospital. Some programs make it a practice when on travel to carry an envelope containing this information, along with signed, permission-to-treat statements. In the event of an emergency, the envelope can accompany an injured person to the nearest medical center. With all relevant material available, a patient can begin receiving treatment while another person completes the necessary paperwork.

Remember that medical bills are between the health care provider—the doctor or hospital—and the patient—the student or staff member. Avoid too much involvement in that transaction. Experience in the field has shown that it is too easy to become embroiled in billing disputes between patients and doctors, to the detriment of all involved. In order to maintain the good graces of local medical providers, you will need to make sure that all bills are paid in a timely manner. However, your goal should be facilitating payment, not providing it, with the above-mentioned exception of critical or acute care.

Finally, if a third party is injured as a result of an incident involving your student, there is some debate about whether you or your student should pay for medical care. In some cases, offering to pay for treatment may be considered an admission of guilt. Seek a legal opinion from your institution's attorney in this instance, preferably as part of your program planning.

After the Crisis

Immediately following a crisis, you should process any applicable workers' compensation forms. In most cases, these papers must be filed within 24–48 hours of an injury. This paperwork should be filed even for a minor injury requiring limited medical attention. Occasionally, a seemingly minor injury later develops into a chronic problem that leads to a claim, even several years later. Your institution is much better protected if you have filed the proper paperwork at the time of the initial injury.

You also will need to help students complete any claims for property or vehicle damage incurred. Claims for third-party injury should also be filed promptly. In both cases, an appointed insurance investigator will assess damages. Remember: if the insurance carrier is ultimately paying the bill, it is the carrier's decision whether to settle a third party claim or not, regardless of the impact such a decision might have on your program.

Summary

- Help students arrange to pay their bills as soon as is practical, but don't pay their bills yourself unless absolutely necessary;

- Have a student to whom you have advanced money sign an IOU;

- Help students reach their parents or insurance company for reimbursement; facilitate wiring money or cashing traveler's checks;

- Make sure a student's bill is settled before she returns home, or payment may never be made. In extreme cases, you may wish to consider withholding grades until a bill is paid in full. Failing to pay a bill can and has damaged program and institutional reputations with local physicians and hospitals. Avoid risking future care because of a patient's delinquent payments;

- Analyze your existing coverage for any holes, gaps, or necessary additions that an incident may reveal, and move to fill them as quickly as possible. This may mean adding new coverage not previously purchased. It may also mean eliminating activities that cannot be adequately insured. The concept of risk management implies a careful balance between risks and their mitigation;

- Write all contact numbers and information down and distribute it in the form of a concise, portable document;

- If you are traveling with a group, carry the contact information with you, just in case. Provide the same information to your students, in case they encounter problems while apart from the program; and

- Post the information in a central location that is readily accessible. Information might also explain when and how to call for assistance, how to handle internal and external communications, what documentation is required, any emergency logistics, and, perhaps, a list of staff phone numbers.

Sometimes a contact number may be as easy as dialing "911," or the local equivalent. In many cases, the local police will act as a clearinghouse for emergency response services. In addition, the U.S. Consulate nearest you often maintains a list of area physicians and other resources you can call. An alternative strategy is to arrange for emergency assistance through your evacuation insurance policy. Often these policies provide a 24-hour on-call dispatcher who can help you locate a doctor or replace a lost passport.

Contact your resources in advance. Familiarize them with your program and your emergency needs. Develop a protocol for when to call them, how to call, and what they will need. A clear list of triggers that will provoke a response should be familiar to all staff. You want to eliminate any confusion about what constitutes a crisis, how staff should respond, and what will be needed by those on the other end of the phone.

Know expected response times and capabilities; know their comfort zones. How long will it take help to arrive? Will they even show up? If they do, what can they do to assist you? What can you do for them? The 911 system has done wonders for American emergency preparedness, but even within the United States, answers to these questions vary greatly from place to place. Overseas, the answers can be even more radical. We have had fire brigades arrive with ladders and hoses in tow to treat a sick student, when what was really needed was a paramedic. In some countries, the response you receive many be neither a fire brigade nor a paramedic.

On-Site Preparations and Coordination With Home Campuses

In most instances, on-site staff must be prepared to shoulder the burden of the front-line response to both individual and group crises. Acting quickly on their own initiative is often an imperative for staff when things are moving fast and student well-being is at risk. Knowing whom to call, where to turn, and how to get assistance, is something that needs to be thought through in advance, and be part of the coordinated response plan.

During a Crisis

In any life-threatening emergency, on-site staff should always contact local authorities and the providers of emergency assistance first, as they are usually in the best position to help. Even if a reliable communications network has been established, as it should be, it is still important for all staff to be familiar with the location of the nearest phone, or to carry one. Many countries now offer viable cellular or pager networks. Satellite phones that cover more remote areas are beginning to arrive on the market, too. Two-way radios can also be useful in some situations. In short, they should use any means or combination of means to communicate effectively. While these days most rapid communication is carried on by e-mail, fax, or telephone, but knowing about HAM radio options is always a good back-up. If communicating by radio or any other open medium, discretion is required to protect privacy. Transmit only information that directly impacts patient care There is no need to broadcast the victim's name or the program name.

Rapid notification is critical. Mobilizing a program's emergency response efforts as soon as possible allows for collaborative problem-solving as the situation unfolds, provides additional logistical support for crisis-related tasks, and immediately creates a larger emotional support network to handle any negative developments. A properly assembled team will also serve to shift the burden of media contact and other external jobs away from those whose attention is focused on the crisis at hand.

It is strongly advised that you name only one contact person on the home campus with whom on-site staff communicates, and that person is ideally identified in advance, as part of your CMP. This is generally the top education abroad administrator, but could be someone else. In any case, it should be the home-campus person who sets into motion the Crisis Management Plan, and, as needed, convenes a crisis management team appropriate to the situation at hand. All parties should maintain a written log of all steps taken and all communications. A written record of all phone calls, discussions, actions, and conversations is important after the event, and also helps track current management efforts more effectively.

Overseas and domestic contacts need to be sure to clarify what each needs from the other: medical care, temporary shelter, transportation, or a search effort, a physical description of a missing person and the place they were last seen, an inventory of stolen property; information on a student's medical history, or whatever else will help. To maximize phone communication, parties should Remain on the line until both parties have everything they; many emergency calls are accidentally terminated by frantic callers before all the necessary details have been provided. There should be no doubt as to the realities of the situation and what is needed to improve it, even if the expectation of immediate help is remote. In Western Europe, an ambulance may be on scene in less than 10 minutes, but elsewhere the delays can be great. The next check-in should be agreed-upon at the end of every contact. Even if no new information is known, the simple passing of time may provide new ideas. Overseas staff should also provide local authorities with contact names and phone numbers for updates and new developments.

Once these communications have been established and everyone is informed about the situation, the crisis response becomes a joint effort. While on-site staff remain on the front line and in the best position to monitor and influence developments, a balance must be found between micromanagement of the crisis by the home campus alone—they may not be in the best position to know what is possible in foreign conditions—and forcing on-site staff to make decisions without the benefit of home-campus information and perspectives. Additionally, on-site staff have ongoing responsibility to the other students with the program, and usually cannot devote 100 percent of their time to the one or more students affected by a crisis. A working consensus on what needs to be done next and whose responsibility it is to do it ideally will emerge, as long as both parties are informed and flexible.

There can be differences of opinion among caring responsible parties, over issues such as the appropriateness of local transportation, the quality of medical care available to victims, whether and when to contact parents, and other complicated issues. Overseas staff must be informed and persuasive when they believe safety is being compromised, and resist making the situation worse by buying into a plan or treatment with which they may not agree. It is possible that a home campus that does not understand local conditions or cultural mores may make the wrong suggestion. Such conflicts should be resolved with the health and well-being of the student as a first priority.

After a Crisis

After an incident, follow-up with local authorities is fairly straightforward. To begin, on-site staff need to help law enforcement officials complete any necessary investigations, whether civil or criminal. Such investigations may include giving statements to investigators, helping to file a police report, or making sure victims visit a local medical center to be examined by a physician. In the case of a sexual assault, the attending physician would typically collect evidence and administer tests for pregnancy, HIV infection, and other sexually transmitted diseases.

Next, on-site staff may wish, or be required, to produce a written report for local authorities, embassy personnel, or crisis counselors involved in the emergency. Such a report would outline the incident, the response, and the key learning for those involved, as seen from your perspective. This is not a finger-pointing activity; instead, its focus must be on developing a better understanding of future crisis prevention and planning. Programs with an existing system of incident reporting and review might choose to disseminate their reports directly to local authorities involved.

Finally, it is important to hold a debriefing on the incident, face-to-face with any involved organizations. Again, the goal of these sessions must be to better prevent and prepare for future occurrences. This direct discussion also allows on-site staff the opportunity to compare its own written report with reports of other parties, and rectify any discrepancies. It is important for legal reasons to draw a subtle but critical distinction between saying that one would respond differently in the future and saying that one responded inappropriately to the crisis at hand.

It can greatly alleviate the stress for all parties to participate in a final meeting with local authorities. It is not uncommon to find that both victims and rescuers alike will need ongoing emotional support in the aftermath of a traumatic event; often, these two groups will have forged a strong bond with each other that makes continued contact helpful and desirable.

Chapter 10

Responding to Overseas Crises That Affect Individuals on Study Abroad Programs

D istinguishing a personal "problem" from a true individual student "crisis" is never easy. One rule of thumb however, is that the perspective of onsite staff is almost always more reliable than are indirect reports via parents or students, especially if those reports are dated. On the other hand, the home campus may have information on the student's background, or other information, that will help in understanding, if not resolving, the problem overseas. In responding to an individual student's real, or perceived, crisis, a natural tendency may be to try to minimize the drama and trauma. Student independence and self-reliance often diminish under the stress of the cross-cultural experience. The last thing a homesick and culture-shocked student wants to hear is. "Oh, it can't be that bad." or "You'll feel better in a few days." But there is no way of telling what is and isn't serious without someone paying close attention and showing appropriate sensitivity.

Caring appropriately is a judgment call, but simply acting more like a concerned parent than a detached teacher can be effective. When a student complains, or through behavior, demonstrates, that there is a strong likelihood that a potential crisis exists, it is important for overseas directors and home advisers to realize that special attention must be devoted toward resolving the situation.

Problems with host families, with local staff or living facilities, or complaints about the director may not become, but they must be thoroughly investigated. If health problems or risky behavior are suspected, particularly substance abuse or abusive friends, the overseas director must feel free to show immediate concern to the student and to advise him directly about appropriate action. If students seem to be having problems with local staff, it is extremely important to determine if the issue is one of cultural difference or truly inappropriate behavior. Often the lines are not clearly defined and lack of sufficient orientation of both students and staff can result in conflicts that can become very unpleasant crises.

Checking on early signs of illness, academic or social problems and following through even when the student is ignoring the problem, will identify and short-circuit potential emergencies. The rule of "escalate, don't minimize" can be quite effective in cases of vague illness, psychological problems, and negative responses to the host culture. A student who is truly too ill to go to class will welcome the opportunity to go home for medical help, while the one who is simply looking for attention will find a way to adjust and avoid being evacuated. Escalation is also effective in short-circuiting dangerous or inappropriate behavior. In order to minimize the chances of having to deal with the victim or perpetrator of a crime, a director is well-advised to give early and firm verbal and written warnings to students who are behaving irresponsibly.

Individual crises, by definition, stem from personal problems that threaten a given student's well-being, and are largely unrelated to what other students are experiencing. On the other hand, what happens to one student and how it is treated can indeed have a profound impact on other students, so working with the affected student's friends, or group in the case of a group program, to provide information, perspective, and counsel, once the crisis has been resolved, may be time very well spent.

At best, some good private counseling with the student in crisis and some time to let this sink in will resolve the crisis, especially if it is related to adjustment or behavioral problems. At worst, the crisis may be due to circumstances beyond the student's or anyone's control, or involve a serious illness or injury, and can threaten her or his continuation in the program. Then, emergency evacuation and return must be considered. In the saddest case, when a student dies, seeing to the repatriation of remains is the very sad duty of overseas staff.

The following discussions explore different sorts of individual crises, and suggest ideal crisis management responses that require a high degree of shared responsibility and coordination between on-site and home campus staff—depending on the nature, phase, and location of the emergency. Some such crises originate in student behavior; others result from conditions and circumstances beyond the student's, or anyone's, control. Again, the operating assumption is that everything possible to prevent the crisis from unfolding has been done, but it has nevertheless happened, and so swift and wise action is mandated.

Personal Crises at Home That Affect Students Overseas

Immersed in their study abroad experience 24 hours a day, students often find little time to focus on the family and friends left behind—which is perhaps as it should be. If things appear normal on the day of departure, students have a tendency to think they will remain so throughout their time away. Living fully in the new environment, tending to academic assignments, and pursuing a host of new extracurricular opportunities, rightly take center stage. Some students experience difficulty effectively organizing their new roles and responsibilities into their lives, and the result can be even little available time for keeping in touch with things on the home front.

On the other hand, ongoing domestic crises, such as a family member's extended or serious illness, will of course cause students great stress when they leave for overseas, especially family members imply that the student really "ought" to be home, to help out. So long as students remain reachable by phone, letter or e-mail, contacts can be initiated by the at-home party, should something calamitous occur. Students' ability to help ease or manage a crisis at home can be severely limited by distance during study abroad. Unless students can reach a comfort level with their reduced accessibility, they risk falling into their own crisis of depression and guilt.

Sometimes the personal crisis at home is actually provoked by the student's absence from the scene. Students abroad often thrive in a newfound sense of independence that can be threatening to parents or friends. Significant others left back on campuses or in hometowns may become insignificant others virtually overnight as students involve themselves in the local social setting. The worst crises of all involve the illness or death of a loved one, especially when it is unexpected. At such moments students need rapid, accurate and caring communication. The role played by on-site staff will vary, depending on how they are brought into the crisis and what is asked of them by the family. Students may need access to a telephone for a private conversation. They may need counseling. They may need help in sorting out the logistics of returning home and/or making an early departure from the program. Above all, they need compassion.

Commonly, programs require students to file itineraries before traveling from the program site for a weekend, holiday, or semester break. Staff must rely on these itineraries to locate students in case of emergency back home. In severe instances, the student will need to leave the program site and return home immediately. Assuming the crisis occurs during the early or middle stages of the time overseas, and the student returns after a short interval, care must be taken to deal with any emotional issues and readjustment, and with missed academic assignments. If the trip occurs near the end of time overseas, returning may not make sense, but arrangements may have to be made to complete all academic work to earn credits.

Physical Health Problems

Successful study abroad, as with anything else, requires sustained good health. The onset of illness abroad or the recurrence of a chronic problem, present special challenges to students and study abroad administrators. Illnesses that might be viewed as routine back home sometimes seem more serious and frightening when abroad, whether or not they actually are. The simplest medications available in pharmacies have different names and appearances, caregivers from home are concerned but unavailable, doctors and hospitals may seem—and be—foreign, all of which can be unsettling to students, and even more so to parents back home. As a result, illnesses may last longer, and psychosomatic characteristics are not uncommon.

Diet

Poor diet can aggravate or cause poor health. While "adventures in good eating" are touted as one of the great attractions of foreign travel, in reality many Americans—and in particular, many American students—are finicky eaters, and do not take the time to sample and learn to enjoy different foods. Even at home their dietary range may be limited, and many of the foods they eat may not be available at the study site. In such situations students may retrench to a shockingly short list of staple foods. In areas where hamburgers and pizza are available, some students invariably eat nothing else. Malnutrition, serious enough in itself, can lead to even more serious illnesses. For students on vegetarian diets, a carefully balanced regimen is essential. If many foods that would satisfy this regimen are unfamiliar or unavailable at their study abroad site, these students who are generally among those most concerned with good health may, paradoxically, find their health at great risk.

Pregnancy

Unwanted pregnancy is a crisis that frequently strikes the college-age population. To a student who suddenly finds herself in this situation, even in the United States, the choices are dramatic and multidimensional, and her decision is possibly the most serious she has had to make to this point in her life. To a student overseas, an entire network of potential support may be missing, including the psychological and spiritual counseling services of the university, as well as access to appropriate medical services within one's own culture. The host country may have vastly different traditions in this area, and as with other crises, students may face an inability to communicate due to language limitations. Abortion may be illegal in the host country, or access to means for ending pregnancy may be severely limited. At the other extreme, abortion may be much more acceptable to the student's host culture than to U.S. citizens. In that case, an American student's feelings of her own impropriety and need for complete confidentiality may not be thoroughly understood. While students may try to deal with their situations without ending their study abroad, program staff need to be aware of how significantly such a crisis, serious enough in its own right, may affect many other aspects of student life, including self-concept, ability to interact with others, and academic success. Many program directors believe that students involved in unwanted pregnancy need to return home to deal with their crisis in a more familiar environment. Others are willing to accommodate to the students' own assessment of what is the best course of action, depending on the local environment and available health care facilities. Questions of confidentiality need to be weighed against questions of medical treatment.

Physical Disabilities/Controlled Illness

Individuals with physical disabilities or a variety of controlled illnesses, whose general health is good, are increasingly traveling and studying abroad quite successfully. They and home campus program staff, however, need to be open and frank with one another from the start in selecting an appropriate program. While all overseas programs need to try to maximize their ability to serve such students, not all sites are well-equipped to do so. Precise student needs must be clear to all concerned, so that the home campus does not send to an overseas site a student who requires greater resources than are available. With proper preparations, the experience of students with disabilities abroad is seldom a crisis. In cases of crises unrelated to the special need, however, the struggle to deal with the crisis can be exacerbated, and requires special sensitivity.

Emotional Health Problems: Severe Depression, Psychiatric Emergencies, Disruptive Behavior, Psychotic Behavior, and Suicide Attempts

Many of the most serious and common crises overseas involve students whose pre-existing emotional problems are exacerbated by the stresses of new living and learning experiences. This especially can be true if some of the motivation for going abroad was fed by the hope that such problems would disappear in new surroundings. Protected by laws and policies regarding confidentiality, students who may be actively in treatment for a variety of mental illnesses can often succeed in gaining acceptance to study abroad programs without disclosing their mental health issues to program administrators.

In well-run programs and large urban areas, students who seek help usually have access to guidance in finding whatever professional help is available at the study abroad site—and sometimes have long-distance access to campus psychological support staff resources back home. These students do experience crisis, but the network of support is usually able to help manage it effectively. Students with serious psychiatric problems may require counseling at a level and regularity unavailable everywhere overseas, and students and parents should be informed as part of the information process that this is so.

Students who hide their illnesses shoulder alone what can become an immense burden. How many do so successfully is never easy to know. Inability to cope, however, can absorb immense amounts of staff time and energy that might have been spent serving the needs of a great many more students. The unfamiliarity of the study abroad environment can be stressful for students with conditions such as manic depression or anorexia nervosa, which may have been under some modicum of control back home. In addition, alcohol consumption can exacerbate mental health problems, and alcohol is a bad mix with many medications.

If the student's mental condition worsens, the resulting crisis can blindside study abroad staff who must then scramble to keep the student safe from herself, ensure the safety of others, and pick up the pieces of shattered relationships with home-stay families, faculty, students, and administrators. Though students may beg to remain abroad, sometimes joined in this plea by parents, the most responsible action in almost all cases is to return the student safely home swiftly, often a difficult task.

Typical Symptoms of Mental Health Problems, from Mild to Severe

- Student misses classes regularly; has trouble keeping focused and directed;

- Student asks to take less than a full academic program;

- Student withdraws from friends and previously favored activities; gives evidence of severe depression;

- Student appears to be missing meals and shows signs of an eating disorder;

- Student is frequently under the influence of alcohol or drugs;

- Student's host family reports unusual behavior, passive or hyperactive;

- Student exhibits severe disruptive (or self-destructive) behavior that appears to have a psychiatric basis;

- Student shows signs of being severely emotionally disturbed: creates disturbances and seems a danger to self or others;

- Student makes a suicide attempt or threat or has spoken with someone about the plan to do so.

On-Site/Home Campus Response Checklist

❏ Director or overseas adviser should talk to the participant and identify as many key people in the situation as possible. Contact should be made with the home campus or U.S. sponsoring institution as soon as the situation is diagnosed as serious.

❏ Information on the actual behavior exhibited and the history of the problem should be carefully collected and a written log needs to be maintained.

❏ The extent of the problems needs to be assessed, as well as the student's support network—family, friends, roommates, etc.; whether or not the student will voluntarily seek help; what professional counsel is immediately available;

❏ If help is available and if the student is willing to utilize it, arrange to have the student seen by a counseling professional immediately. Have the student escorted to the designated location of the appointment, preferably with one or two interested and supportive people.

- *If necessary, arrange and carry out hospitalization.*

- *If possible, arrange consultation between on-site and U.S. campus or family professional personnel.*

- *In some cases, the decision will be made to bring the student home in order to receive appropriate treatment (facilitate this via "International Student Identity Card (ISIC) Traveler's Insurance," and/or "Assist America").*

- *With the student's consent (ideally, obtained in advance) arrange to notify his/her designated emergency contact and other involved parties on a need-to-know basis.*

- *In the absence of consent, work with information that is available from nonprivileged sources in planning follow-up support. If the student's life is in jeopardy, but consent has not been given, it may be wise to contact parents or family nonetheless, considering the moral imperative of doing something that may help.*

- *Prepare to assist and support other involved persons using available resources.*

- *If the student's behavior remains a serious impediment to the educational process or a threat to safety, work with home campus personnel to determine what other measures are necessary.*

❑ If student will not voluntarily seek help and appears to be dangerous to himself or others, the on-site director or adviser should:

- *In all cases, continue to keep a detailed log of all events concerning the situation.*

- *Assess who can be called to persuade the student to seek help (e.g., friend, roommate, or therapist). Work with those people to persuade the student to obtain treatment.*

- *Continue to encourage the student to seek help.*

- *Maintain contact with the home campus and others on the home campus crisis management team, to provide an informed and coordinated response and whatever counseling is feasible for the student's condition. If appropriate, and if such procedures exist in the host country, consider steps to have the student involuntarily committed to the hospital. In most circumstances, however, arrangements will be made to have the student sent back to the United States for hospitalization.*

❑ If the student will not voluntarily seek help BUT does not appear to be dangerous to self and/or others, the on-site director or adviser can do the following:

- *Assess who can be called upon to persuade the student to seek help. Work with those persons to persuade the student to obtain treatment.*

- *Continue to encourage the student to seek treatment.*

- *As soon as the student is stable, contact the home campus to provide information regarding the details of the situa-*

> *tion, and seek whatever counsel is advised by the local campus management team. Again, where possible, consultation between the home campus and overseas site should be arranged.*

> • *Establish behavioral limits and carry them out to the extent that the student will cooperate.*

> • *If disruptive behavior continues, overseas personnel should notify and brief the home campus to discover the need for other emergency measures as may be appropriate, including suspension from the overseas studies program.*

A Serious Example

A student's mental crisis abroad can overwhelm program staff who are unequipped to cope with it. One student, treated at home for depression and suicidal tendencies, hid her condition and began a semester abroad. After a horrifying period in which the student left suicide notes and vanished from sight for two weeks, the Resident Director arranged emergency counseling and an immediate flight home. En route to the airport under escort, the student fled, this time not to be heard from for many more weeks. During this time, school administrators in the United States and the host country walked a narrow line as they balanced concern for the student's well-being with the reality that they were helpless to assist her. Concerned over liability, the school formally declared to the parents that the student was no longer their responsibility, since she was no longer a "participant" and since the school had made its best effort to return her to the United States. At the same time, they offered to share whatever information might come their way concerning the student's whereabouts in an effort to get her home. Ultimately the student contacted the counselor and returned home, to the relief of everyone involved.

Guarding confidentiality important, but concern for a student's welfare is more important. Given the choice of keeping information confidential versus keeping students safe, opt for safety. Such action will be in the best interests of the student and your program. Crises rarely end with all parties satisfied, and legal action against a program or university can result from great dissatisfaction. Program administrators and legal advisers to such programs generally agree that it is preferable to be accused of denying students their rights than to be accused of not keeping students safe.

Serious Injuries or Death Due to Accidents or Criminal Assault

Typical Problems

- Travel accidents (private auto, bus, train, etc.);

- Recreational injury (e.g. skiing, mountaineering, scuba, etc.);

- Serious illness (AIDS, hepatitis, malaria, etc.);

- Drug overdose; or

- Fainting spells, loss of consciousness.

On-Site/Home Campus Response Checklist

❑ Assist the student in finding appropriate medical care in a hospital/clinic that you trust. Assess the extent or severity of the accident/illness, usually by talking with the physician treating the student. Keep a log that will include notes regarding the circumstances leading up to the accident/illness, the outcome of any discussions with the attending physician, notes from conversations with home campus personnel, and the course of the medical treatment as it progresses.

❑ Contact the home campus and brief appropriate parties about the student's condition, with all due attention to maintaining the privacy of the injured person.

❑ Depending on the severity of the injury or illness, contact the person designated by the student as his emergency contact.

❑ In consultation with any attending physicians, monitor the emergency situation as it develops and provide updates to the home campus. In some cases, the student may need to be evacuated in order to receive appropriate medical treatment.

❑ Obtain a second opinion regarding any necessary medical treatment administered to the student. In some cases, arrange contact between with the host country physician treating the student and the home campus or family physician.

❑ If appropriate, inform the home campus to prepare for media inquiries.

❑ Inform the student's professors at the host university, etc. that the student will be absent from classes.

❑ Provide appropriate information and reassurances to other program participants.

❑ In the unfortunate case of a student's death, in-place protocol needs to be activated.

The sheltering, *in loco parentis* environment many students experience at their chosen college or university may give them little relevant experience in recognizing those who would do them harm. Other students quite adept at survival in New York City or Washington, D.C. turn naïve when they take up residence in Madrid or Harare. Many students who at home would never hitchhike, leave doors unlocked, or give their address to a stranger, do these very things as soon as they are abroad. It is as if there is something not quite real about being overseas, as if these places are magically without the same sort of dangers found in the United States.

Fortunately most student experiences with crime are minor: an unwatched backpack stolen from the seat of a train, a protruding wallet picked from a pocket. Traveler's checks and credit cards are easily replaced, passports and plane tickets are as well, though not as easily.

A more difficult area is that of social relations, bound up in the complex subject of learning to live in the local culture. Making friends and meeting locals their own age are important matters to students abroad. American students, unwillingly and usually unknowingly, are often prejudged by others in cultural terms. Are they as free and promiscuous as the Americans on Baywatch or other U.S. television programs well known to viewers around the world? Probably not, but individuals in the host country may assume they are. If local males act on that assumption, at what point do American females realize how they, their words, and their actions are misconstrued? Early awareness can halt an incident at the level of cultural misunderstanding. A later one can leave a student vulnerable to sexual assault. At this point, victimized students discover that local norms and laws may be enormously different from the sexual harassment and assault policies in place at their home schools.

In virtually all cases, students on study abroad are disadvantaged by insufficient language ability and lack of familiarity with host-country legal systems when reporting crimes. In the often lengthy prosecution of those crimes, students are further disadvantaged by the temporary nature of their residence overseas. The result is that only the most serious transgressions, involving the most persistent students and their supporters, stand any chance of being punished. In the majority of cases, students returning home must simply put the incident behind them unless they are willing and able to make themselves available to prosecutors during the usually lengthy period of investigation and trial. Unresolved criminal actions against students are one of the most powerful negative consequences of a period of study abroad. Many crimes are never formally reported.

Crime exists in all countries and all cities. With this in mind, it is important to include information on steps to avoid becoming a crime victim while studying abroad. However, there are many study abroad students who do become victims of petty theft or other crimes, either at the study abroad site or in the country or countries that they will visit while taking part in the study abroad program.

Institutions should inform students how to respond to crime whether they are in the more secure presence of responsible adults, or when they're traveling on their own. Students who became victims of robbery and rape in Guatemala, faced the criminals who assaulted them, with the help and support of the sponsoring U. S. institution. The students actually returned to Guatemala months after the program ended. Although most instances of theft will not result in such a formal group response, administrators should be familiar with the steps necessary to report crimes abroad.

When students become victims of crimes, it is important that institutions be ready to offer psychological support. Study abroad programs should know how to seek counseling support for students who have been victims of crimes, to assist them in moving forward or possibly returning home, if the effects are serious enough. The United States government, in Title II of the *Student Right to Know and Campus Security Act,* requires institutions to collect crime statistics, report them to the federal government, and inform students of individual campus statistics.

Legal experts believe that institutions are required to collect statistics on campus crime (murder, rape, robbery, aggravated assault, burglary, and motor vehicle theft) and to make that information available to students, employees, and applicants upon request. One source advises the following:

"Data must be provided about crimes that take place on college-owned or college-controlled property in a 'reasonably contiguous geographic area' as well as property owned or controlled by student organizations (such as fraternities). Data on arrests for weapons, drug abuse and liquor law violations on campus must also be provided.

"Institutions must also publish an 'annual security report' that includes campus policies regarding procedures and methods for reporting crimes, access to campus facilities, housing security procedures, arrest authority of law enforcement personnel and their relationship with local police, and descriptions of crime prevention and security awareness programs.

"Providing data to potential litigants about prior criminal activity on or near campus; may make it difficult for college to claim that it was unaware of prior criminal activity. This increases forseeability of violence against students.

"On the other hand, provision of crime data to students may permit colleges to argue that students were aware of the risk and should have taken additional precautions." (McMullan, S. (1997). Institutional Liability for Overseas Study Programs. *Law and Higher Education: Issues in 1997. Vol. I,* Paper presented at the Eighteenth Annual National Conference on Law in Higher Education, Stetson University College of Law, Clearwater Beach, Florida.)

The *Student Right to Know and Campus Security Act* adds some minimum standards to the way institutions inform students about campus crime, and suggests that this law also applies to overseas study. Such information can assist administrators in putting in place policies and procedures to limit the possibility of crime and inform students how they can limit their exposure to crime. Further, when crimes occur, all students need to be made aware of the threat. The director's decision on how to do this will involve a number of factors: the size of the program, the degree to which students already know of the incident, and the feelings of the student victims about maintaining whatever level of confidentiality still remains. Strategies could include a posted bulletin, in-class announcement, or a general meeting. Students can and should go to the police when there is reason to, with staff company and support. They should be encouraged to contact their parents if they desire to do so.

Overseas staff and programs must be advocates for their victimized students, and must seek to defend and protect students to the extent possible. They should also be willing to meet with parents, who frequently come to the study abroad site to aid their son or daughter and who need a sympathetic ear. This does not mean, however, that they need to advocate for students in the investigation and punishment of crimes. Students and their families remain the key players in deciding how aggressively to pursue legal rights. Program staff can give them moral and psychological support, but should draw the line short of actively representing students in their quest for justice.

Victimization from Sexual Aggression, Abuse, and Harassment

Sexual assault that takes place overseas is different from overseas petty crime and may have a tragic effect on students. The federal *Student Right to Know and Campus Security Act* puts into place domestic regulations about how to prepare students for the possibility of sexual assault and how to respond if this occurs. Many believe that it also suggests strongly that institutions should implement specific policies and procedures for responding to sexual assault overseas. This law requires the institutions to include within its annual crime statistics report a description of institutional policy regarding sexual assault. It involves the following provisions:

- Describe the programs in place to promote awareness of rape, acquaintance rape, and other sexual offenses.

- Create procedures to follow if a sexual offense occurs, including whom to contact, the importance of preserving evidence and to whom the alleged offense should be reported.

- Provide information on student's option to notify proper law enforcement authorities, and an institutional statement on assistance to be provided in such circumstances.

- List on- and off- campus counseling, mental health, and other student services for victims of sex offenses.

- State that an institution will change a student's housing and academic situation after an alleged offense if reasonably available.

- Specify sanctions that may be imposed for a sex offender.

At the very least, institutions sponsoring overseas programs need to ensure that sex crime policies (regarding referral to counselors and medical professionals, procedures for reporting a sex offense, the handling of disciplinary actions, and notification of options for changing living situations after a sexual offense has occurred) are known and available to students.

Typical Problems

A student is a victim of rape, attempted rape, or other violent sexual assault.

On-Site/Home Campus Response Checklist

- ❏ Talk to the person reporting the crime, and determine the identity and location of the victim.

- ❏ Clarify with the student the degree to which he wishes to involve local and university police.

- ❏ Discern any obvious physical and emotional disturbance.

- ❏ If there is obvious physical injury, make sure the student is taken to a hospital or clinic that you trust for urgent care.

- ❏ If there are signs of obvious emotional disturbance, consult a psychologist or psychiatrist and provide immediate support to victim.

❏ Inform the student of the laws and procedures for dealing with sexual assault in the host country, which may vary from those in the U.S. For example, in the United States it is important to preserve the evidence of a sexual assault to be used as evidence in court.

❏ If there is no obvious physical injury, have the victim consent to being transported to the hospital or clinic of choice.

❏ Contact the home campus so they can inform the crisis management team and counseling center and other appropriate offices. With the student's consent (given previously via a release form, or now), inform the student's parents or designated emergency contact.

❏ Begin writing and maintain log as crisis proceeds.

❏ Provide regular briefings to the home campus.

❏ If overseas director or home campus are contacted by a representative of the media, do NOT give release student names or speak on behalf the institution until a coordinated media response is written and approved.

If the victim DECLINES assistance, the on-site director should:

❏ Escort or transport the victim to home or a designated location.

❏ Inform the victim that she will be contacted later to see if she requires assistance.

❏ Provide the victim with phone numbers of a hospital or clinic; psychologist or psychiatrist; and any other rape crisis resources that may exist, as well as a law enforcement authority.

❏ Contact a local psychologist/psychiatrist, brief him/her of the situation, inform him/her that the victim has refused assistance, but that the victim may be contacting him/her.

❏ Contact the home campus to obtain advice for dealing with the crisis, inform emergency contacts, and aid the student in activating his/her support network.

❑ Begin writing a log with a clear notation of the circumstances surrounding the offer of assistance and the student's refusal to accept such assistance, updated as needed.

❑ Provide regular briefings to the home campus.

Additional suggestions:

• Know the institutional policies with respect to sexual assaults and ask counsel to review their applicability to the institution's specific overseas program.

• If applicable, to the overseas program, ensure that the policies and complaint procedures are included in student materials and are known to the institutional contact people dealing with students.

• Do not adopt a laissez-faire attitude toward any complaints; ensure that they are quickly investigated and resolved properly

Responding to Lost or Missing Persons

Typical Problem

Student is reported missing by roommate, other program participants, host family, or professor.

Usually, such students turn up in a day or so. They may have wandered off on their own, with another student, or with a new local friend, failing to follow directives not to do so, especially without informing someone of their whereabouts. But especially if previous student behavior suggests the potential for something more serious than wanderlust—serious substance abuse problems, depression, or dangerous risk-taking—it is a mistake not to begin to react at the earliest indication that something serious may be happening.

On-Site/Home Campus Response Checklist

❑ Program staff should contact institutional authorities (if applicable), asking them to check clinic and hospital admissions and city records; it is possible the student has been admitted to a facility.

❑ Begin keeping a log of information and actions taken, updated as the crisis progresses.

❑ Contact home campus and/or U.S. sponsoring agency to inform it that the student has been reported missing.

❑ Maintain contact with roommates, host family, landlord, close friends, and other members of the student group, seeking and relaying-on all pertinent information that turns up. . If the student lives off-campus, talk with the student's roommate, or host family, and neighbors. Ask them to contact you immediately if the student returns.

❑ Contact the student's professors to determine when student was last seen. Gather information on any unusual behavior that may have been exhibited.

❑ If the student has not been located within 24-48 hours of the first report of disappearance, file a report with the local police.

❑ Re-contact home campus, and suggest convening of crisis management team to be ready to coordinate appropriate actions. These actions may include contacting the student's designated "Emergency Contact" person. Appropriate follow-up to be planned.

❑ If applicable, work with overseas and home campus to coordinate appropriate actions and follow-up.

❑ Provide appropriate information and reassurances to other program participants.

❑ Once the student has been located, inform appropriate persons on-site and on home campus. If necessary, activate other protocol, for serious accident, illness, or death.

❑ If contacted by the media, do NOT give the name of a student or speak on behalf of the program without contacting the home campus before you respond. You may, together, wish to develop a common response.

Serious Student Misbehavior

All schools and most programs have policies governing student conduct and the consequences to be applied when rules are broken. Based on laws and legal concepts common in the United States, these policies may involve the active participation of home campus officials, including the Dean of Students, and student organizations including a Judiciary Board. The processing of infractions is a collaboration among these campus-based groups. Study abroad programs, which rarely have their own codes, routinely apply those from the larger campus when incidents occur overseas, and the result can often be a miscarriage of the justice that the policies are supposed to ensure.

A recent incident can serve to illustrate potential difficulties: Two pairs of friends, of different ethnic background, finding an opportunity to rent a flat for four, move in together. In a dispute over a stereo, each set of friends makes accusations against the other. The dispute heats up, and by the time the four flat-mates go to the Resident Director, verbal threats of bodily harm have been made. Neither side wants to back down by moving out of the flat, and at the landlord's contract was signed by all four parties. So the threats escalate. Racial slurs are found on a bulletin board at the school, and one of the flat-mates admits writing them "as a joke." All four students call their parents, and the parents in turn appeal to the study abroad office on the home campus to do something.

Clearly much inappropriate behavior is going on. Battle lines have been figuratively drawn, and no one is interested in compromise. Most programs reserve the right to terminate a student's participation when inappropriate behavior becomes egregious. In fact, however, termination rarely occurs. Part of the problem lies in the ineffectiveness of campus policies that were not designed for study abroad. If the dispute just described had occurred on a home campus, a number of actions could have been taken. First, a formal complaint could have been lodged by either pair of friends against the other. Second, the university could have acted to suspend the students who made the threats or wrote the racial slurs. In a privately-owned apartment, the matter of the contract could have been left to the students and the landlord to sort out among themselves.

The incident occurred on study abroad, so how are the consequences different? In the first instance, few programs abroad have fully functioning locally based systems to file and respond to formal complaints. There is no Dean of Students, usually no student government of any kind, and no formalized way to lodge complaints. In the second instance, while it would be possible to suspend a student who admits writing racial slurs, a violation of school policy, there may be no way within the regulations to send the student home, since in this case the flat does not belong to the university. Thus the students would remain abroad and their problem would not be solved. These students were told that they could press their case against each other (and ultimately against the program, since none of the students was satisfied) by filing complaints whey they returned to the campus. It is possible they did this, although the matter dropped off the study abroad office's radar screens once the students returned to the United States.

What, though, if the student is from a different school than the one operating the study abroad program? One student submitted a final paper that the professor judged was plagiarized. Though the incident took place abroad, the crisis it provoked occurred entirely on domestic soil: the professor advised the student, then back on her campus, that he was giving her a failing grade for having cheated on the paper. Unable to bring her case to his own school's academic judicial board (since she was no longer a student of that school), he and the study abroad office submitted the evidence of academic dishonesty to her home school, which ultimately declined to sanction her for an offense committed while she was "on leave." Slipping through the crack between two systems, the student escaped more serious consequences.

If on-site staff represent a host institution, its code of acceptable student behavior applies and takes precedence over a student's home campus rules. Whether or not the director reports back to the home campus on incidents of student misbehavior may be an individual judgment. In instances when students are enrolled in a program run by another U.S. institution, the rules of the sponsoring institution, not the student's home institution, usually prevail. But in this instance, on-site staff may need to inform both institutions about the situation and the reasons for the actions taken. Obviously, in situations where students are enrolled in programs sponsored by their own home college or university, the rules that govern conduct, adjudication, and punishment are those imposed by the home institution. In all these variations, the key is to make sure that students are thoroughly informed about what is and what is not acceptable behavior, and what the consequences are for failing to abide by the rules.

Student Criminality

Institutions should make clear to students that the legal policy and procedures in many countries around the world are very different from those in the United States. In the United States, individuals are considered "innocent until proven guilty." However, in most countries around the world, if the local legal authorities consider that you are guilty of a crime, someone will be considered guilty of that crime, unless they can prove their innocence. As discussed below in the section on violation of drug laws, being a US citizen will not shield a student from criminal charges or jail time. It is therefore important for program directors to have a basic understanding of the foreign legal system and provide students with guidance on avoiding situations where they may violate the law.

The most difficult law enforcement crises occur where some local laws and customs are at odds with U.S. legal traditions. Students may believe that "it's a free country," at least for them, when in fact certain freedoms are seriously curtailed. A recent news story reported American students jailed in Burma—then immediately expelled, to their great good fortune— for wearing "Free Burma" T-shirts and passing out pro-democracy leaflets. While they were not actually on a study abroad program, their experience was not unlike that of some study abroad students. On one African program, in what ultimately was classified a "misunderstanding," two female students were jailed late one night as prostitutes. In fact they were looking for a taxi at the end of a club outing. Their dress, however, was "provocative," and in perhaps their biggest defiance of local mores, they were unescorted by males.

More serious offenses, those involving theft, serious bodily harm, or repeated antisocial behavior, place students at serious legal jeopardy. The U.S. consulate is called, more to ensure fair treatment under the law than to argue for leniency. A local lawyer is needed. The luckiest of students under these circumstances are expelled from the country, sent home on the first available plane. The study abroad experience is at an end, and the student is likely to be distressed and humiliated. Further consequences may await him/her back on campus, depending on the nature of the offense and the identity of any victims.

Criminal activity overseas is not defined by U.S. law, but rather any activity violating the laws of the country where a study abroad program takes place. Ignorance of the severity of local laws is never an excuse for violating them, nor will being a foreigner relieve a violator of local laws or assure any special attention. Some countries may even make it difficult to contact a representative of the US. Government. In the case that a representative of the United States is contacted, the victim may be surprised to find that person is powerless to help.

The U.S. Consular Officer CAN:

- Visit students in jail after notification of their arrest;

- Give students and directors a list of local attorneys, but the U.S. Government cannot assume responsibility for the professional ability or integrity of these individuals;

- Notify family and friends and relay requests for money or other aid if authorized by the student;

- Intercede with local authorities to ensure that U.S citizens' rights under local law are fully observed and that one is treated humanely, according to internationally accepted standards;

- Protest mistreatment or abuse to the appropriate authorities.

The U.S. Consular Officer CANNOT:

- Demand immediate release from jail, or get anyone out of jail or the country;

- Represent anyone at trial, or give legal counsel;

- Pay legal fees and/or fines with U.S. Government funds.

Typical Problems

Student is arrested for theft, assault, or drug possession.

On-Site/Home Campus Response Checklist

- ❑ Quickly assess the situation by obtaining as many details as possible. Determine who, what, when, where, how and why. Begin logging details of the crisis situation, and maintain it as the crisis develops.

❑ Immediately contact the U.S. Embassy Consular Officer. Ask the officer for referrals to lawyers, and provide this information to the student. The Consular Officer will also work to ensure that the student's human rights are not violated.

❑ As soon as possible, contact the home campus to brief it about the situation, possibly convening the crisis management team, including legal counsel, to initiate contact with the U.S. Embassy Consular Officer.

❑ Convene the home campus crisis management team as a resource, and provide recommendations as appropriate for continuing action.

❑ The on-site director should visit the student wherever he/she is being held, reassure the student, and explain the legal procedures of the host country. Also, ongoing contact needs to be maintained with the U.S. Embassy Officer assigned to the student.

❑ The on-site director provides regular updates (at least on a daily basis) to the home campus and crisis management team until the crisis has been resolved.

❑ Plan media contact as described previously.

Serious Alcohol Abuse

A recent Gallup poll shows that in the United States, college students are the group with the greatest proportion of drinkers. An estimated 85-95 percent of college students consume alcohol routinely and 20-25 percent have problems related to drinking that negatively affects their life. Statistics further indicate that one in 10 people who drink will become dependent. Many alcohol abusers, especially younger ones, use illicit drugs as well. According to the American College Health Association (ACHA) publication, Alcohol: Decisions on Tap, recent campus statistics show that alcohol is involved in:

• About two-thirds of all violent behavior;

• Almost half of all physical injuries;

- About one-third of all emotional difficulties among students;

- And just fewer than 30 percent of all academic problems.

Alcohol abuse therefore may be the most serious home campus problem that accompanies students who study abroad. Beyond the physical effects of such abuse, students encounter serious difficulty as they confront host-country values and attitudes related to drinking. The classic European example is well known: American students with histories of binge drinking arrive in countries with low or no minimum drinking age, overindulge, and through their uncontrolled behavior, become embarrassments to themselves and to their study abroad programs.

Still, the differences in minimum drinking age can be significant: If twenty-year-olds over-imbibe and turn violent in a host-country pub or club, they are doing so in a setting where they would not have legal access back home. For many students, an arrest for disorderly contact may be their first such brush with the law. Their treatment may range from mildly disagreeable to horrifying, depending to a great extent on the host country and its legal institutions. Program staff are called, often in the middle of the night, and students are often amazed to find that they as Americans are indeed subject to the laws and penalties of the land.

Local home stays sometimes can provide students with good role models for responsible drinking—French families whose members have a glass or two of wine at every meal, for example. More extensive efforts to promote moderation run certain risks: university programs can serve alcohol legally at student functions in London, for example, but who is at fault if students drink to excess and then, failing to look right, step into the street and are run over? Liability for sponsoring institutions looms large these days, and many programs are increasingly wary of staging gatherings that involve alcohol.

Each program director heading overseas with a group must have a clear understanding from the institution as to what the alcohol policy should be on the overseas program, factoring in the ages of the students, home campus policies, where the program takes place, and other variables. This policy should be articulated to students before departure, after arrival, and whenever it seems relevant to remind them. Directors of overseas institutions and programs receiving U.S. students are put in a more ambivalent situation if local laws, institutional policies, and alcohol standards differ markedly from U.S. practices—as they are likely to in most countries—especially if students come from a wide variety of U.S. campuses that themselves have different codes of acceptable and unacceptable conduct. Often, despite the best efforts at informing students, the crisis situation arises when a student or several students act in a way that puts at risk their own health and safety or the well-being of the program and of others. Habitual drinking to excess represents a crisis, and usually needs to be addressed by expulsion from the program, if warnings go unheeded.

Drug Use

Drug use and abuse continue to be significant problems in U.S. colleges and universities. In the American College Health Association (ACHA) publication, *Alcohol and Other Drugs: Risky Business,* the National Institute on Drug Abuse (NIDA) cites the following statistics:

- By their mid-20s, nearly 80 percent of today's youth have used an illicit drug.

- One in 18 high school seniors have tried crack and by age 27; and nearly 40 percent of young adults have tried cocaine.

Many of the students going abroad tend to be adventurous or risk-takers; others are simply interested in "partying" or "going native." It would be naive to assume that all study abroad students are drug-free prior to going abroad or will not begin to experiment with drugs once they arrive abroad. It happens that U.S. students, new to a foreign culture, sometimes violate local laws, whether knowingly and assuming they will not be found out or unknowingly, forgetting what they were told. In most cases involving the arrest of a study abroad student, the student is simply engaged in the kind of behavior that might be commonplace at home—and quite possibly illegal here as well. As noted above, it is essential that administrators, faculty, and students participating in study abroad programs be made aware of the possible severity of punishment for drug violations abroad. In spite of this, however, overseas and domestic administrators, faculty, and students need to be prepared to deal with possible violations of drug laws abroad by U.S. students.

In some countries, possession of drugs can result in a legal sanction as severe as life in prison or death. Many countries do not have a legal distinction between the personal use and possession of drugs and the distribution or sale of drugs. By contrast, in some countries, citizens may be able to legally carry or sell drugs. However, the same possession or sale of drugs may result in severe legal penalties for a U.S. citizen. According to R.D. Dawood in his book, *Travelers' Health: How to Stay Healthy All Over the World* (Random House, 1994), "Some countries like Turkey and Thailand conduct the specific policy of applying the full force of their laws against foreign nationals, who are highly visible as well as being more vulnerable. . ... A single cannabis cigarette in Greece means prison for one year plus one day, minimum." According to the U.S. State Department's publication, *Travel Warnings on Drugs Abroad:* "During 1991, 3,050 Americans were arrested in 105 foreign countries. Of these, 1,271 ended up in jails because they assumed they couldn't get arrested for drug possession. From Asia to Africa, Europe to South America, Americans are finding out the hard way that drug possession or trafficking equals jail in foreign countries."

There is very little that anyone can do to help if students are caught overseas with drugs. It is both the home campus responsibility to tell students what the drug laws are in a foreign country before they go, the on-site staff responsibility to repeat this when they arrive, and the student's responsibility to take this counsel. *"I didn't know it was illegal"* will not get anyone out of jail. Of all Americans arrested on drug charges in 1991, marijuana was involved in 77 percent of the cases. Many of those jailed possessed one ounce or less of the substance. Once someone is arrested, the American consular officer cannot get them out. If a student is arrested on a drug charge, it is important that everyone knows what can and cannot be done.

Death of a Student

There is nothing more shattering for all concerned than the sudden death of a student, whatever the cause. Not only does a death have an impact on friends and family like no other calamity, but its shock waves of grief and disbelief are usually felt both overseas in the student group and on the home campus for a long time afterwards. Of all crises, a student death requires the most sensitive and complex response. There is much to do and say both overseas and at home, and coordination between here and there must be close, well-planned, detailed, and efficient.

On-Site/Home Campus Response Checklist

❏ On-site director must verify the identity of the student. Gather as much information about the circumstances surrounding the student's death as possible. Begin logging all information.

❏ On-site director contacts home campus with news of confirmed death and as much other information as is available at the time. Home campus convenes crisis management team.

❏ Home campus notifies the student's designated "emergency contact," in person, if possible, and offers other appropriate support. Home campus must work with the on-site director in assisting the family with details: transportation arrangements, accommodations, and arranging for a meeting with the physicians.

❏ On-site director must inform the U.S. Embassy or Consulate.

❏ On-site director must work with the home campus to coordinate a plan for dealing with the situation. An emergency network is needed to offer appropriate support to all involved parties, such as close friends, roommates or housemates, the host family, other program participants, and the person who may have discovered the body. Once the network is in place, the on-site director can begin to inform the student's roommates or housemates and close friends.

❏ Home campus should notify appropriate offices and personnel and make sure that all the appropriate paperwork is completed and that all appropriate contacts have been made. A letter should be sent to the campus community if deemed appropriate.

❏ Media response. See information above.

Chapter 11

Responding to Overseas Program Crises

M
ost study abroad crises affecting entire programs are unexpected, though, in retrospect, the premonitions may seem simply to have been overlooked. Program crises can take many forms: transportation disasters, medical epidemics, natural catastrophes, political upheaval, social unrest, or even dysfunctional leadership. Such calamities are generally caused by factors beyond the control of those responsible for study abroad programs, be it the home campus or organization, or the overseas institution or agency. Chaos can result with staff, participants, and others associated with the program. Crisis resolution demands ample and accurate information, plus much time, energy, and tact.

General threats to entire programs are dramatically different from crises involving only one or two individuals. The first question for both on-site and home campus staff to ask and answer is often, how to get past the initial shock and sort out real versus perceived dangers to the program. This process requires having all emergency planning and communications systems in place, and the means of gathering reliable facts and informed perspectives. Making the wrong decisions on site or upon instructions from home cannot only endanger students and bring their overseas experiences to an end, but can also raise legal implications and complications. In all situations, the primary considerations for international educators are the safety and the well-being of all participants.

Some in the legal profession have advised that program staff should be attuned to doing the right thing, regardless of confidentiality issues and what they perceive to be other constraints on their actions. Lawsuits cannot be prevented. Though laws vary from nation to nation, group program disasters involve more than one nation. The complexity of national and international laws, and the general right of people to file a lawsuit regardless of liability and/or the situation can result in lengthy legal struggles. Some issues to keep in mind:

- You may be working with, and dependent on, guidance from at least two national governments, perhaps more.

- High levels of security may interfere with the gathering of information.

- A disaster plan may be in effect at the crisis site and involvement may be restricted to official personnel. You and your staff may have no control over what is happening.

- Be in immediate touch from the home campus base with family and friends of those involved in the crisis, and establish a contact system to alert and update them immediately to new developments.

- Beware those people who wish to capitalize on a crisis (media, insurance people, those who prey on victims, etc.;) and communicate only with those officials you know; suggest that any family and friends follow the same procedures.

Ultimately, the 'best' action is one that 'does the right thing.' There is no one correct decision for all situations. By gathering sufficient information, checking with other programs that operate in the destination, and by evaluating all aspects of the situation, on-site staff, in conjunction with the home campus crisis team can make the best decision for the program. Assessing a 'real' versus a 'perceived' crisis is critical. Cancellation is not inevitable but may, after sufficient deliberation, be the appropriate course of action.

Travel Crises

Most U.S. study abroad professionals are unfortunately very familiar with recent major and well-publicized travel disasters. The Pan American plane crash in 1989, the night-time bus accident in India in 1996, the 1998 bus hijacking in Guatemala, each are examples of crises that occurred when students were in transit as part of their overseas experience. Each directly impacted entire programs, even if some participants were more directly affected than others. Like other such tragedies, the short range jolt was one of shock and horror, and the long-range reverberations—personal, legal, programmatic—are still being felt by grieving parents and family, as well as by program sponsors.

Any such event can create immediate hysteria among participants and those people in both the home and host countries who have relationships with the program and the participants. While such situations are complex and chaotic enough on their own, responding to them can be further complicated by worldwide media such as web sites, wire services, and TV networks like CNN, broadcasting often the worst-case scenario reports instantaneously, to seemingly everywhere. Such immediate, attention-grabbing, and often intentionally sensationalistic "news" alerts may reach families and friends prior to the notification of home campus program staff. Such publicity can only stir up emotions on all sides, and complicate crisis management.

In addition, when lawyers become involved, and as aggrieved parties cite negligence, communications between all parties become more difficult and a lot of time and money is involved before a legal resolution is found. Increasingly, campus legal counsel advise that extracurricular travel excursions within study abroad programs represent one of the biggest areas of exposure to potential accidents and subsequent liability claims from American parents, so that the best legal strategy is to eliminate, or at least reduce, the number of such trips. Even arranging international travel for students is sometimes seen as having legal implications for program sponsors. Since there can be no study abroad program without travel, some institutions urge using foreign carriers rather than American ones, especially at times of terrorist threats against U.S. citizens.

At no time is that more true than when participants are injured or killed. However singular the travel accident, there is often pressure to cancel the program and bring participants home quickly, whether this is the 'right' decision or not, in the long run. The role of on-site and overseas staff is to make sure that all relevant information is factored into this decision.

Medical Crises

Medical epidemics that impact entire programs are rare, in part because program approval is generally not authorized for countries where major health hazards are known. Campuses can research medical issues with their medical center staff or the Centers for Disease Control in Atlanta. Most programmatic medical crises occur only when precipitated by events that happen after a program has begun. Cholera, typhoid, malaria, dengue fever, flu, and severe gastrointestinal disorders are examples of medical conditions that can arise suddenly and can impact entire programs, especially when prophylactic medications haven't been prescribed or taken as recommended.

When medical crises affect study abroad, program leaders need to evaluate the severity of the illness, the availability of medical care and medications on-site, the prognosis for recovery, and the probability that illness will spread. All factors must be assessed, in collaboration with host country medical personnel and in the home country. Again, in the United States, the Centers for Disease Control may be the best possible resource worldwide for treatment and evaluation of the situation. Other sources include the International Red Cross, the International Association for Medical Assistance to Travelers (IMAT), and in-country equivalents that also provide valuable assessment of current conditions facing short-term visitors without immune system defenses.

Proper hospitalization and medical evacuation insurance can cover situations where ill participants who require immediate emergency care are unable to travel independently to their home country or to a nearby nation that has adequate medical treatment available. The cost of adequate insurance becomes insignificant in comparison with the costs that can be incurred with a medical evacuation. When programs are affected by severe medical afflictions, the general crisis response plan should be followed. This means utilizing pre-established communications links between the overseas site and the home campus, so that information can be gathered from multiple sources, and can be shared and discussed in the process of decision-making.

Some issues to keep in mind:

- Home country medical personnel may have limited knowledge of the actual medical situation and how it manifests itself in the host country.

- Home country medical personnel may not have accurate information on the medical treatments available in the host country.

- Home country medical personnel may have only textbook knowledge of medications and their actual effect on the crisis at hand.

- Host country medications and medical facilities may be very limited and not up to home country standards (or in some instances may be far better than is known by U.S. colleagues).

- Host country medical personnel may be preoccupied with their own country residents and may not be available to treat foreign nationals.

- Communication with the crisis site may be difficult, if at all possible.

- Your college/university/organization may have to fly in both medications and medical staff, if transportation to the site is possible.

- Immediate treatment overseas may be the most prudent approach, whether or not the decision is to bring the group home.

- Medical evacuation may be the best solution, when the affected students are stable enough to permit travel.

- The media will be on the scene almost immediately, to talk with family and friends (media spin effect).

The challenge to on-site and home campus staff is to take the lead in making informed institutional decisions for the health and welfare of program participants.

Natural Catastrophes

Earthquakes, hurricanes, floods, famine, drought, and other natural catastrophes can easily devastate a program site and close a program quickly. They also can be less severe or take place in a large country where students are living and learning far from the disaster site. Most Americans have such a poor sense of geography that a flood in the northwest corner of Brazil can lead them to assume that all of Brazil must be under water! Therefore, confirming the event and assessing the situation in-country are the critical factors in developing an action plan.

Gathering accurate information is crucial. Obviously, access to valid and current information is easier if you have established good communications links beforehand with overseas staff, provided these are in working order. If students are attending a foreign university or are enrolled in a program sponsored by another institution, it may be much harder to learn what you need to know.

It may take several hours or days to gather sufficient information in order to develop the best way of proceeding. Imprudent action can be as detrimental to program participants as excessively delayed action. In the meantime, parents, friends, the institution/organizations Board, administrators, legislators, and other interested parties will demand information and action. Trained public relations staff can help by planning media announcements and messages provided by phone to concerned inquirers.

Earthquakes, hurricanes, and floods may preclude program staff from traveling to the disaster site. Relying on the assistance of service agencies and in-country personnel may be the best course of action. Famine and drought usually provide sufficient advance notice so that program participants can leave the site prior to the crisis. Program staff in the home country and the host country should monitor these situations and terminate programs before a situation becomes a full-blown crisis.

As with other crises, gathering adequate and accurate information, convening the crisis team, developing a response plan, and communicating with families, friends, and the media are the important steps in reacting to the crisis.

Some issues to keep in mind:

- In natural catastrophes, communication with those at the crisis site often is cut off.

- Your college, university, or organization may have to rely on host country governments, the home government's foreign affairs offices, the Red Cross or its equivalent, short-wave radio operators, and other creative forms of communication to obtain desired information.

- Transportation to the crisis site by home country personnel may not be possible for several days.

- Intense panic from family and friends occurs quickly.

- The host country situation may be one of devastation, which may be emotionally traumatic for program staff who might be able to travel to the site.

- Evacuation of injured participants and repatriation of remains may be necessary.

- If evacuation and repatriation are necessary, the college, university, or organization will need to become familiar with procedures for those actions in the host country, and their compatibility with procedures and legal requirements in the home country.

Political and Social Crises

Political and social unrest—civil war, armed strife with neighboring countries, political terrorism and conflict—is sometimes predictable as a potential threat to programs taking place in unstable areas. It is also the case, however, that many programs taking place in such areas—Israel, Northern Ireland, Guatemala, etc.—have excellent safety records, largely to the on-site staff's ability to keep abreast of the current situation, to prepare students properly for how to avoid risks and protect themselves, and at distancing operations from dangerous regions and hotspots.

Thus, "safety" can be as much a matter of program preparations, as of location per se. Modern terrorism erupts anywhere, and not just in regions where social and political tensions are high—witness the bombing of the World Trade Center in New York City a few years ago. Its reach can come about as a direct result of action taken by a government toward either an in-country group or another nation itself. That said, if a situation is evaluated as inevitably threatening, the location should not be selected for a program until stability returns.

In 1990, political upheaval in the Middle East brought terrorist threats against Americans in Italy. Six American university programs in Florence, Italy, received letters threatening unspecified retaliation against American students if the United States were to take military action against Iraq, signed by a previously unknown organization identifying itself as the Secret Revolutionary Popular Movement. Although the police characterized the threats as a scare tactic, similar to other threats made against American-linked firms in Europe during the outset of the Kuwait crisis, patrols increased at the American university office locations and the programs rightly perceived themselves to be in the midst of a very real crisis, that could not be ignored. Some decided to close, others considered closing, while all took extraordinary security procedures to warn and safeguard students and staff. Numerous other examples exist.

The 1998 bombings of the US Embassies in Kenya and Tanzania, followed by U.S. military retaliation in Afghanistan, and the continuing instability in the Middle East and numerous other parts of the world, demonstrate that the threat of political violence and terrorism remains a constant concern to the American public, especially those who travel overseas. However sporadic these outbursts, no program or sponsoring institution can afford to look the other way, and readiness to respond prudently and expeditiously must be part of any planning.

Apart from being the possible intended victims of harm, programs and individuals can at times get caught in the crossfire of warring factions. This sort of very dangerous limbo can isolate program participants, such as those students who were studying in the China interior during the Tiananmen Square uprising. In times of severe crisis, the program staff and participants may not be able to contact the embassy or consulate of their own country, nor may they be able to communicate outside the nation. At other times, innocent bystanders may be arrested and jailed. In rare situations, program participants may be directly involved in the unrest.

"Terrorism" is defined in Title 22 of the United States Code, Section 2656f(d). That stature contains the following definitions:

- The term "terrorism means premeditated, politically motivated violence perpetrated against noncombatant (...in addition to civilians, this includes military personnel who at the time of the incident are unarmed and/or not on duty....) targets by subnational groups or clandestine agents, usually intended to influence an audience.

- The term "international terrorism" means terrorism involving citizens of the territory of more than one country.

- The term "terrorist group" means any group practicing, or that has significant subgroups that practice, international terrorism. The U.S. Government has employed this definition of terrorism for statistical and analytical purposed since 1983 (U.S. State Department, *Patterns of Global Terrorism: 1997,* URL: www.state.gov/www/global/terrorism/1997/Report/intro.html)."

In preparing for worst-case scenarios of terrorism, institutions should educate themselves (administrators, faculty, staff, students) as thoroughly as possible not just about overseas locations but also with regard to U.S. government counter-terrorist policy. As noted by President Clinton after the terrorist attack in Luxor, Egypt: "Once again, we are reminded of the painful truth: Terrorism is a global threat. No nation is immune. This is why all nationals must redouble our commitment to fight this scourge together (U.S. State Department, *Patterns of Global Terrorism: 1997,* URL: www.state.gov/www/global/terrorism/1997/ Report/intro.HTML). Campuses should explore whether their insurance policies include coverage that will assist in responding to an act of terrorism and/or a terrorist threat and consider purchasing institutional liability insurance that includes coverage for terrorism and kidnapping. When integrated into the institution-wide insurance policy, the cost could be limited.

Some issues to keep in mind:

- Assess the severity of the unrest and the intended target of the unrest by contacting the home country foreign affairs office, the home country overseas Embassy, and other relevant agencies;

- Consider the in-country culture and how you might use that knowledge to respond to the situation;

- Establish a communication chain that can be easily implemented;

- Devise an evacuation route that will assure the safety of all participants (i.e. small group travel, as opposed to all participants on a bus heading for the airport);

- Use various routes of travel and modes of transportation for the small groups that are evacuating;

- Choose departure ports that are known to have a high level of security as a gathering and evacuation point;

- Keep your evacuation plan strictly confidential— from program participants, family, friends, the media, everyone except those who MUST know in order to implement the plan;

- Maintain anonymity of all program participants, in both the home and host countries;

- Check with the home country Embassy/Consulate in the host country, to ascertain locations (restaurants, bars, theaters, bookstores, tourist establishments, etc.) where your country nationals and tourists tend to 'hang out' and advise program participants to avoid those locations;

- Advise program participants to dress as much like in-country residents as possible;

- Have a plan to finance an emergency evacuation. Some programs require program staff to carry a corporate American Express card; others have an unlimited line of credit with travel agencies.

- Panic can quickly set in with family, friends, and the media. Again, have in place a comprehensive crisis management plan.

When contact with program participants is impossible, campuses should consider their options. An earthquake in Japan; political unrest in China; or war in Bosnia are situations where communication channels are unavailable and contact within a nation is interrupted.

Most situations of this type become a media event. There will be pressure on the home campus to get information and report on it. Three areas need consideration. The first area is preparing the program director or the overseas program agents to handle the situation independently, if necessary. Since the actual emergency cannot be predicted, the program director should have basic emergency response skills and a general process for handling program crises individually.

The possibility of limited or no contact from the home country should be discussed between home campus and on-site staff, before students depart. The first priority is the safety and well-being of students. If on-site staff is able to reach all the students, gathering the students together, taking roll, assessing their well-being, and escorting them to a safe location should be the first priority. Once these steps have been accomplished, on-site staff should contact those in charge of the emergency—Red Cross, government agents, etc.

The home campus must handle incoming calls from panicked family and friends, newspaper and television reporters, federal government agents, and other interested parties. It may initially have no information to report on the participants and, yet, everyone will expect facts and a plan. Honesty and brevity, not conjecture, are the best policies. Most colleges and universities, and program-sponsoring organizations, have a public affairs staff who are trained to handle the media and not emotionally involved in the situation. They can calmly and effectively respond to all media inquiries and may be a good choice to interact with family and friends. They can provide guidance on how to handle the situation and may be the most effective staff to carry out this component of crisis response.

Leadership Dysfunction or Incapacitation

Many study abroad programs run by U.S. colleges and universities, especially those of a semester duration or less, depend on one faculty leader to teach, supervise, and care for a group of students, perhaps without additional assistance. Minor hitches and obstacles are to be expected—the failure of arranged transportation to show up for a program trip, for example—without dire consequences.

Planning for overseas study, however, rarely focuses on the potential for disaster as it relates to anyone but the student. But what does the home campus do when the key administrator overseas suddenly is unable to perform his or her duties? When that person fails or becomes incapacitated, group well-being is in peril. What if this person suddenly and unexpectedly falls ill? What if he or she has a serious travel accident? What if you ascertain that this person has a habitual addiction to prescription medication that limits his ability to perform required duties? What if you discover, after a program begins, that your on-site staff person has a well-hidden drinking problem that abruptly interferes with his work? Who fills in for the key administrator—without the students feeling the impact of the loss? What can be done in advance to prepare for such a crisis? How, in short, does the home campus minimize the impact of staff dysfunction?

Staffing crises can occur on study abroad programs. Consider these unexpected events:

- A resident director of a semester program unexpectedly died of a heart attack, during overseas orientation;

- A faculty member leading a short-term program abroad failed miserably in his leadership role; students complained that he was unavailable; rumors spread that that he was drinking in a local tavern most days, occasionally with students;

- A resident director of a semester program was hospitalized while on vacation in a secluded location, missing the first three weeks of the spring programs, forcing his staff to oversee orientation, open bank accounts, coordinate travel plans/group excursions, and more. (To complicate matters, the airlines would not permit him to fly until his doctor could provide a clean bill of health.)

- A resident director suddenly fell ill and was unable to lead the program; a quick replacement, whose résumé appeared to be stellar, was appointed, but didn't perform the duties of the job well; students and parents called with vociferous complaints.

Given these true examples of what can happen, the home campus crisis management plan must address the issue of how to assist or replace a dysfunctional overseas leader. It should include provisions for the training and readiness of a back-up leader—or provisions for program cancellation and the completion of interrupted course work on the home campus. Where and when there is more than one on-site staff member overseas, the policy should clearly state lines of succession and assure that staff who may take over have appropriate credentials and training.

This, in turn, means that the home campus needs to understand the full role and responsibilities of overseas leadership. Student evaluation of staff and faculty performance should be built into programs at regular intervals and informal lines of communication should be maintained. Where faculty behavior is at issue, department chairs and deans should retain authority to advise, correct, and reassign program leaders. Obviously, the approach taken will differ some depending on program length. When the program is ongoing, operates throughout the academic year, and employs a semi-permanent overseas resident, a different response to dysfunction is required than in the case of a faculty member leading a short-term program overseas. In the first instance, a temporary solution might have to be found, such as sending a short-term replacement overseas while recruitment for a replacement takes place. In the second instance, if a substitute in not immediately available, the program might have to be canceled.

Given the time pressures to come up with an effective and expedient solution to this program crisis, it is important that the home campus maintains an up-to-date job description for the on-site staff position abroad and is able to answer questions about day-to-day responsibilities, major challenges, likely compensation package, and the like.

Campus colleagues who should be involved in resolving this crisis might include:

- Dean/Provost—to keep them informed and quickly gain their support.

- Human Resources/Personnel Department—to notify them of an illness/injury that might require disability benefits; to check policy on handling issues of incompetence [Note: policies regarding tenured faculty and unionized employees may require special attention.]; to identify legal issues, such as employment laws that might govern the employee's status overseas; to identify temporary help who can aid your local office requires additional home office support.

- Finance Department—as you are certain to require additional funds for emergencies related to the crisis.

- Public Relations Department—to keep them updated; they do not want to be caught off guard in the event that the media, colleagues or parents call them for information.

In the interim, it is important for those who are troubleshooting, trying to put the pieces of a sometimes large puzzle together, to have a program manual or guidebook to refer to. This manual should include a detailed calendar that outlines what tasks are handled each month. The written manual also functions as a training tool during times of planned transition. It can easily be updated, allowing any staff turnover to take place more efficiently and effectively.

In addition, the home campus needs to:

* Know the key people in your overseas director's rolodex: This is the best guide to your overseas support network. How can these key contacts help you?

* Maintain contact with the on-site director's local colleagues, a tremendous source of information and support. During difficult times, they are likely to point things in the right direction.

* Prepare domestic and overseas staff for such a crisis: If the primary campus administrator needs to go overseas immediately, can other local staff fill in? Where are their skills limited? What are reasonable expectations? Will they be compensated for additional work, particularly if the additional workload is ongoing due to a serious crisis abroad? Are they willing to be available during severe crises? What are the limitations?

* Keep a pending file: This file should have clear notes with dates and times of ongoing conversations as well as a daily "to do" list that will help your staff through the transition.

* Communicate with students and parents: Inform them that the situation is under control. They are your clients and those who are most directly affected by the crisis. Put their minds at ease by letting them know that your main concern is student safety and the continuation of the program.

* The study abroad program administrator also needs to communicate the status of employee abroad to the campus human resources department. If the employee is not going to be available for an extended period of time, this department is responsible for sharing college policies and disability information in a timely manner. If the employee is a tenured faculty member, other issues need to be addressed.

Cancelling Programs

A program provider's second worst nightmare, after death or serious student injuries, is having to cancel a program. Sometimes programs are cancelled for what might be perceived because of pressures institutions face when crises occur. Intense media attention on terrorists in Egypt caused many colleges to cancel programs even when their own knowledgeable on-site personnel could demonstrate that simple precautions would make Cairo as safe as any other major city, possibly safer.

In the present litigious climate, it is tremendously risky to continue programs in places where someone might say later, 'You should have known it was dangerous.' If, after careful deliberation, the decision is made to continue a program after the original safety profile that is consistently shared with students and their parents, has been altered significantly, it is extremely important to give students an option to leave the program without penalty. This revised "informed consent" procedure allows students to make their own decisions about the risks of the program under the new conditions.

In countries where universities may close for a time unexpectedly, should there be occurrences such as student or staff strikes that lead to closing classes, the crisis management plan should always include a return-to-the-home-campus option, or a secondary site with provision for individually hired faculty. In the case of more general national emergencies—natural disasters, political turmoil, etc.—in instances when American students are directly enrolled in host universities, it is assumed that personnel at a host university will follow the crisis management processes recommended in the chapters of this book addressing foreign student services. Knowing this in advance is always worth the time of finding it out.

Perhaps the most visible and immediate crises for study abroad are those that arise suddenly and unexpectedly, such as terrorist activities directed against Americans, political unrest, or natural disasters. When danger is perceived, the first impulse is often to flee, to evacuate the group. Ironically, unless the U.S. State Department has directly ordered evacuation of all Americans, the safest course may be to stay put and lie low, particularly if local staff can find accommodations in residential areas away from tourist attractions and city centers. In most cases, as noted above, programs or parts of programs may have to be canceled if a leader cannot continue and an equally qualified substitute is not available. The same may be true if carefully checked-out travel arrangement fall through and substitutions are on questionable carriers or in unknown locations. Overall, it is better to cancel a program and take a financial loss than to continue and risk problems from hasty decisions. If a decision is made to continue with new arrangements, students should again be given the option of dropping out without penalty.

Program Cancellation Criteria and Policy Recommendations

Program cancellation—calling off the program prior to departure of participants—and termination of a program—recalling a program prior to the closing date—need careful assessment. Usually these decisions are challenges, as various stakeholders have differing views. Again, the basic criterion for program departure or continuance is the safety and health of all participants.

Canceling a program prior to departure requires much informational input and courage. Gathering sufficient information to make a decision may be a challenge. Assessing the situation both at the point of arrival at a site, and at the program site itself, are critical. Can the program be carried out with little-to-no threat to program participants?

Stakeholders have much invested and will want to assure that their interests are considered. Stakeholders may include:

- Participants, who have already paid out significant funds;

- Family and friends;

- Travel agents and transportation firms;

- Overseas agencies and institutions;

- College/university/organization Board of Trustees and CEO;

- College/university/organization financial offices;

- College/university/organization legal counsel;

- Insurance agencies;

- Faculty and/or program sponsors;

- Home and host country governments;

- State and provincial governments; and

- Politicians.

Home campus administrators may feel pressure both to cancel and to continue the program. Coping with conflicting and contradictory opinions is always a major challenge, especially when student health and safety has to be balanced against all the reasons for running the program in the first place. Some campus stakeholders will focus on the money spent on the program to date and will insist on recovering all of the expended funds. Some stakeholders will focus on public image. Others will pressure the program staff to meet its commitments. Additional personnel will be obsessed with legal concerns. And some stakeholders will be concerned exclusively with the potential risks to safety and health, the bottom line.

Termination of a program in progress requires similar evaluation but may be an even more difficult decision to make. In part, this is because students overseas seldom want to come home if they feel (either naively or because they are better informed) the situation does not threaten them. But their on-site views may be in direct contrast to those held by their parents, who may be less well-informed but are concerned and worried by anything they do not fully comprehend. Once a program is underway, program stakeholders may have even more contradictory positions. Gathering information and making the decision, however, should still follow the steps enumerated above.

Additional concerns of academic programs are the completion of courses by participants and the impact of termination on their financial aid. Obviously no responsible international educator would advocate for the continuation of a program that is in danger on the basis of preserving the academic credit and financial aid provided to students. This is why contingency plans should be in place to enable students to complete their academic work, to the best of the institution's ability, so that they do not lose credit or financial aid eligibility.

In assessing the decision to cancel or terminate a program, staff should consult:

- Home country government travel advisories;

- Home country travel advisories

- Travel advisories of other nations, as a supplement to home country advisories;

- In-country Embassy/Consulate;

- Program director assessment;

- Partner university/organization assessment;

- Advice of other university programs at the overseas location;

- Risk management firm advice;

- University/organization insurance company advice;

- Travel agencies;

- Aid agencies (e.g. Red Cross; IMAT; NGO's);

- Legal counsel;

- Medical advisers.

Program staff should evaluate the information using the following criteria:

- Safety of program participants;

- Assurance of basic needs (food, water, health care);

- Probability that the crisis will subside;

- Ability to evacuate safely and responsibly (airport choice, transportation to the airport, airline choice, covering the cost of transportation, maintaining secrecy of the plan, dealing with participant and family anxiety; masking the national identity of participants; laying out behavior criteria for participants) if necessary;

- Medical and legal implications of program continuance/cancellation/termination.

If a program must be cancelled, there remains much to do after the students and leaders return to campus. In any case, a huge number of practical questions arise about housing, academic credit arrangements, registration for new course-work, tuition refunds, insurance, and the like. If the emergency is real, there may be significant individual and group emotional trauma to deal with. Involving the experienced campus counseling center and others who have been through such experiences, to provide empathy and therapy to those who need it is can be essential. When the worst has happened, its impact can be long-lasting and profound.

APPENDIXES.

Resources and Forms

Appendix A

Resources for Chapter 1

Gray, Francine du Plessix, *Soviet Women: Walking the Tightrope.* New York: Doubleday, 1990. ISBN: 0385417330.

Dragus, Juris G; Pedersen, Paul B.; Lonner, Walter J. and Trimble, Joseph E., editors, "Dilemmas and Choices in Cross-Cultural Counseling: The Universal versus the Culturally Distinctive," *Counseling Across Cultures,* Third Edition. Honolulu: University Press of Hawaii, 1989.

Larson, Wendy Ann, editor, *When Crisis Strikes on Campus.* Washington, D.C.: Council for Advancement and Support of Education, 1994.

Siegel, Dorothy, *Campuses Respond to Violent Tragedy.* American Council on Education: Series on Higher Education, Oryx Press, 1994.

Appendix B

Resources for Chapter 2

Andersen, Sharon Rezec, reviewing the situation at the University of North Dakota following the flood.

Charles, John, referring to the previously mentioned earthquake in California, and the situation at California State University.

Cumps, Carol, University of Massachusetts-Amherst.

Flores, Alfred, Jr., as reported to author, concerning the flood of July 28, 1997 in Fort Collins, North Dakota, which wiped out a significant part of the city and the campus.

Green, Judith, concerning Hurricane Fran in 1996.

Larrance, Anneke J., St. Lawrence University, New York.

Majchrowicz, Danuta, Arizona State University, discussing routine preparation for heat problems.

Mason, Ruth, Gustavus Adolphus College.

McClellan, Chris, Lower Columbia College, Washington.

Moline, Carol, Gustavus Adolphus College.

Pearson, John, Bechtel International Center at Stanford University, Stanford, California, reported that after the 1989 Loma Piada earthquake (which did almost $250 million worth of damage at Stanford alone), a Stanford faculty member who is himself foreign and an expert on earthquakes, gave a talk entitled "Shake, Rattle and Roll" for international graduate orientation programs for two or three years afterwards.

Pierce, Nancy, St. Lawrence University, New York.

Rabaey, Julie Ann, Gustavus Aldolphus College in Minnesota.

Rogers, John, reviewing the situation on the University of Iowa campus after the August 1993 floods.

Rose, Julie Kyllonen, University of Western Illinois.

Smith, Heather, University of North Carolina—Wilmington.

Theis, Mary, Clarkson University, Clarkson, New York.

References

The Federal Emergency Management Agency (FEMA) website, http://www.fema.gov, offers fact sheets and provides many suggestions for homeowners. The recommendations provided in this section were modified from FEMA

Quesenberry, John D; Coppis, Carla E.; Thiesse, Steven A.; "Responding to a Disaster: An Administrative Perspective, *International Education Forum,* Volume 13, No. 1, Spring 1993.

Appendix C

Resources for Chapter 4

Prevention

Reading List

Carden, A. I., and Feicht, R. (1991). "Homesickness Among American and Turkish College Students." *Journal of Cross-Cultural Psychology,* 22, 418-428.

Church, A. (1982). "Sojourner Adjustment." *Psychological Bulletin,* 91, 540-572.

Kennedy, E. (1977). *On Becoming a Counselor: A Basic Guide for Non-Professional Counselors.* New York: The Continuum Press.

National Institute of Mental Health (1987) *Medications.* Rockville, MD.

Pruitt, F. J. (1978). "The Adaptation of African Students to American Society." *International Journal of Intercultural Relations,* 2, 90-117.

References

Alexander, A. A., Klein, M. H., Workneh, F., and Miller, M. H. (1981). "Psychotherapy and the Foreign Student." In P. B. Pedersen, J. G. Draguns, W. J. Lonner and J. E. Trimble (Eds.).

Pedersen, P., Lonner, W. J., and Draguns, J. G., Eds. (1976). *Counseling Across Cultures.* Honolulu, HI: University of Hawaii Press.

American Psychiatric Association (1994). *Diagnostic and Statistical Manual of Mental Disorders* (Fourth Edition). Washington, DC.

DeArmand, M. M. (1983, April/May). "Mental Health and International Students." *NAFSA Newsletter,* April/May. Washington, DC: NAFSA: Association of International Educators.

Van Tilburg, M. A. L., and Vingerhoets, A. J. J. M. (1997). *Psychological Aspects of Geographical Moves: Homesickness and Acculturation Stress.* Tilburg, The Netherlands: Tilburg University Press.

Zwingmann, C. A. A., and Gunn, A. D. G. (1983). *Uprooting and Health: Psycho-Social Problems of Students from Abroad.* Geneva: World Health Organization, Division of Mental Health.

Eating Disorders

Resources

Australia: The Anorexia and Bulimia Foundation, 1513 High Street, Glen Iris, 3156 Victoria, Phone: 613-885-0318.

Canada: Bulimia Anorexia Nervosa Association C/O Psychological Service, University of Windsor, Ontario NQB 3PH, Phone: 519-253-7421.

New Zealand: Women with Eating Disorders Resource Center, P.O. Box 4520, Armagh and Montreal Streets, Christchurch, Phone: 643-366-7725.

United Kingdom: Eating Disorder Association, Sackville Place, Magdalen Street, Norwich, NR3 IJU, Phone: 603-621-414.

United States: American Anorexia and Bulimia Association (AABA) 293 Central Park West #1R New York, NY 10034, Phone: 212-501-8351.

Academy for Eating Disorders, Division of Adolescent Medicine, Montefiore Medical Center, 111 East 210th St, Bronx, NY 10467, Phone: 718 920-6781, Fax 718-920-5289.

National Association of Anorexia Nervosa and Associated Disorders (ANAD), Highland Park IL 60035, Phone: 847-831-3438.

Anorexia Nervosa and Related Eating Disorders Inc. (ANRED) P.O. Box 5102, Eugene OR 97405, Phone: 503-344-1144.

Eating Disorder and Prevention (EDAP) Suite 803, 603 Stewart Street, Seattle, WA 98101, Phone: 206-382-3587.

International Association of Eating Disorder Professionals (IAEDP) 123 NW 13th Street, #206, Boca Raton, FL 33432, Phone: 407-338-6494.

National Eating Disorders Organization (NEDO) 6655 South Yale Avenue, Tulsa, OK 74136, Phone: 614-436-1112.

Footnotes

Fasting Girls, Joan Jacobs Brumberg, Harvard University Press, Cambridge, Massachusetts, 1988, p. 12.

Recommended Reading

Culture and Weight Consciousness by Mervat Nasser, Routledge Press, 1997. This book explores the incidence of eating disorders in a number of different cultures, including Asian, African, and European.

Appendix D

Resources for Chapter 5

Relationship Violence

Bennett, Vanora. "Russia's Ugly Little Secret: Misogyny," *The Los Angeles Times,* December 6, 1997.

Perlez, Jane. "Uganda's Women: Children, Drudgery and Pain," *The New York Times,* February 24, 1991, p. 10.

Stillman, Alan D, Assistant Dean of Student Affairs/International Student Adviser, New England College, Henniker, Hew Hampshire, in e-mail, January 1998.

Cumps, Carol, Director, Office of International Programs, University of Massachusetts, in email January 6, 1998.

United Nations web site: www.un.org.

Rape and Abortion

American College Health Association (ACHA)
P.O. Box 28937
Baltimore, MD 21240-8937
Phone: 410-859-1500
Fax: 410-859-1510
http://www.acha.org

U.S. Dept. of State Overseas Citizens Services
2201 C Street, NW

Washington, DC 20520
Phone: 202-647-4000 (24 hrs)
Phone: 202-647-5225
http://www.state.gov/

Gay Men's Health Crisis Hotline (GMHC)
119 West 24th Street
New York, NY 10011
Phone: 212-807-6655
Phone: 1-800-243-7692 (toll-free)
http://www.gmhc.org

CDC National Prevention Information Network (NPIN)
http://www.cdcnpin.org

National Organization for Women (NOW)
105 East 22nd Street
New York, NY 10010
Phone: 212-260-4422
Phone: 202-331-0066 (Washington, DC)
http://www.now.org

Planned Parenthood
810 7th Avenue
New York, NY 10019
Phone: 212-541-7800
Phone: 1-800-387-4394 (toll-free)

Centers for Disease Control and Prevention
1600, Clifton Road
NE, Atlanta, GA 30333
Phone: 404-639-3311
http://www.cdc.org

Health Check for Study Work and Travel Abroad (CIEE)
205 E. 42nd Street
New York, NY 10017-5706
Phone: 212-666-4177

Phone: 1-888-Council (toll-free)
http://www.ciee.org

Kennedy Center for International Studies
Brigham Young University
P.O. Box 24538
Provo, Utah 84602-4538
Phone: 1-800-528-6279 (toll-free)
http://www.byu.edu

Race and Racism Issues

Anti-Defamation League
http://www.adl.org

The Asian-American Legal Defense Fund
71 W 23rd Street, New York, NY 10010-4102
212-966-5932

National Multicultural Institute
http://www.nmci.org

Speak Out
http://www.igc.org

Appendix E

Resources for Chapter 7

References

Althen, Gary, "November 1, 1991: The Killings in Iowa," *NAFSA Newsletter*, April-May 1992, pages 30-31. Washington, DC: NAFSA: Association of International Educators.

Olson, Barbara, "Community Volunteers in the Iowa Campus Crisis," *NAFSA Newsletter*, January 1992. Washington, DC: NAFSA: Association of International Educators.

Durkheim, E. (1951) *Suicide*, The Free Press, New York.

Schneidman, E. (1985) *Definitions of Suicide*, John Wiley & Sons, New York.

For information about shipping remains to foreign countries, visit U.S. Department of State web site for current details: http://www.state.gov/.

Appendix F

Crisis Response Checklist

[Adapted from Institute for Shipboard Education/Semester at Sea documents]

1a. Specific information to be collected from the site

What happened?

Where did it happen?

When did it happen?

Who was involved?

Who are the witnesses?

Who has been contacted?

What action, if any, has been suggested by authorities at the site?

1b. It is critical to get detailed information regarding names, times, places, witnesses, etc.

Status of the participants:

Where are the participants?

What is the physical condition of the participants?

What is the mental health of the participants?

What communication system has been established among the participants?

What information needs to be communicated to the participants?

Do the participants have any immediate needs?

2. Specific contact information

    Who contacted the home university/organization?

    When did the contact occur?

    How was contact made?

    What was discussed?

    What plan was developed?

    Who was to take what action?

3. Double-checking facts

    What agencies/organizations need to contacted?

    Who will contact each agency/organization?

    When will the agency/organization be contacted?

    How will the gathered information be communicated?

    Who will collate information?

    How will the Crisis Team receive the information?

4. Action plan

    What action needs to be taken?

    What are the legal issues to be considered?

    Who needs to be contacted?

    What financial arrangements need to be made?

    What legal action needs to be taken?

5. Post-crisis follow-up:

    What debriefing is needed and who should be included?

    What post-trauma counseling is needed?

    What letters and other forms of communication need to be undertaken?

What legal action should be reviewed and initiated?

Who will gather all information?

Who will write the report?

6.   Who develops the Crisis Management Plan?

On-site program staff

- identify on-going issues which may become crises
- provide information about health and safety contacts
- develop realistic "invisibility" or evacuation plans
- provide emergency back-up

Provider staff

- develop policies and procedures manual
- develop preventative measures
- design orientation for students
- identify realistic processes
- train short-term staff/leaders
- gather official and unofficial information on program site
- coordinate distribution of information to those who would have to act in emergency

Home campus study abroad staff who regularly send students on your programs

- concur on student selection criteria
- concur on behavioral expectations
- develop own policy on refunds, bringing students home in mid-term

Faculty supervisors, department chairs, deans

- concur on leader selection criteria
- support faculty leader training
- concur on performance/behavioral expectations for faculty leaders
- develop policy for completing credit if student is sent home or program is canceled.

Student affairs personnel

- concur on student selection criteria
- develop policy on housing returnee(s) in mid-term.

Bursar and registrar

- concur on refund, registration and credit issues arising from program cancellation or return of individual student.

Risk management office, legal office/college lawyer, institutional insurers

- help to set criteria for assessing risk of site or activities. (safety profile)
- contribute information on individual and institutional liability

Higher administration institutional policy committees

- approve plan and include policy in appropriate manuals.

Appendix G

Natural Catastrophe/ Disaster Resources

In addition to relief services, the **American Red Cross** provides practical and helpful awareness and educational information. The International Federation of Red Cross and Red Crescent Societies include over 170 national societies around the world. Phone: 1-800-HELP NOW or 1-888-853-6846; http://www.redcross.org

In partnership with IBM and CNN, the **American Red Cross** maintains a web site with disaster information: http://www.DisasterRelief.org

The **Committee on Earth Observation Satellites (CEOS)** shares disaster information: www.ceos.noaa.gov.

The **Federal Emergency Management Agency (FEMA)** is an independent agency of the U.S. government that reports to the President. FEMA provides relief services and on on-line library. Phone (helpline): 1-800-462-9029; http://www.fema.gov

National Voluntary Organizations Active in Disaster (NVOAD) is a partnership of over 30 volunteer organizations to provide information to the public about cooperative efforts of disaster response organizations in the United Sates. Links are provided to other relief agencies; http://nvoad.org

The **National Weather Service-National Oceanic and Atmospheric Administration** provides publications and information on various natural hazards; http://www.noaa.gov.

The **Salvation Army** is an international evangelical Christian religion with a presence in 100 countries. Phone: 1-800-752-2769; http://www.salvation-army.org

The **Spire Project,** overseen by Community Networking, provides general travel information with links to travel advisories in English; http://cn.net.au/country.html

The **University of Wisconsin-Extension, Division of Cooperative Extension** provides a disaster handbook on floods, fire, drought, tornadoes, winter storms, and community/family issues that can be downloaded; http://www.uwex.edu

The **U.S. State Department** links to embassies and offers State Department advisories; http://www.state.gov.

The **World Meteorological Organization** coordinates global scientific activity to allow increasingly prompt and accurate weather information; http://www.wmo.ch

Appendix H

Phases of Disaster

The University of Wisconsin-Extension, Department of Cooperative Education has published "The Disaster Handbook." In this handbook, four phases associated with the aftermath of disasters are described.

Historic Phase. This period usually occurs at the time of impact and in the period immediately after. Emotions are strong and direct. People are called upon to respond to demands for heroic action to save their own and others' lives and property. Altruism is prominent, and people expend major energy in helping others survive and recover. The most important resources during this phase are family groups, neighbors and emergency teams of various sorts.

Honeymoon Phase. This period generally extends from one week to six months after the disaster. For survivors, even with the loss of loved ones and possessions, there is a strong sense of having shared with others a dangerous, catastrophic experience and having lived through it. Supported and often encouraged by the influx of official and governmental staff who promise many kinds of help, the victims begin clean-up. There is anticipation that more help soon will be available. Pre-existing community groups and emergency community groups are especially important resources during this period.

Disillusionment Phase. This phase generally lasts from about two months to one or even two or more years. Strong feelings of disappointment, anger, resentment, and bitterness may appear if failures occur and the promises of aid are not fulfilled. Outside agencies may need to leave, and some of the local community groups may weaken. Also contributing to this stage may be the gradual loss of the feeling of "shared community" as victims concentrate on rebuilding their own lives and solving their individual problems.

Reconstruction Phase. The survivors they come to realize they will need to solve the problems of rebuilding their own homes, businesses, and lives largely by themselves and gradually assume responsibility for the tasks. This phase generally lasts for several years after the disaster. The appearance of new buildings replacing old ones, the beginnings of new construction, and the development of new programs and plans all serve to reaffirm residents' belief in their community and their own capabilities. If these signs of progress are delayed, however, the emotional problems that appear may be serious and intense. Community groups with a longer-term investment in the community and its people become key players during this phase.

Appendix

International Student Information Forms

INTERNATIONAL STUDENT INFORMATION FORM
MOUNT IDA COLLEGE

Name_____Date Fall Semester 2000
          last name   first name

Resident Student_____   Commuter Student_____

Local Address _____

_____

Local Telephone Number   email
____(____)_____

Country of Citizenship_____Country of Birth_____

Major _____BS degree?_____Associate degree?____

Permanent Address in **HOME COUNTRY** _____

_____

Telephone Number: Country Code_____ City Code_____ Number_____

IN CASE OF EMERGENCY, NAME OF SOMEONE IN THE **UNITED STATES** THAT
WE CAN CONTACT

NAME_____TELEPHONE NUMBER_____

ADDRESS_____

****

IMMIGRATION INFORMATION

Passport Information   Visa Information
   Country Issued By_____   Visa Type_____

   Passport #_____   Place Issued_____

   Date Issued_____   Date Issued_____

   Place Issued_____   Expiration Date_____

   Expiration Date_____   Single Entry__Multiple Entry_

FORM I-94

Admission Number_____ Admission Date_____

Permission to Remain Until_____

I-20

Expiration Date_____

259

INTERNATIONAL STUDENT INFORMATION FORM

Lillian and Emanuel Slutzker Center for International Services

PART A   *Notify the SU Student Records Office (106 Steele Hall) or SUNY-ESF Registrar's Office (112 Bray Hall) of revisions in PART A.*

Social Security (Admission) Number   Last (family) Name   First (given) Name, Middle Initial   Gender

Date of Birth   City & Country of Birth   Country of Citizenship   OIS Use Only

SCHOOL: **LEVEL:**   LOCAL TELEPHONE NO:
☐ SU   ☐ GRADUATE   area code
☐ SUNY-ESF   ☐ UNDERGRADUATE   LOCAL ADDRESS:
                                        Box #   Residence Hall   Room #

PROGRAM(S) _____
                                        House/Bldg. #   Street   Apt #

                                        City/Town   State   Zip Code

RELIGION: | **MARITAL STATUS:** | *Please add information about dependents in PART D.*

PART B

YOUR E-MAIL ADDRESS: |
HOME COUNTRY CONTACT PERSON: **EMERGENCY CONTACT PERSON IN THE U.S.:**
☐ Mr.   ☐ Mr.
☐ Ms.   ☐ Ms.
  Contact Person's Name   Contact Person's Name
Does this person speak English? ☐ Yes ☐ No   *Does this person speak English?* ☐ Yes ☐ No
Relationship: ☐ Parent ☐ Spouse ☐ Other   *Relationship:* ☐ Parent ☐ Spouse ☐ Other

Mailing Address   Box #   Residence Hall   Room #

City/Town   Providence/State   House/Bldg. #   Street   Apt #

Country   Postal Code   City/Town   State   Zip Code

                                                 Tel. No.
Telephone (with country code and city code)   area code

PART C   *Refer to your immigration and health insurance documents to verify data in Part C.*

IMMIGRATION DATA: ▸ Visa Classification: | *Is J-Visa student subject to two-year home stay?* ☐ Yes ☐ No
                        F-1, J-1, etc.

▸ Form I-20/IAP-66:   I-20#10; or   I-20#5, or
                      IAP-66#   IAP-66#3
                      Issue Date   IAP-66 Program Number (J-1 only)   Completion Date

                                                          ☐ "D/S" or
▸ Form I-94:   ☐ ____ / ____ / yr
           I-94 Departure Number   I-94 Entry Date   I-94 Departure Date

▸ U.S. Visa:
           Visa Number (Not Control Number)   #/entries   Visa Issue Date   Visa Expiration Date

▸ Passport: |
           Passport Number   Passport Issue Date   Passport Expiration Date

SPONSOR TYPE(S): ☐ Personal/Family   ☐ University Assistantship   ☐ Home Government
                     ☐ Private - Home Country   ☐ University Fellowship   ☐ U.S. Government (i.e., AID)
                     ☐ Private - U.S.   ☐ University Scholarship   ☐ Int'l Agency (i.e., IIE, LASPAU, UN)
HEALTH INSURANCE TYPE(S): ☐ Haylor, Freyer, & Coon (**HIGS**)
                              ☐ S.U. (**BC/BS; Univera; Healthsource; United Health**)
                              ☐ Medical Evacuation & Repatriation (Int'l S.O.S.)
                              ☐ Other: Policy Expiration Date

PART D   DEPENDENTS CURRENTLY IN THE U.S. (Use Additional sheet if needed)

Spouse
           Last (family) Name   First (given) Name   Date of Birth   Country of Citizenship
☐ Son
☐ Daughter
           Last (family) Name   First (given) Name   Date of Birth   Country of Citizenship

Student Signature in English   Student Signature as appears in passport   Signature Date

Appendix J

School Agreement Forms for Study Abroad

Cornell Abroad

Agreement/Release Form

Cornell sponsored programs: Berlin Consortium, Denmark International Study Program (DiS), Early Childhood Education Practicum in Göteborg, Sweden, Kyoto Center for Japanese Studies, Cornell Nepal Study Program, EDUCO (Emory, Duke and Cornell in Paris), Michigan-Penn-Cornell Program in Seville, Spain and the 17 universities in the United Kingdom

Cornell Abroad requires that <u>all</u> students sign this form as requested to indicate agreement <u>before</u> departure

The following agreement is designed to protect all participants in programs abroad: students, faculty members, Cornell University, and agencies & individuals cooperating with Cornell University.

The signed agreement/release must be received at Cornell Abroad, 474 Uris Hall, prior to departure from the United States.

*Cornell Abroad has no access to student health records. Accordingly, **if you have any physical or mental health, consultation with a medical professional in this country before departure** to discuss the potential stress and difficulties attendant in the overseas experience **is strongly encouraged.***

PROGRAM OR UNIVERSITY NAME AND LOCATION:_____

1. My participation in the above program is entirely voluntary and will require transportation to and habitation in the country of _____ and may involve subjection to risks relating to or arising out of program activities;
2. I understand that there are risks inherent in such activity and I have been apprised of such risks and agree to assume all said risks and responsibility for my health, safety, and property while participating in this program;
3. I release Cornell University, its officers, agents, and employees from any and all liability, damage or claim of any nature whatsoever arising out of, or in any way related to my participation in this program, including but not limited to the medical authorization given to Cornell University, acts of God, acts or omissions of any third parties (including but not limited to common carriers, hotels, restaurants, or other firms or agencies), except such as may directly result from the negligence of Cornell University, its officers, agents, or employees;
4. I indemnify and hold Cornell University harmless from any damage or liability incurred by Cornell as a result of any illness I may suffer, including the costs of any medical care, or any injury or damage to the person or property of others which I may cause, or from any financial liability or obligation which I may personally incur, while participating in the program;
5. I understand that the University reserves the right to make cancellations, changes or substitutions in cases of emergency or changed conditions or in the interest of the study abroad group. Should the University cancel the program, full refunds will be made unless the cancellation is due to political, natural, technological or other catastrophes beyond its control in which case Cornell University will be able to refund only uncommitted and recoverable funds;
6. I also understand that the following refund policy is applicable if I withdraw from the program for any reason: the <u>$300 tuition deposit</u> billed on the Bursar bill for Cornell sponsored programs is <u>non-refundable,</u> charges may be incurred for housing costs and the usual Cornell tuition refund policy applies to the balance of the comprehensive study abroad charge. A student who receives Cornell University financial aid should understand that signing this agreement signifies commitment to repay any awards received for the semester from which he/she has withdrawn and that these charges will appear on the bursar account;
7. I understand that because of the exigencies of its billing cycle, Cornell University reserves the right to determine the date

on which foreign currency may need to be purchased for payment of tuition and any other charges billable to my University Bursar's account. Due to fluctuations in the price of foreign currencies, Cornell Abroad reserves the right to adjust program charges;

8. I understand that Cornell University requires that all students be covered by appropriate accident and medical insurance and that they be financially responsible for such expenses. In addition, I understand that the payment for medical expenses may have to be advanced and reimbursement sought later from the carrier. Cornell University also requires that students planning to operate a motor vehicle obtain liability and collision insurance that will cover them in the applicable foreign countries. It also recommends that students insure their property from loss and theft;

9. I understand that all students are subject to Cornell University regulations (including but not limited to the Code of Academic Integrity and the Cornell University Campus Code of Conduct), the host university's or program's regulations and guidelines, and laws of the host country and that in the event of violation of these, academic failure, or behavior which is detrimental to the student, other students, or the program, the director of the program shall have the right to dismiss the student from the program. Cornell University is not responsible for the defense of a student accused of a violation of the laws of the host country and is not responsible for the payment of any fines or other penalties resulting from such violations;

10. As a participant in this study abroad program, I pledge to conduct myself in a manner that reflects favorably on Cornell University;

11. I understand that the manufacture, distribution, possession, use or sale of controlled substances as defined by New York State or Federal Law, or the laws of my host country is prohibited during study abroad. I understand that I will be directly subject to the laws and legal procedures of my host country as applied to the use, possession and distribution of illegal drugs and these will likely be strictly enforced by local authorities;

12. I further understand that I am solely responsible for ascertaining the lawful age for the possession or consumption of alcoholic beverages in my host country and for my conduct in compliance with local laws as enforced by local authorities;

13. I agree to complete all the academic work required by my program or university before the end of my study abroad term, semester, or academic year, whichever is applicable, and to remain on site until that date. I understand that the only exception to the foregoing may be earlier departure in the event of a medical or personal emergency, or in the event that I have completed all my examinations within a stated examination period at the end of the term, semester or academic year.

14. I certify that I am at least 18 years of age or older.

PRINT NAME:_____

SIGNATURE:_____ DATE:_____

COMPLETE & RETURN THIS FORM TO:
CORNELL ABROAD, 474 URIS HALL, ITHACA NY 14853
TELEPHONE:(607)255-6224 FAX:(607) 255-8700
E-MAIL: CUAbroad@cornell.edu

STUDY ABROAD AGREEMENT

This is an Agreement between the undersigned study abroad Participant and the University of Nebraska-Lincoln ("the University"). **Read carefully, sign, and return to International Affairs.**

This Agreement incorporates by reference all informational material distributed by the University regarding the Participant's specific study abroad program, including the attached cost information. These materials address a general description of the program, eligibility requirements, cost, registration procedures, award of credit and related topics. The Participant agrees to: (1) read and understand all material distributed and agrees to be bound by it; (2) attend all pre-departure orientation meetings; (3) maintain the eligibility standards established for the program; and (4) consult with the U.S. Department of State Travel Advisory Service and Center for Disease Control as specified in the distributed materials.

The University reserves the right to make such alterations in the program as may be necessary or appropriate, consistent with the goals of the program. While the University tries to maintain the stated program itinerary, activities, and costs, it may make modifications in the event of unforeseen or changed circumstances, such as changes affecting safety, changes in program expenses, currency fluctuations, tuition increases, room and board increases and changes in the academic calendar or course offerings at the host institution. The University shall not be liable for damages or other results caused by events beyond its control.

Should Participant fail to pay any fee or debt owed to the University or any host institution arising in relation to Participant's involvement in or actions taken in the course of the program, the University may place a "hold" on Participant's University records and ability to register until the debt is satisfied in its entirety, in addition to any other recourse available.

The Participant agrees to have sufficient funds for personal expenses and for return transportation, if applicable.

The University may cancel the program should the University determine circumstances require such cancellation, in which case the Participant shall receive such refund as the University in the exercise of its reasonable efforts is able to recover for the Participant.

The Participant understands that living in or traveling through a foreign country may involve certain health and personal risks, including terrorists attacks and other acts of violence, and the Participant accepts those risks. He or she agrees to exercise reasonable and prudent care while abroad with regard to food, substance use and abuse, threats to physical safety and political instability.

The Participant authorizes the on-site program coordinator (whether an employee of the University or host institution) to seek and obtain medical treatment in the event the Participant does not have the capacity to do so.

The Participant is required to be covered by adequate health and accident insurance applicable in the program locale and to the program activities, including medical evacuation and repatriation of remains benefits. The Participant understands that any sickness and accident insurance provided by the program may or may not cover pre-existing conditions up to a particular amount and he/she will read the insurance information provided for details of the coverage in effect. If the University or host institution should pay for Participant's medical or other personal expenses, Participant shall reimburse the payer for the expense.

The Participant understands the essential elements of participating in the program and has read the program Health Sheet. The Participant represents that he/she is able to fully take part in the essential elements of the program. If the Participant believes that he/she is in need of a reasonable accommodation in order to fully take part in the essential elements of the program, the Participant represents that he/she has contacted the University's 504/ADA Coordinator and completed an accommodation evaluation in such a reasonable time-frame so as to allow for satisfactory evaluation of the requested accommodation and adequate time to implement the accommodation, if any. The Participant has informed the study abroad coordinator and the program coordinator of any accommodation to be provided as a result of that evaluation. The Participant has disclosed to the study abroad coordinator and the program coordinator any health condition, to the extent that it may affect the Participant's safety and welfare or that of the other program participants. If in the course of the program, the study abroad coordinator or the program coordinator should determine in his/her good faith judgment that the health, safety or welfare of the Participant or others, or the integrity of the program, is jeopardized by the Participant's health condition, the Participant agrees to withdraw from the program and return to the U.S.

The Participant agrees to abide by the rules and policies of the University and the laws and regulations of the host country and the host institution. The Student Code of Conduct shall apply to student Participants throughout the course of the program. The University may remove the Participant from the program should the University determine that the Participant's actions, conduct or behavior impede, disrupt or obstruct the program in any way, subject the University to risk of liability, or jeopardize the Participant's health or safety or that of the other program participants. Termination from the program shall result in a forfeiture of all program fees and a loss of academic credit where applicable.

The Participant understands that he/she is a non-degree student at any host institution involved. The University may terminate the Participant from the program if he/she fails to enroll or ceases to be enrolled at the host institution, withdraws from the program or violates the host country's or institution's laws, regulations or rules. Termination for such cause shall be without refund.

The Participant is responsible for ascertaining the applicability of credits to be earned through the program to his or her degree requirements.

While the University may assist with or arrange for transportation in connection with the program, Participant agrees the University shall not be liable for any injury, accident, delay, or irregularity, or any loss or damage to baggage resulting from strikes, lockouts, weather, government regulations, sickness or other causes. The Participant is urged to purchase trip cancellation and baggage loss insurance.

The Participant shall obtain a valid passport or proof of citizenship and all other necessary travel documents prior to departing the U.S. (Non-U.S. citizens are especially advised to thoroughly understand the particular entrance requirements of those countries he or she plans to enter, as well as re-entry into the U.S.)

The Participant consents to the University's use of his or her name, photograph, likeness, and comments for publicity or promotional purposes, as the University in its sole discretion may determine.

The Participant will indemnify, hold harmless, release and forever discharge the University, its Board of Regents, its officers and agents, either in their individual capacity or by reason of their relationship to the University, for all claims or demands the Participant, his or her heirs, representatives, executors or administrators, may have against the University by reason of any accident, illness, or injury or other consequences arising or resulting directly or indirectly from the program, any air flights or other travel associated with the program, any provision of medical care, or by reason of the actions or negligence of other parties which may result in injury, death, property damage or other loss to the Participant.

This Agreement shall be governed by and in accordance with the laws of the State of Nebraska. Any claim brought arising from a claim under the terms of this Agreement shall be brought in a forum of proper jurisdiction and venue located within the State of Nebraska. This Agreement takes effect upon receipt by and signature of International Affairs.

I have read and fully understand the terms of this Agreement and, in consideration of participation in this program, agree to the provisions thereof, including the payment and withdrawal/refund policies.

_____
Signature of Participant

_____
Name (printed)   ID Number   Date

If the Participant has not yet reached his/her 19th birthday, this agreement must be signed by his/her parent/legal guardian.

_____
Signature of Parent/Guardian   Name/Relationship (printed)   Date

_____
University of Nebraska-Lincoln, Authorized Signatory

abroad.ckm rev 12/20/99

SYRACUSE UNIVERSITY
DIVISION OF INTERNATIONAL
PROGRAMS ABROAD

FORM #2: Conditions of Participation

Name _____

last   first   middle initial

SS# _____ / _____ / _____

Country of Study _____ Semester and Year _____

2" x 2" Photo
(attach with tape)

Circle your program

A&S / Arc / Pre-Arc / Art / Drama / Hum Dev / Info Std / Mgmt / Pub Comm /
Speech / SWK / Option II / Option III / Direct Placement

NOTE: If the student participant is under age 21 OR if a parent or guardian is responsible for paying the tuition and fees, BOTH the student and responsible parent or guardian must sign. See the back of this form.

1. I (we) have read the information contained in the acceptance packet and, in consideration of the acceptance by Syracuse University's Division of International Programs Abroad of the student named above, understand and agree to the conditions under which the program is offered.

2. I (the student participant) agree to conform to the Syracuse University Code of Student Conduct and Statement of Student Rights and Responsibilities which are published in the Syracuse University *Study Abroad Handbook*.

3. I (we) accept financial responsibility for all University tuition, fees, and charges associated with expenses for the program, and understand payment is due prior to the time of departure. I (we) understand if payment is not made prior to departure, the University may bar me from participation in the program.

4. We release Syracuse University and its officers and agents from any and all claims and causes of action for loss of or damage to property, bodily or personal injury, loss of companionship or support, or death sustained by me or third parties arising out of any activity or travel conducted by or under the control of Syracuse University, unless the loss, injury, or death is caused by the negligence of Syracuse University.

5. Syracuse University reserves the right to cancel any program or course at any time when deemed appropriate due to unforeseen circumstances.

6. Refunds for tuition and fees will be made in accordance with the current refund policies of the Division of International Programs Abroad, relating to involuntary withdrawals, as stated in Syracuse University's publication *Tuition, Fees, & Related Policies* in effect for the corresponding year.

7. If students under 21 years of age leave the host city overnight, such travel must be approved by the student's parent or guardian. Approval shall be deemed granted by execution of this form. In addition, the University requests, but does not require, that students inform a DIPA overseas staff member of such travel plans.

8. I (we) certify that the student will be covered by health insurance valid outside the United States and sufficient to cover medical expenses during her/his participation in the DIPA program.

9. Occasionally a student may require hospitalization or other medical treatment. Except in a true emergency, most physicians and hospitals will not render medical treatment to a minor without the consent of a parent or guardian, or to a non-minor without the individual's written consent. Please complete either (a) or (b), whichever is applicable.

(a) **Minor** (under 21):
I (we), the parent(s) or legal guardian(s) of _____, born _____, 19____, appoint the representatives of Syracuse University in the host country for the program identified above to act on my (our) behalf in authorizing any unexpected medical, dental, or surgical care or hospitalization for my (our) child (ward).

(b) **21 Years of age or over** (as of date this form is signed):
In the event that I, _____, born _____, 19____, am incapable of consenting to medical treatment, I appoint the representative of Syracuse University in the host country for the program identified above to act on my behalf in authorizing any unexpected medical, dental, or surgical care or hospitalization for me.

Continued on next page ☞

Name _____
       last   first   middle initial

10. In giving this release and agreement, I (we) understand that travel, living and study outside the United States involve risks that are beyond the control of Syracuse University. I (we) understand that the social, cultural, political, religious, governmental, health care, legal (both civil and criminal) and other systems, as well as the geophysical characteristics of foreign countries may be different, in subtle and/or significant ways, from those in the United States. For example, behavior that might be illegal, or socially or culturally unacceptable or offensive in the United States may not be illegal and may be normal or acceptable in certain foreign countries; behavior that is considered normal or acceptable in the United States may be illegal or socially or culturally unacceptable or offensive outside the United States; in some countries political unrest and/or upheaval may be expected; police, fire and other governmental systems may be inadequate in certain countries; the quality and availability of health care may be very different than what is typically available in the United States; and different parts of the world are susceptible to different geophysical forces, including hurricanes, earthquakes, floods, tidal waves, tornadoes, volcanoes, and other natural disasters. I (we) acknowledge that we have fully considered these and other risks of participation to our satisfaction. I (we) also acknowledge that participation in this program is optional and that participation would not have been permitted without this release and agreement.

My (our) consent to the terms of this agreement is indicated by my (our) signature below.

Participant's Signature_____
                                                            Date

* Parent/Guardian's Signature _____
(Required if student is under 21 years of age)   Date

* Parent or guardian signature is required if the student is under 21 years of age or if the parent or guardian is responsible for paying tuition, fees, and charges.

Return this completed form to: Division of International Programs Abroad
                                      Syracuse University
                                      119 Euclid Avenue
                                      Syracuse, NY 13244-4170

Appendix K

Criminal Classes of Deportable Students and Scholars

	Aggravated Felonies	Crimes Involving Moral Turpitude (CIMT)[3]	Multiple Criminal Convictions	Domestic Violence	Drug Offenses
Definition	Ever-expanding, enumerated list of crimes appearing in the statute below	Act or omission which are contrary to moral laws and customary rules of right and duty between people	Same as one CIMT	Conviction for domestic violence, stalking, child abuse, child neglect, child abandonment, OR violation of a protective order	Violation of any law relating to controlled substances[5]
Statute	INA[1] s.101 (a)(43)	INA s.237 (a)(2)(A)(i)	INA s.237 (a)(2)(A)(ii)	s.237 (a)(2)(E)	s.237 (a)(2)(B)(i)
Bar to Readmission	Lifetime[2]	10 years	10 years	10 years[4]	10 years[6]
Waiver Available	None	Full pardon by the President or Governor	Same as one CIMT	None	None
Effective Date	Convictions on or after 11/18/88	Conviction within <u>five years</u> of admission	Convictions <u>anytime</u> after admission	Convictions after 9/30/96	Conviction anytime after entry
Requisite Period of Incarceration	Varies by crime	Conviction where a sentence of more than one year <u>may be imposed</u>	None	None	None

1- "Immigration and Nationality Act"
2- Unless Attorney General has consented to readmission
3- "Crime Involving Moral Turpitude"
4- Unless aggravated felony, then bar is lifetime
5- Except single offense for possession of less than 30 grams of marijuana for one's own use
6- Unless aggravated felony, then bar is lifetime

Appendix L

When an International Student Dies

University of
Nebraska
Lincoln

International Affairs
International Place
420 University Terrace
P.O. Box 880682
Lincoln, NE 68588-0682
Phone (402) 472-5358
FAX (402) 472-5383
email: iaffairs@unl.edu
http://www.iaffairs.unl.edu

WHEN AN INTERNATIONAL STUDENT DIES

The tragic death of an international student whether caused by illness, a car accident, suicide, homicide or a recreational activity brings with it unusual circumstances which necessitate cooperation among various professionals and departments on campus. Although there is time to prepare in the event of a lengthy terminal illness, most deaths are unexpected. Consequently, it is important to review this information periodically to be prepared to act at the time of tragedy which is almost always accompanied by a high levels of anxiety.

I.   **Record Keeping**

What happened? Record all details about incoming information, such as: place of death, cause of death, witnesses, etc.

Look at student file for emergency contacts, information on the student's family, sponsoring organization (if any), Lincoln Friend, student's age, photo, health, history, religion, etc.

After the notification process (described below) compile a contact list of all people who will need to be reached in subsequent hours, days, weeks, months: include name, address, title, phone number, fax number, e-mail address (e.g. the coroner, the country embassy or nearest consulate, the family of the deceased, the police officer).

Collect campus and local newspaper articles/reports for files and for the family.

II.   **How and when do we contact the immediate family?**

Immediately notify the Dean of International Affairs (   ), the Associate Dean of International Affairs (   ) and the International Student and Scholars Advisors (   ).

Consult with the Vice Chancellor for Student Affairs (   ) regarding notification. UNL has a "Notification Procedure to be Followed in the Event of the Death of a Student" (attached). Although the Vice Chancellor is designated to notify the family, it may be either impossible due to language proficiency or culturally preferable for the notification to be made by someone else (the embassy, the sponsor, a relative, the supervising professor, an international administer, etc.) The Vice Chancellor will make the decision in connection with International Affairs.

Generally, this notice must be given quickly and if possible, in person. Determine if the circumstances of death should be disclosed to the embassy, the media, to the public, to friends, to the student association, etc. Determine if a family member can be reached by telephone and if he or she understands spoken English.

University of Nebraska–Lincoln   University of Nebraska Medical Center   University of Nebraska at Omaha   University of Nebraska at Kearney

III.   **People and Offices to Be Notified**

    Administrative and advising staff in International Affairs
    Vice Chancellor for Student Affairs (see "Notification Procedure ..." as to how other
        student campus officers are notified and are to respond)
    Lincoln Police
    University Police
    General Counsel
    UNL Public Relations
    Sponsoring organization (if any) ... it may have its own notification procedures
    Exchange coordinator at home institution (if any)
    Local clergy of student's religion (if any)
    Lincoln Friend (if any)
    Major advisor or supervising professor
    Embassy or consulate ... (will have advice on cultural protocol
    Student association (if any)... will have advice on cultural norms and expectations
    Mature, proficient interpreter (if needed)
    Insurance company ... utilize insurance clerk at UNL Health Center (2-7435)
    The U.S. Immigration and Naturalization Service
    Volunteers

IV.   **Information Management/Coordination**

Designate a single individual to act as media spokesperson. Make certain everyone knows who the spokesperson is. Be sure to keep that person up to date.

Call an emergency, high priority meeting of key people including campus police, international affairs staff, association leader and closest friend or friends. Consider including Lincoln Friend (if any), depending on relationship, and major advisor or supervising professor.

Determine through team discussion what kind of information can or should be given to the press or friends of the deceased. Keep in mind that confidentiality or culture may influence this decision. You may receive calls from the local and international press. Rumors spread quickly. Avoid speculation in formal and informal discussions.

Record details. Collect newspaper and other accounts and reports. Verify information if necessary.

V.   Care for Concerned Students and Friends

Make a list of all those people who will need special counseling as result of the crisis. Plan professional grief counseling for small or large groups. (Virtually everyone associated with the deceased will experience some level of guilt, depression or anger and may want to gather to discuss the circumstances.) Find a comfortable location to meet and make facial tissues available.

Alert the Psychological Consultation Center to the death. Arrange with the Center to provide individual or group counseling if requested. Perhaps arrange for a counselor to be present at the hospital or funeral home.

Work with the student association to identify specific friends or family that may need support.

Consider offering counseling support through the Residence Hall staff, religious organization, etc., as appropriate.

VI.   Burial, Cremation, Repatriation of Bodily Remains, Memorial Service

Refuse a request for an autopsy if it will render the remains impure for a religious burial or cremation. Consultation with family and/or members of the student's religious group is essential before a response is given.

Ask clergy and Lincoln Friend (if any) for advice on funeral homes. Have someone collect information on costs of cremation or burial in order to give some options to the family.

In some instances the family may not believe that the death occurred or that the deceased is the person identified. If possible, a photograph of the body should be taken and sent to the family along with newspaper clippings of obituary notices and other articles relating to the death, police and accident reports and printed materials distributed at a funeral or memorial service.

Whether or not they travel to the U.S., parents may need to decide quickly between burial, cremation and repatriation of the bodily remains. They may also want to view the body and request that disposition not be made until they arrive.

Repatriation of remains requires calling airlines, the mortuary and the State. It may be necessary to have a death certificate, a Statement of Non-Communicable Disease and funeral home assistance. If the family is not here, it may be appropriate for a friend or someone from the University to accompany the remains home.

If the body is to be cremated, check to see if it must be embalmed first. No special permission is needed to carry cremation ashes on an airplane in the U.S. There may be laws with regard to bringing ashes into certain countries. Questions should be directed to the embassy or consulate of that country in the U.S. Check with foreign airlines to determine if special permission and documentation is needed to travel with ashes.

For a memorial service:

1. Determine appropriate protocol from friends from home country and/or those of the student's religious persuasion, embassy or consulate, etc.

2. Advise who will arrange the service (family, friends, student association, academic department, etc.).

3. Find clergy/chapel. You may want to have the service videotaped. For some cultures (e.g., Japanese) it may also be appropriate to display an enlarged photo of the student.

4. Invite relatives, friends, Lincoln Friend (if any), home country nationals, faculty and others. Be certain there is representation from International Affairs and, if advanced undergraduate or graduate student, from department.

5. Prepare a formal program and order of service (see attached). Observe culturally appropriate religious rituals (with or without flowers) for the service. Incense and white mums, for example, are sometimes used in Buddhist services.

6. Videotape the service, using an unobtrusive tripod. Save or give a copy of the videotape to the family.

VII. Handling the student's belongings/business matters

Obtain a death certificate for the family.

Arrange a refund of the student's unused airline ticket for the family.

Contact the health insurance/car insurance agent for information on coverage/refunds. There may need to be discussions or negotiations between the insurance company and the hospital. It may be helpful to ask the Director of the University Health Center to assist in this process.

If the student's remains are to be repatriated, the insurance company generally must give its approval before the body is released from the hospital.

Find out what, if anything, can be done with personal possessions of the deceased. Legally, an immediate family member or authorized representative must handle the arrangements. In some circumstances, police or legal procedure may require that belongings be held for a specific period of time. Recommend appropriate places for donations.

Make arrangements to settle the student's personal matters...bank accounts, outstanding bills, rent, disposition of furniture and car.

Collect, pack and ship belongings, or have them ready for the family to take with them.

If the student lived on-campus, contact the Residence Director in the Residence Hall. If the student lived off-campus, contact roommates or the landlord.

VIII.   Accommodating the family of the decreased

When the Family Travels to Lincoln

If the student's parents/relatives decide to travel to the U.S. you will need to plan for their airport pickup, lodging, itinerary, restaurant meals, and local transportation. Type their schedule for each day. Parents will want to meet with their child's close friends some hours after their arrival. Arrange for a mature translator to accompany them.

On occasion, it may be necessary for the family to obtain a visitor visa to the U.S. In order to expedite visa issuance, it may be helpful to call the U.S. embassy or a U.S. consulate in their country and/or fax a letter explaining the situation, the student's immigration documents and a physician's letter.

Nearby off-campus housing will reduce some of the transportation problems. Possible housing includes: The Cornhusker, 333 S. 13th (474-7474); The Holiday Inn, 141 N. 9th, (475-4011); Clifford Hardin Center For Continuing Education, 33rd and Holdrege (472-2949); Great Plains Budget Host Inn, 27th and "O" (476-3253); and Town House Mini-Suites, 18th and "M" (475-3000). It is a good idea to leave food/fruit/tea/flowers in their room.

On-campus housing may be available on a case by case basis. Guest housing is always available during the summer.

Designate someone to correspond with the family during the next several months.

When the Family Is in Lincoln

If the student's family is already in Lincoln, be ready to assist as requested. Identify one international staff member as the principal contact. Correspond with the family during the following months.

Appendix M

Funeral Service Leaflets

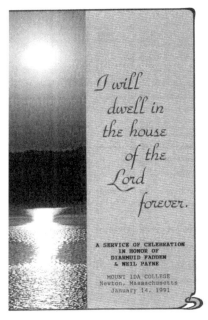

I will dwell in the house of the Lord forever.

A SERVICE OF CELEBRATION
IN HONOR OF
DIARMUID FADDEN
& NEIL PAYNE

MOUNT IDA COLLEGE
Newton, Massachusetts
January 14, 1991

A SERVICE OF CELEBRATION
IN HONOR OF
DIARMUID FADDEN & NEIL PAYNE

MOUNT IDA COLLEGE
Newton, Massachusetts
January 14, 1991

PRELUDE . . . . .Marlys Saltzer

THE LIGHTING OF THE ALTAR CANDLES . . . . . . Edmund Botchway

OPENING WORDS . . . . .Rabbi Robert M. Miller
Temple Beth-Avodah

STATEMENT OF CELEBRATION. . . . . . .Rev. Richard H. Glessner
Chaplain of the College

REMARKS FROM MOUNT IDA SOCCER TEAM CAPTAIN. . . .Joseph Dunne

THE SERVICE OF CANDLELIGHT. . . . .Members of the Soccer Team

READING . . . . .Christophe Goff
President of the Class of 1992

CHORAL SINGING. . . . . .Members of "The Mount Ida Singers"
Beatrice Maier, Director

"Da Pacem Domine," Melchior Frank
"The Peace," Roger Emerson

KEYNOTE ADDRESS . . . . .Dr. Bryan E. Carlson
President of the College

READING . . . . Rev. Michael Doocey
Mary Immaculate Church

READING . . . . .Rabbi Robert M. Miller

CHORAL SINGING. . . . . . .Members of "The Mount Ida Singers"

"Let There Be Peace On Earth," Miller & Jackson

A TIME FOR SHARING. . . . . .Members of the Audience

CLOSING REMARKS . . . . .Rev. Richard H. Glessner

PRAYER TO CLOSE INDOOR CEREMONY. . . . .Rev. Michael Doocey

THE EXTINGUISHING OF THE ALTAR CANDLES . . . Edmund Botchway

POSTLUDE. . . . . .Marlys Saltzer

PROCESSION TO THE SOCCER FIELD (weather permitting)

PRAYER OF DEDICATION. . . . . . . .Rev. Richard H. Glessner

TRUMPET TRIBUTE . . . . Christopher Baillargeon

"Call To the Colors"

THE RAISING OF THE COLORS . . . . . . Dr. Jacqueline Palmer
School of Science & Allied Health

Mount Ida College remembers also in our prayers--

Sandra Sutherland Fox, Ph.D. (NCDE)
recently deceased

Naseraldee Asadallah, member of the Soccer Team
from Kuwait, disappeared in Iraqi invasion

Mount Ida college gratefully acknowledges the presence today
of--
The Consulate General of Great Britain
represented by
Kathleen Tunsley, Vice Consul

The Consulate General of Ireland
represented by
Geoffrey Keating, Vice Consul

Kenneth A. M. Kapansa

Born 4/13/54 Mufulira, Zambia
Died 7/28/94 Syracuse, New York
Ph.D. School of Education
Syracuse University
Syracuse, New York
USA

Remember now thy Creator
in the days of thy youth, while
the evil days come not, nor the
years draw nigh, when thou shalt
say, I have no pleasure in them;
While the sun, or the light, or
the moon, or the stars, be not dark-
ened, nor the clouds return after the
rain:
            ECCLESIASTES 12:1-2

To every thing there is a season,
and a time to every purpose
under the heaven:
            ECCLESIASTES 3:1

Lord make me an instrument
of thy peace
Where there is hatred,
Let me sow Love;
Where there is injury, Pardon;
Where there is doubt, Faith;
Where there is darkness, Light;
Where there is despair, Hope;
Where there is sadness, Joy.

Divine Master, grant that I
may not so much seek to be consoled
as to console;
to be understood as to understand;
to be loved as to love,
for it is in giving that we receive,
it is in pardoning, that we are pardoned,
and it is in dying that we are born to eternal life.

Kenneth A. M. Kapansa

Kenneth Kapansa came to Syracuse in 1989 to pursue a Ph.D. in Education. He recently earned his doctorate degree from the School of Education, while enrolled in the Teaching and Curriculum Program. After which, Kenneth chose to gain practical and research experience when offered an assistant professor's position in the Elementary and Secondary Education Department at SUNY Oswego in September of 1993. Ken's plans were to rejoin the staff at the University of Zambia, in Lusaka, Zambia, after completion of his educational objectives and practical training experience, where he was a faculty member at the School of Education, Department of Language and Social Sciences, before coming to the United States.

Kenneth was born in Mufulira, Zambia in 1954 to Mary Kang'Ombe and Aaron Kapansa of Mansa, Zambia. He is survived by his wife: Moira Nalungwe Kapansa, his sons: Kasenga and Chilembo, daughters: Pwasha and Bupe, four brothers and two sisters of Mansa, Zambia and relatives in Zambia.

Kenneth will be missed by many and we hope his legacy will be realized by future students.

Appendix  N

Sample Notification of Death Letter to Campus Community

SYRACUSE UNIVERSITY

OFFICE OF INTERNATIONAL SERVICES
DIVISION OF STUDENT AFFAIRS

November 2, 1989

Dear Student, Friend and Member of our International Community:

We have all been saddened by the recent death of fellow student,   .
The sudden, senseless tragedy has made all of us anxious, concerned and more aware
of our vulnerability.

Some students have asked about memorial services, news coverage and other issues.
The OIS has sought to be culturally sensitive in all areas of this tragedy. Therefore, at
the request of   parents, no personal information was given to <u>any</u> media.
Friends, faculty and others were asked not to discuss her personal life with reporters.
Her family was very relieved to find that those wishes had been respected.

In addition, the visit to Syracuse of her parents upon learning of the death of their
daughter demanded our total attention to their needs and desires. If we, at the OIS,
seemed to pay less attention to the needs of other students, we ask your understanding
of these circumstances. We can only assure you that all energy, cultural sensitivity and
university resources were devoted to the   family and the members of our
Japanese student community in the week immediately following her death. It is
important for you to know that the Chancellor, himself, was personally involved in the
arrangements and facilitation of all efforts on behalf of   death.

The School of Management and the Dean of Hendricks Chapel are working with the
OIS to plan a memorial service during the week of November 6-10 for those students
and friends who knew   . Details are available at the OIS, at the School of
Management and at Hendricks Chapel. If you wold like to talk with an adviser at the
OIS, or with a counselor at the Health Center, or with a member of the religious
community about your own grief, worries about safety or ideas for insuring the safety
of our students, p free contact our Office, Hendricks Chapel or the Health Center.

The answers to questions about why such tragedies occur are rarely satisfying. Our
feelings of anger and vulnerability are normal responses to such events. We can only
hope to support each other in our grief and continue to live in the sprit of love and
understanding common to the humanity we all share. I invite you to come and talk
with advisers, counselors or others who are concerned and caring. We will all gain
strength in our shared effort to build a new tomorrow.

Very truly yours,

Patricia A. Burak
Director and the entire staff of the Office of International Services

310 Walnut Place / Syracuse, New York 13244-2380
Tele: 315-443-2457 / Fax: 315-443-3091 / E-mail:OIS@SYR.EDU / URL: http://sumweb.syr.edu/ois